A Future Beyond the Sun

a love story

'Man must himself by his own resolute efforts
rise and make his way to the portals
that give upon liberty, and it is always
at every moment in his power so to do.
Neither are those portals locked
and the key in possession of someone else from whom
it must be obtained by prayer and entreaty.
That door is free of all bolts and bars
save those that man himself has made.'

Mali Klein

First published 1997

Published by Fisher Miller Publishing
Wits End, 11 Ramsholt Close,
North Waltham, Basingstoke,
Hants
RG25 2DG
United Kingdom

Printed by Redwood Books

Perfect bound

ISBN 1–899077–04–9

A catalogue record for this book is available from the British Library.

Photo acknowledgements

The photograph on the front cover was taken by Mali Klein on 14th May, 1994, at Lacoste.

The cover photograph of Greg and Mali Klein is used with permission from Sue Feast, Photographer.

The author and publishers wish to thank the following for permission to use photographs for which they hold copyright:

Gillian Holmes (Greg and Mali in Lacoste; Gudrun, Greg and Mali in Lacoste, March); Elaine Johnson (both wedding photographs); Donna Klein (Veterans' Administration Hospital, Richmond); Greg Klein (Mali and JBJ in Gruyères); Mali Klein (Skaftafell National Park, Iceland; Agios Giannis, Limnos; Greg and cats, Rhodes); Nick Pearce (Gudrun, Greg and Mali in Lacoste, May)

Cover design: Ann Miller

Publisher's note

At the time of publishing, different countries use different measures.
The appropriate units have been used for each country. Please note that
8 kilometres ≈ 5 miles, 1 litre ≈ 1.75 pints, 1 cm ≈ 0.4 inches or 1 inch ≈ 2.5 cm.

The author and publishers have made every effort to contact copyright holders of material reproduced in this book. Any omission will be rectified in subsequent printings if notice is given to the publishers.

I wrote this book for me and for Greg, beloved husband, for Ānando, beloved husband and teacher, and for Charles, also a teacher.

Acknowledgements

My love and gratitude to:

Sasha, Sophie and Michael for our time in Lacoste; Con and Effi Cazoulis for Limnos; Gillian and Mike for being there; Don for our Apple Mac, without which neither Clouds nor this book would have been possible; my mother and Elaine for giving up so much house space to Clouds; Sheila in Canada for her constant encouragement; Debbie and Susan in California for keeping me sane and reminding me that anything's possible; Jane and her wonderful garden; Kittisaro and Mary Thanissara for not forgetting; Noy for her years of support for Ānando and for looking after me so well in Thailand; Jef, Jan and Judy in Lacoste; Betty and Paul in Eguilles; Lóa and Birgir in Hafnarfjördur; Ingibjörg and Jón in Reykjavík; Nick Papadimitriou for the best supermarket in Lardos; Sue for the photographs; Pauline for the laughter; Janey, Joan and Ann as a great production team; Dinh Truong Phuoc in Hoi An.

Last but not least, all the staff in the VA hospitals in Richmond and Hampton who worked so hard for us, the girls in the hospitality house in Richmond and everyone connected with The Friends of the Vietnam Veterans' Memorial (FVVM), Washington DC.

Thank you.

A Review

... Loving and learning and living in the moment, Greg and Mali teach us valuable lessons through the full gamut of their emotions. Their insightful dialogue remains forever etched within our hearts.

Sheila Snow, Ontario (Author of *The Essence of Essiac*)

Part One

Clouds
Together

Chapter One

He told me I had beautiful eyes. No one had ever told me that before until this man who became my beloved in the splendour of the Indian summer of his life. Twice I saw the signal flash as he came walking down the road from the monastery. The shadows became the silhouette of his head and shoulders with the pack over his arm. He walked quickly around to the car door. Suddenly he was there, sitting beside me, taking immediate possession of my hand. The silence alive with his excitement, his breathing, he settled into the seat, stretching out legs that were clearly outlined in the dark navy sweat pants. At last the robe was gone.

'Let's go,' he said.

The clock on the dashboard read 11.33. I edged the car forward, driving slowly without lights until we were safely under the railway bridge and then out on to the main road and away from Kandersteg. All along the twisting, winding road I drove in a dream, guiding the wheel with my left hand. He covered the other with kisses, delicately, lips and fingertips, feeling, tasting, enjoying, pushing up my sleeve to touch my wrist and the tender skin on the inside of my forearm.

'Pull over soon, I want to kiss you,' he said.

But it was not yet midnight and the villages in southern Switzerland in those last few minutes of Saturday, June 6th 1992 were still well lit. There was nowhere obvious to stop beside the road.

'Don't worry, my love, we have all the time and space in the world. We will be in Gruyères by one o'clock. Nothing and no one can take you away from me now,' I said.

And so it was. We drove over Jaunpass past the avalanche warning signs, through the narrow opening on to what remained of the damaged road, to come down at last to see the little medieval town of Gruyères and the castle still flood-lit against the top of the hill.

I had bread and chocolate and apples in the car but he was too excited to be hungry. Eager to be alone with me, closing the front door of the hotel quietly behind us, creeping up the stairs and treading softly along the thickly carpeted corridor to Room Ten. Laughing he put down the pack and picked me up, relieved that I was light enough to be swept gracefully over the threshold into our warm, waiting room.

My little travelling shrine was already set up on the table at the end of the bed. Candles and incense sticks lay unlit before the Buddha-rupa, an assortment of carefully selected new clothes hung in the wardrobe, towels and my favourite musky shower gel laid out in the bathroom. The bed turned back. Waiting.

'This is so correct,' he murmured as he held me that first time. I felt him trembling, urgent against me and my own response came swift and strong but he was less than two hours out of the monastery and without the usual rites.

'Come Beloved, to the tub! We have to wash away the monk and perform the ceremony, do we not?' I said.

Our natural respect for ritual lasted through our simple disrobing formality, to explode after twenty years and a lifetime of waiting in an almost instantaneous, atomic, mutual orgasm. I wrapped him round tenderly, not letting him move, holding him, feeling his weight over me as we lay coupled together in the warm, drowsy peace, in the world that was our room, our bed.

'I wanted to make love to you all night,' he murmured. 'I wanted to last longer for you. Are you disappointed in me? Tell me truly.'

'Beloved you, I am complete! I waited so long for you, only you. Look at me, do I look dissatisfied?'

'No, you look wonderful. That's why I wanted to make love to you all night. I can't understand why I am so tired.'

'My love, think about the last twenty-four hours, the last twenty years for that matter. Haven't you been under just a little bit of stress? And as for our love-making, I am very flattered that you appreciate me so well. You are neither unhealthy nor elderly and after twenty years of celibacy I expected nothing less. Believe me, Beloved, it was wonderful! You are wonderful!'

He looked at me carefully, intensely, relaxing as he saw my sincerity, the love shining in my eyes. Smiling, covering my lips, my face with little, murmuring kisses, at last he snuggled down into my arms, his head against my breast, drifting into sleep.

Sometime in the night I was woken up by the pressure of his arms as he slept, still holding me so tightly as if he was afraid I would be gone in the morning. I stroked his head, feeling the softness of his hair already almost half an inch long, the hard ridge of his skull covered in scar tissue where it had been broken by the bullet so many years ago and the vulnerable concavity, akin to the fontanel that had aroused all my paranoia when my children were first born. Kisses followed my fingers, he shifted a little, murmuring contentment. 'This is so right,' I thought.

'I'm so glad I love you,' I whispered. 'I'm so glad you love me.'

We made love again as the first light was showing through the chinks in the curtains and this time he was more satisfied with himself. He didn't know me well enough yet to be completely free from doubt.

Breakfast finished by nine thirty and we were hungry enough to be out of bed by eight forty five and into the shower. He laughed as he wandered naked around the room, examining all the new things I had brought for him.

'I completely forgot to be shy with you,' he said.

'Well, it's a bit too late for that now,' I said. 'Are you shy, really?'

2

'Yes I am. Remember I was brought up Catholic. I was always self-conscious even with steady girlfriends although I did my best not to show it. I'm really surprised at myself now, especially after twenty years of monastic conditioning. I'm also very glad.'

'So am I,' I said, reaching out for another kiss that threatened to become complicated until we looked at the clock. Typically I had remembered to bring all of his things and virtually none of my own. I went down to breakfast in the black silky top and Levis that I had worn the night before. He bubbled his way down the stairs in uninhibited delight with a golden earring in his left ear, wearing a pale cream and green silk shirt, green socks to match and a pair of stone-washed Levi 501's that fitted him perfectly.

We found a cosy corner at a big circular table all to ourselves. He ordered breakfast. Croissants and toast, hot milk for me, hot chocolate for him. He looked at the cutlery, hesitating before he picked up the knife. He saw me watching him.

'Don't forget I've been using a spoon for the last twenty years,' he said. I offered him the butter and the jam and he only just stopped himself from making the gesture of acceptance. We laughed together in pure pleasure. But as I cut into my bread, the knife made a slight scraping sound against the plate and he winced.

'What's the matter?' I said, surprised suddenly to be looking at Ānando, his eyes veiled, that so well remembered look, inscrutable, detached.

'My monastic conditioning. The sound of the knife on the plate, it offends me.'

'I'm sorry, I didn't realise. I don't usually crash through my food.'

He relaxed and smiled again.

'It's all right. It's the result of twenty years of eating without touching the sides of the bowl with the spoon. Old habits die hard.'

'It's not such a bad habit. I promise I'll try not to do it again.'

'Do you mind?' He seemed to need reassurance.

'No, really I don't,' I said.

From the beginning of our association, from the time he told me on tape that he didn't want to be a Buddhist monk any more, maybe even before then, I had decided never to allow myself to expect anything from him unless it was the unexpected. Any presumption on my part could only result in frustration or disappointment. In relating to him I would have to be content to take one day at a time. It was impossible to predict what would come up in so intricate a situation with a man of such complexity.

It was ten o'clock before we were back in our room. I suddenly remembered that I was supposed to be telephoning my daughter Gudrun, left biting her nails in England, to announce mission accomplished.

'I've got him,' I said.

I could hear the relieved voices in the background.

'Everything's just fine. We forgot to ring earlier, we were very distracted. Now ring Gillian, she'll be waiting to talk to Ajahn Santikaro.'

I put down the receiver. For one long moment I allowed recognition of the eruption that had already begun in England fully into consciousness.

'Can you feel it? It's like a hot wave,' I said.

'It's inevitable but that's there and their own conditioning reacting. We are here and us and that's much more interesting to me right now,' he said.

And I could see that he had genuinely and quite deliberately put it out of his mind. He was right of course. No amount of wondering or imagining would do anything for the situation other than to confuse it still further.

Money came next. I emptied my pockets and my bag on to the bed and handed him every coin and note I had.

'There you are, it's all yours. I'll help you if you need it but I would be very glad never to have to look after the money again. I've always had to be so responsible and it would be wonderful to have time off,' I said.

'Willingly! It's important to me to have you completely dependent on me. I need it in our relationship.'

'Nothing suits me better, believe me.'

'You won't feel insecure without your own money?'

'If I do I shall just have to learn not to be. Besides where would it come from? You don't want me to work and I have nothing of my own save the money in the bank in Iceland that we are to travel with.'

'Yes, I'm glad to have that but it will be the last. I don't want you giving any time or attention to anyone else ever again, only to me. I need it, I need you. Shall you mind not doing the healing and the counselling?'

'No, my love. The Gods have given me something else to do. They have given me you, Beloved.'

'And I have you and I am so grateful, so very grateful.'

'Promise me, promise me you will never leave me again. I couldn't bear it. These past weeks have almost killed me,' I said.

'I promise I will never leave you again,' he said smiling, kissing me.

'And you will never shave your head again?'

'I have absolutely no intention of shaving my head ever again. That's finished with. Besides, you would have to give your permission for me to do it.'

'Really? Then we're quite safe. You will never have my permission to go back into the monastery as a monk.'

— �֎ —

It was raining when we went out but it didn't matter. Nothing mattered. I showed him the red paint mark on the wall where I reversed the hire-car in a hurry the week before. We sat out a heavy shower in a niche in the castle ramparts. By mutual consent we went back to bed for the afternoon.

'I want to take you out for a special dinner tonight,' he said. 'Do you have any idea where you would like to go?'

'I haven't a clue. There are plenty of little restaurants here in the town. But I want to do a healing session on you before we eat.'

4

'Shall we do it now?' he said, getting up. 'Do I have to wear anything?' he added with a grin.

'No, you don't have to, but I want to concentrate and without clothes you are too much of a distraction.'

He pulled on underwear and a tee-shirt and sat himself down on the floor in front of the shrine. His back was perfectly straight, his legs folded neatly around themselves into the lotus position. The sheer elasticity of his body and movement fascinated me. I went through the simple technique in which I had been so well trained that manifested individually in each of the healers. For me it had developed as an ability to see through my hands, visualising my clients almost as a colour X-ray when I touched them.

I was shocked at what I saw now. The imbalance of energy, the deeply-rooted trauma, his weariness of spirit. I closed my hands gently around his head and saw a disturbingly large, dark green coloured mass of energy just behind the scarring of the gunshot wound. It was deep within the brain and moving inwards, spreading slightly towards the left side of his head from the centre. I had never seen or heard of anything like it before and I could only conclude that it marked the lingering trauma of the wounding. I made the final passes over his head, kissing him tenderly on the back of his neck to bring him back fully into consciousness.

'Mmm, that was wonderful,' he said. 'Did you see anything?'

'Exhaustion, stress as you might expect. A bit of a mess really. There's a peculiar dark green stain around the gunshot wound to your head and a distortion of energy just below the waist level with the scars on your back. Have you had any kind of a brain scan in the last few years?'

'No, it never seemed necessary. What does it mean?'

'I don't know. I can only think it must be the imprint of old trauma.'

'Still, after all these years?'

'It can take more than one lifetime if it is severe enough. Maybe it would be a good idea to have you scanned if we go to America, just to be sure.'

He shrugged, dismissing the idea immediately.

'That's hardly necessary. I can see well enough. I think the field of vision defect has grown larger in the last two or three years but I can still see what I can see well enough. I used to have occasional headaches but nothing in the last few months. I feel perfectly well in myself, especially since last night and this afternoon.'

Immediately we were tumbling on to the floor, pulling the quilt and pillows off the bed. Clothes scattered over the carpet.

We were late for dinner. Sitting side by side at the table in the hotel restaurant; he would always insist on sitting next to me at table, never opposite, so that he could feed me from his plate, steal from mine, knees touching, the warm strength of his thigh secure against mine. But I detected a momentary anxiety in him as we climbed back into bed. I snuggled down under his arm, wrapping myself around him, stroking the soft brown hair that was so perfectly symmetrically scattered across his chest.

'Cuddle me,' I said, 'hold me, talk to me.'

'What about?'

'I can feel anxiety in you Beloved, and I think I know why. We are not performing bears you know. You have made more than enough love to me in the last twenty-four hours. I know we have lifetimes to make up for but it doesn't have to be all at once.'

He smiled and held me closer.

'Thank you for that. You are very good for me.'

'Let's go to sleep. Already I love sleeping with you, I sleep so well, I feel so safe.'

'Yes, it's strange. It's as though we have always slept together. I am still amazed at how relaxed I am with you.'

'I'm not. It's meant to be this way.'

But for all our good intention, sleep did not come so easily while the eagerness, the fascination was so strong. It was long after midnight before we slept again.

We had to be out of the hotel by eleven the following morning and on the road to Italy by way of the Grand St Bernard tunnel. We had to go shopping for shoes as he only had the walking boots he had on when he left Kandersteg. I followed him into the bathroom to find my toothbrush already set out with a ball of toothpaste squeezed neatly on to it. He was standing naked in front of the large mirror in the bathroom, lathering his face and shaving with a swift, well-practised hand. I was fascinated, standing behind him, watching his reflection in the mirror.

An old art-student never dies. My skilful eye saw beyond the hollow-eyed, hollow-cheeked, haggard face, the skin, surprisingly soft but hanging too loosely on a stressed and almost emaciated body. I saw a beautiful bone structure, strong and well made, clear, dark grey-blue, sometimes almost black eyes, that lower lip that was much too attractive for a monk and a beautiful line from the back of his head down a slender neck, and that almost too vulnerable throat, to broad, sloping shoulders. Nothing that a few weeks of love and food wouldn't put right. His legs were a constant source of delight to me. So straight and strong. 'The best legs in the Sangha!' so I insisted. And already on his head a thick covering of hair that was much more brown than he had dared to think possible. I had thought him to be of less than medium height but now suddenly I found myself walking beside someone easily a head and shoulders taller than me. He seemed to be growing in front of my eyes as he stood straight and proud with the long burden of the robe gone from his body and mind.

He rinsed his jaw, patting it dry with the towel.

'Am I shaved well enough for you?' he asked, smiling back at me 'I don't want to give you a red chin.'

'You are perfect,' I said. I meant it. He was so neat and precise in his movements, and so very masculine.

'You don't think I am fat, do you?'

'How can you say that?' I answered in complete amazement. 'There should be a lot more person inside this skin. You have got to gain weight! It has to be twenty pounds at least.'

'What!' He was horrified. 'I'll be fat!'

'That is absolute rubbish! It's going to take a lot more than that to make such a thin person fat.'

'We'll see about that. We'll have to negotiate. Do you really think I am so thin?'

'Look at yourself!' He looked at himself hard in the mirror, turning this way and that, anxious, worried.

'I'm not unattractive to you, am I? I do please you, don't I?'

In answer I ran my fingers down his back and to his loins, caressing, arousing an instant response.

'Do I look unattracted by you? Do I feel unattracted by you? Do I seem displeased?' I said softly.

Grinning, he turned around to me.

'Indeed you do not.'

It was so exciting, this discovering, this uncovering, this tender revealing. Physically, intimately, emotionally, spiritually he was everything I had always wanted. In the days, the nights, the weeks, the months that followed, I gave him back his manhood. He gave me my woman. And something more. The child within each of us, freed from the burden of youth and the natural obligation to our parents or our peers. Complete and without pretension as neither of us had been before.

— ✳ —

It was still inclined to rain as we left Gruyères. But the sun was shining in Italy as we set up the tent at the campsite in Aosta. As it happened, we stayed only for one night. The shops were nothing special and we wanted to go back to the mountains. Perhaps to Arolla in Switzerland, the highest camping place we could find on the map. We packed up the tent and the car, instantly the perfect work team and revelling in the ease and the lightness between us. Wearing tee-shirts and jeans we drove back towards the Grand St Bernard Pass on a beautiful morning of sunshine and flowers and happiness, taking the road over the mountains that was just opened for the summer season.

We were back in sweaters and coats as we crossed the border high up at the snow line. Greg insisted on stopping for hot chocolate and milk in the restaurant but my attention was immediately on the floor to ceiling display of polyester St Bernard dogs of all sizes and designs that we had to pass to get to our table. In my days of loneliness I had always travelled a little white teddy bear around with me, never feeling at all threatened by Ajahn Ānando's desanas about people who needed a cosmic teddy bear. In unmitigated revenge, I had given him one for his own use and contemplation for his last birthday, complete with a miniature citrine and aquamarine string of mala beads around its neck. But my Sveinn Magnus had been given to Gudrun when I left England and even in my present state of bliss I felt the gap. With one last lingering look, I took myself to the table where Greg was already holding out a chair for me. He saw me settled and then went off to place the order.

'Greg?' He stopped and turned.

'Yes?' I was almost too embarrassed to ask.

'Greg, I want a dog.'

A look of consternation came over his face. I could see that he hadn't understood what I meant.

'One of those out there on the stand. Only a little one, please, the very smallest,' I pleaded.

He was so relieved.

'I thought you wanted a real one! I was just about to ask you how on earth we were going to live in a tent with a dog!'

'Can I have one, please?'

Without another word he vanished into the back of the shop. Ten minutes later a mug of hot milk appeared on the table in front of me beside my very own polyester St Bernard, all six inches of him with a brown, felt barrel tied around his neck. He had to be Jean Bernard Jacques. JBJ, destined to a life travelling in pockets or peering out of the top of my bag, to be squeezed by Customs officials in airports and regularly to appear in restaurants and photographs regardless of any ridicule that Greg might be inclined to heap upon his head. I refused to be insulted. I was only delighted. He was easily one of the best of the dogs on the shelf and not even the smallest.

We three went down into the sunshine again driving our little grey car into the lushness of the green of the early summer. Cows standing knee deep in grass nodding their heads, clonking their bells, flicking their ears at the flies. Snow still dazzled the highest peaks to fall patching on the lower slopes that tumbled over the stones into flowers. Golden buttercups and vetch, the pink and purple and cream of the cow parsley and the blue of the forget-me-nots. A sweet, clear air, fresh on the wind from the snow, spiced the heat of the sun on the green. It was all so new. We were so new. It was wonderful.

'You are a very good driver,' he said for no particular reason as we drove up one of the steep, winding mountain roads. Glancing at him I saw that he was looking at my hands on the wheel rather than at me.

'You mean that you know I have to drive and you don't mind but you would really rather be driving yourself,' I said, laughing.

'You're right. Can I here? There's no one around.'

'All right but only on the side roads, promise me? And if you feel tired or bothered tell me right away, okay?'

He was so pleased. He was immediately out of the car and holding the passenger door open for me to get in. He drove to Arolla, bubbling with happiness so that he could hardly sit still but always careful of what he was doing, compensating for his loss of vision. After the first few kilometres I could relax and enjoy his pleasure, watching him and allowing myself time and space to indulge in the delight of this new peace, this new freedom.

What did I know of this man? Ānando, now Greg again and determined to be known hereafter as Greg. In some ways he had never been a monk but I knew that he would always be a monk. The monk, the man, the Marine, they were all my inheritance. His time as Ānando had passed but he was the sum total of all that Ānando had been. And Greg, past and present.

I had taken both Greg and Ānando into my heart. Essentially the man who presented himself to me as a lover, a companion in spirit, possibly a husband, but who was also possessed of the finer qualities of the monk, the indelible etching of twenty years of monastic training and conditioning.

'Don't let me throw the baby out with the bath water,' he said to me now. 'It's in me to reject it all as a natural reaction, in anger, but I don't want to do that. Help me to keep all that was good of Ānando alive.'

— ✳ —

I first saw him on the morning of November 9th 1989 when, reluctantly following a persistent summons from some other dimension, I drove myself to the Buddhist Monastery, at Chithurst in the heart of rural southern England, in time for the single, daily meal.

'When you have passed your driving test you will go to Chithurst,' said a voice in the middle of my head.

'Why? What on earth do I have to go there for? I have enough to do with the healing training, I have no time for another religious community.'

'When you have passed your test you will go to Chithurst.'

I took the test on November 1st 1989, consoling myself as I drove back to the test centre, having almost killed a cyclist, with 'Oh well at least I won't have to go to Chithurst now.' No one was more amazed than I when I was told I had passed.

'You will go to Chithurst.'

'I don't want to go to Chithurst.'

'You will go to Chithurst.'

After eight more days of procrastination that was actually becoming guilt – 'Why should I listen to this? It's got me into trouble enough before, do I need more?' – I found myself standing in the monastery kitchen watching the silent monks passing along the line of lay people waiting to fill their bowls. My mind was reeling with the peculiar power that charged the whole atmosphere. I didn't really notice him as an individual then even though he was the first to be served and was seated directly in front of the golden Buddha for the meal.

'I'm not bowing to a statue,' I thought, kneeling upright on the floor, rigidly obstinate while the others touched the boards with their foreheads. 'I'm not bowing to a man either.'

It was only later that I realised that a major source of the power lay within the Abbot himself. It emanated from him so that I only had to put my nose inside the door to be able to tell whether he was in the building or not. Much later I realised that he was mostly unconscious of it and of the effect he had. In that alone, coupled with his natural charm and the position he was in, he was dangerous.

I didn't speak to him until exactly five months later, after I had been going to the evening meditation for some weeks. He was standing alone in the hallway in a shaft of reflected light from the stairwell, watching me drag some heavy bags out of my car and in through the door.

'What is this?' My first thought, as I came under the scrutiny of that peculiar stillness. Originally one of the four monks under Ajahn Sumedho to bring Theravadan Buddhism to England in 1977, he was undoubtedly one of the Sangha superstars whether he liked it or not. I was already well used to the other senior monks who were dynamic but more traditional in their practice. But I could see at once that he was something very different.

His face was closed, masked. The eyes, accentuated by the lack of eyebrows, were slightly hooded, veiled. No one could close their eyes quite like Ajahn Ānando. He could have been cast in bronze and gilded, so complete was that almost reptilian stillness that was barely broken by the slow turning of his head. He was always tanned. How he managed that in an English winter I never knew. And he shaved off well. Even the initially startling dent was centrally placed on the back of a small, well-shaped head. Impeccably robed, the curious cat-like grace of his movement honed and polished by years of Tai Chi, and with his neat, slightly pointed ears he looked somehow off-worldly and in possession of an exotic unreality that was more in accordance with the ceremonial of the High Priest than a Buddhist monk.

Naturally attuned to the proprieties of ritual, he demanded complete attention and respect for the formality of the monastic discipline. No one dared to be late for morning and evening chanting. But when approached by an individual in need he gave his time and attention unstintingly, far more at ease in a more personal approach than in relating to larger groups.

Teaching never came easily to him. The intensity of his self-consciousness was always acutely aware both of what he considered to be his lack of formal education and of the brain damage he fought so hard to disguise. Yet on the increasingly rare days when he could relax into rhetoric, his eyes would light up with an infectious enthusiasm, his hands gesticulating expansively to emphasise a point. Few could resist the compulsive charisma of Ajahn Ānando on days like that. His policy of choosing not to speak rather than to say something trite often had a greater effect than he knew. What he didn't say was often more potent than what he said. But in his own, critical mind, he often confused personal feelings of inadequacy with his natural ability to listen.

10

He had the gift of silence. He was not inclined to push easy answers on anyone who came to talk to him. In the silence they found the space to answer their questions for themselves. Despite himself he liked to be admired because he thought of himself as essentially not admirable. People found him intriguing, infuriating, sometimes intimidating, often attractive, often inspiring. Many loved him, others were completely unmoved by him. Paradoxically he never fully realised the debt of gratitude so many felt towards him.

He was too far over the top for me. Attractive neither as a monk nor a man. In conversation, when I found myself stimulated into direct and almost casually cheeky comments towards him and his time-softened East Coast drawl, I decided that it would be better for my practice to avoid him, which I managed successfully for the next eighteen months. I had Ajahn Khurovedho and Ajahn Santikaro to talk Dhamma with. I didn't need any kind of relationship with the Abbot, even as a teacher. Yet within a few weeks of observing the subtle reactions within the community, I had caught on to the pain and the loneliness of the man behind the Robe and I knew that, although the others were more immediately my friends, I would support Ānando if ever the need arose. But it was mostly an unconscious decision at that time.

I worked in the monastery garden once a week all that summer, carefully dressed in my baggiest trousers and least revealing shirts that only usually saw daylight in the stables at the farm where I lived. Having ensured that my clothes were completely forgettable and with not a trace of perfume anywhere upon me, I made a consistent effort to play down any attraction I might retain in looks or behaviour as inappropriate to time and place. I drew the line at mascara. I had been wearing it since I was eleven years old and saw no reason to stop now. I attended evening meditation regularly, enjoying being there and to be able to talk to the monks and as I began to get to know the nuns, at last I felt I had found a place of peace and refuge in Chithurst. In some ways it reminded me of the happiest times of my childhood when visiting my grandparents who had lived only a few miles away in the next village. The garden looked out on to the same hills that I had always seen standing by the front door of their little cottage.

And now I was sitting beside him as he drove us high into the mountains in Switzerland. I was watching him handling money, ordering food, eating three meals a day. I was suddenly in this new and intimate relationship with Ānando whom I had already known as Greg for several months. As a lay woman I had learnt to defer to him as the Abbot with the utmost respect, which the events in the monastery of the previous autumn had done nothing to tarnish. That period had been difficult for me too. Trapped on the inside, knowing too much, being forced to question all that I valued in the monastic community as a refuge. Heart-torn at having to watch the diminishing of the power and the light that had been Ānando. Yet increasingly impressed by his courage and uncomplaining dignity in the face of criticism and shame.

The evening after he had given me the tape telling me he didn't want to be a Buddhist monk any more, he was lingering in the lane as I came hurtling down the hill towards the monastery, coming early to put my cushion out in the shrine room before the evening sitting. I was still in shock, the tape carefully hidden in my bag and never out of my sight. I was terrified of it being discovered before I had had time to erase it.

'I don't want to be a Buddhist monk any more. I want to live with you and through that relationship find out what love is really all about.'

I had reversed the cassette player and replayed it six times before the words began to sink in. I was stunned. What had happened? Was that the reason for all those strange questions about the cost of living these days? He wanted to live with me? Certainly it was not an unattractive idea when I really thought about it. Life was suddenly accelerating to light-speed and beyond.

Almost too late I saw him in the glare of the head lights and jammed on the brakes. The car skidded to a halt beside him and I wound down the window.

'I could have killed you! I didn't expect to see anyone out here!'

He didn't answer immediately. He stood looking down at me, nervous, fiddling with the edge of his jacket, the handle of the car door.

'Did you listen to the tape?'

'Yes.'

'How did you respond?'

'I was shocked and then I was pleased.'

'Why were you shocked? Was it so unexpected?'

'Yes it was. It was the last thing I expected to hear.'

'But you were pleased?'

'Yes, I was pleased. I am pleased.'

In the dimness of the side lights of the car I could see the stillness come over him. The silence growing, intensifying, screaming between us. Few people used the lane at that hour and the darkness with its whisperings and night noises folded us into anonymous security. Each waiting for the other to speak. Unbidden, the words came tumbling out, outrageous when he reflected on them later.

'But are you mine?' he asked me.

'Yes. I am your woman,' I said.

Without hesitation or time to consider. Whatever made me say that?

'I can't believe I haven't kissed you,' he said.

He raised his hand in a helpless, almost hopeless gesture.

I knew the rules very well. I had read the Patimokka but I had supported him in his overwhelming misery and isolation for so many months. His pain had become my pain. In answer I reached out. Slowly, tentatively, closing my fingers around his. A white-hot electricity flaring between us as he made his first direct physical contact with a woman after twenty years. I was

12

surprised at the strength of the gripping, returned pressure of his hand. But the warmth, the softness of his skin. Was the rest of him like that too?

'So what do I call you then?'

'You can call me Greg,' he said.

It was the evening of Sunday, March 1st. I knew there was no going back. In those few short moments we had done something final. We were committed. In all my weary years of marriage I had never been anyone's woman. Briefly I had experimented with it once, but I was not 'property' material. I had never been with anyone I could completely respect. I turned the key in the ignition, I was expected elsewhere before the evening sitting.

'It's all right,' I whispered. 'I love you.'

He turned and vanished into the darkness. Over the stile and across the field back to the monastery. The next afternoon he left for Thailand, making a tape for me as he showered and packed. Sealing it innocently in a used, brown envelope, he had the audacity to ask Gillian, a longstanding lay supporter and a friend to both of us, to give it to me as she delivered him to the airport.

The next two weeks were very difficult for me. I had answered with my heart but my head took over in the cold light of the following morning. My freedom, so elusive for so many years and planned and prepared for the coming summer, was threatened in the least expected but most controversial way. Chithurst would never be the same without that commanding, arresting presence. What could possibly alleviate such a sense of loss? And hadn't it been I who had consistently and publicly said 'Never, never get emotionally involved with a monk because they are, without a doubt, absolutely crazy?' What kind of emotional suicide was I letting myself in for? He was one of the most extreme. Probably the most demanding and under that impressive facade, passionate, volatile, vulnerable and emotionally so frail. And brain damaged. How much was he really affected by that head wound? Caution, self-preservation told me not to build either hopes or dreams around him. Not yet. He could change his mind any time and he had to be given every chance to do so. I didn't want to have to live for perhaps the rest of my life under the shadow of his remorse and regret. If he left the monastery, it had to be of his own volition. Until then, for my own sake as much as his, I would do my best neither to persuade nor influence his decision.

By the end of the first week my heart was running ahead again, knowing that at any moment it could be completely broken but willing to take the risk while I waited for him to return. Waited to see whether he had already changed his mind. He telephoned within two hours of landing at Heathrow. Both of us reassured to hear the other speak, listening carefully, anxiously for subtle tones and nuances. Both very much aware of the fragility of this new relating.

Instinctively I was always protective of him. He had given me his confidence knowing it would be safe with me. There would be no more breaking the rules. If our time together was to come it would come and then there would be time enough. Neither could there be any vacillation on my part. I had given my word and I would answer to him and only to him. Nothing and no one else mattered. My children were grown up and deep into their own lives. Even Gudrun at sixteen had a space entirely of her own. I was so tired of trailing around behind their teenage energy, feeling no longer necessary or needed.

Desperately I wanted a life where I could pursue my spiritual practice in freedom, uncluttered by sullen criticism and other people's demands and desires. This man, this monk, was perhaps the only human being I had ever met who could share that kind of life with me. Only time would tell. Meanwhile I would watch and wait and see what happened as I had done all my life. Following a dream, my dream. I had always known that one day I would meet the one man who would be my completion, my fulfilment. Could he be the one?

Looking at him now, with the scandal blowing sky high in England and already faxing its way around the world, I dared to hope. For the first time in my life I felt cared for and cared about. Lavishly, attentively. I had been so used to driving him around, holding doors open for him, bowing to him. Now he was driving and holding doors open for me, the car door, in the hotel, holding back a queue so that I could go first, pulling out a chair for me to sit at the table, pouring water into my glass. Glancing over me with a quick appraising eye before we went out to be sure that I was perfect.

'Lipstick, Mali! Don't forget! And we must get you some good nail polish.'

It didn't need a lot of money. Just care and meticulous attention, united with the growing power of an all-consuming love.

Chapter Two

We were very careful and polite with one another during those first days taking one day at a time. He had been years in command, nothing changed. Everything was negotiable except for one thing. He was the boss and I didn't want it any other way. We were always talking as though we had eons to catch up on and I was only temporarily astounded into silence when he asked, in all seriousness, how I thought I would make it through the menopause. Managing to keep a reasonably straight face I answered equally seriously, bearing in mind the extreme practicality of the question in consideration of my rather dangerous age.

It was on the tip of my tongue to ask him the same question in regard to the male equivalent but I had soon noticed that he found it very difficult to laugh at himself and I wondered how my teasing, slightly sacrilegious sense of humour would go down. Accordingly I kept a firm clamp on my mouth until habit got the better of me and I answered one of his pronouncements using his full name without thinking.

'Gregory, please!' I said, accenting his name with a delicately quirky twist in tone, ending in a squeak.

I waited for the axe to fall. Several endless seconds frozen and then he was laughing and by the next day he was calling me Nutt after a Burmese Goddess, or so he said, and his 'golden witch', and I was saluting orders with 'Yes Sir!' Another barrier had fallen, another fear departed.

'Grow old with me Mali,' he said, over and over again.

He dreaded infirmity in old age. 'Old, white-haired and blind'. His worst nightmare. The ever-present horror of the darkness, blood and darkness. And rarely mentioned but often hinted at, a deeply ingrained fear of going insane. Dying was a more welcome alternative. He had last looked into the face of death on the battlefield and deep within himself he did not associate dying with peace. Rather with an agony of blood and fear, surrounded by the screaming wounded. He still reacted strongly to the smell of his own blood.

During the last winter retreat at Chithurst he had insisted that I make a tape for him about death, telling him about my perception of death and its reality for me. I could tell him only what I had seen for myself, about what appeared to be true for me. I told him about my nursing experiences, helping my father to die, the horses I had had shot. Seeing my grandparents meet beyond death when I was a nineteen year old student, at the time fashionably anarchistic with no interest in death whatsoever. I had hardly known where to begin but eventually I managed to fill a ninety-minute tape that seemed to satisfy him, even to impress him. I didn't know why. My assessment was hardly in accord with standard Theravadan views and teaching.

'Old age, sickness and death'. In Buddhism the three outward symbols of mortality that he had reflected upon and given desanas on for so many years but still feared.

'That is why I'm here. You have to help me,' he said.

'Why? How?' My mind, wavering in an instant of helpless perplexity.

He readily admitted he could hardly bear anything that in any way suggested personal criticism.

'Please don't criticise me Mali,' he said. 'My self respect has been so low for so long. I have no reserves.'

'But what would I criticise you about? Have I criticised you?'

'No you haven't. You have never been anything less than kindness itself, caring and passionate, and so good for me but I have to tell you. I need to tell you how I'm feeling.'

'Always tell me, I'll try not to be hurt. Kisses in excess help a lot. Let's practise!'

Doubt, the paradox, raised its head very early on. I would be on my back purring, sticky wet and smelling of sex, contemplating the perfect synchronicity of our love-making and he would come crashing through my rose cloud.

'Do I satisfy you? Do I really?'

'Oh no! Here we go again, the good old monastic doubting mind.'

'I can't help it.'

'Do I honestly look dissatisfied? Do I smell dissatisfied? Look at me, I'm laying here positively voluptuous with your love-making and you dare to even think I'm not satisfied? Kiss me this instant Gregory Klein! Accept your punishment and lay back and take it like a man while I devour you!'

And doubt died until the next time under my lips and laughter and the deep intimacy of my finger tips.

'You are so good for me, so good for me. You know, I never realised you were so funny,' he said.

We were finding we had so much in common. Literature, music, rock and baroque, although I had yet to convert him to Bruce Springsteen. Vegetarian food that was simple, nutritious and basically raw. Big, fast motorbikes. Interrelated views on religion and politics, not that either of us were overly interested in the latter, and refreshingly mutual ideas on what was peace and what was pleasure. He could skate, I couldn't. I could ride horses, he couldn't. We vowed to teach each other some day when there was more time, when we were less obsessed with each other. Would it ever happen?

Then it was my turn.

'Tell me truly. Do you have any regret at leaving the monastery? Have you felt any remorse? Do you feel any remorse?'

He closed his eyes, sitting silent and still. Ānando again even in jeans, considering carefully before he answered.

'No, I have no regret whatsoever at leaving. I have never for one moment regretted the time I spent in the monastery. Certainly I don't feel it was a

16

waste of time. I'm sorry for any pain my method of leaving may have caused but then there was no other way as things were. I have no desire to be a monk again. It would have been very different I think if I had no sense of purpose, if I didn't think we had a purpose. But I feel that we have something to do in this world together, you and I, and I want to find out what it is.'

'Promise me you will tell me if you change your mind in any way?'

'Of course. I couldn't help but tell you.'

Even our biological rhythms were in accord. We played and cooked and walked and packed in a constantly encircling dance, weaving one around the other in a perfect harmony punctuated only very frequently with a lingering kiss. We continued the formal observance of ritual at meals, preparing them together, laying the plates and cups out carefully on the grass, saying grace before we ate. Always, from the very first meal, making the practice of offering the other the first spoonful of food from the plate.

'Holy Ones, bless us and keep us safe,

keep us healthy,' he would add with a suggestive grin,

'Protect us and guide us,

continue to open our hearts to each other

in love and devotion,

and to all Beings.

Sadhu.'

It was still natural for me to offer him each bowl of food. It was a gesture of respect I wanted to continue, enjoying the formality and grace of it. He deserved nothing less. Morning and evening meditation went to the winds in the interests of making love but I did remember to set out the little shrine at the back of the tent every time we set up camp. After twenty years of men and robes he was intrigued to be surrounded by female underwear, as if two or three pairs of my wisps of knickers washed and hanging on rails or in corners represented being surrounded. He had been accustomed to being waited on for the last ten years so he was quite happy to give me his laundry too and when it had dripped enough, to lay it across the back shelf of the car to dry in the sun as we drove along.

A single cloud crossed my horizon one evening while he was standing in a call box talking to his mother and elder sister in America. He wanted me to be with him but as the conversation went on, the tone of his happiness reminded me of all that I had left unsaid in England and never could say. Not wanting to infect him with my wretchedness, I excused myself and went to sit on a step on the shadows of a building nearby.

Only Greg knew exactly why I had walked out on that last misery of a marriage. No one else did and it was not a subject that I cared to air in the general mêlée of views and opinions. How was it for my children now? They might be grown up but it's still tough when your mother's name is on too many lips and few of them with compassion. I would be able to talk to Gudrun for a little while longer but there would be no picking up the phone and talking to the boys again for a very long time while they were living where they were and with whom. Their father and I had always remained friends since our divorce but now a second and acrimonious divorce loomed on the horizon, unfortunately unavoidable. Even though it was I who was the petitioner, by my own choice and my absence, I would go undefended in the public eye.

With that and my latest escapade, it was inevitable that I would be the target of a lot of anger, jealousy and suspicion from all sides. My beloved was the Ajahn, controversial but much loved. Already I was designated 'the blonde' who had driven the car. The situation would have to be left to scream itself out and considering the fragility of our emotional reserves, of the two of us it was better that the worst of the antipathy be directed at me rather than at Greg, or 'my Lord' as I called him now.

'You have to call me that in front of my mother,' he said laughing.

'Why?'

'Because being American she will so appreciate it!'

'I might be calling you something else by then.'

'Well as long as it's appreciative I don't mind,' he said.

'Could it ever be anything else, my Lord?' I said, with a mocking, loving little bow and a kiss.

'I want us to have rings,' he said. 'Before we go back to England if that's possible. I think it's important to have them as a token of our commitment to one another and it's important to me to have you wearing a ring that I have given you. Is there enough in the budget to buy two gold rings? I have no idea what they cost. I have never bought any before.'

'I should think we can afford them as long as they are plain and without stones and as long as we don't buy them in Switzerland. We could go to the nearest town in France for a night and see what they have there. We may even find you some shoes as well.'

'I've always wanted a gold ring. Do you mind wearing yours on the third finger of your left hand?' he said.

It was one of those potentially difficult moments when any hesitation on my part would blight his newly blossoming self-respect.

'No. Not if it comes from you,' I said.

— ✳ —

On Thursday, June 11th, the fifth day of this lifetime of love, we headed towards France, stopping in a lay-by beside a river to prepare our simple midday meal of bread, cheese and vegetables. The road was quiet for the time of day. Nevertheless we sat beside the car facing the water that came rushing with all the cold urgency of the mountains melting into summer. We had started out early and we were hungry. We were always hungry. Sometimes for food, always for love and love diverted us again with the salad half chopped and the cheese still sweating in a polythene wrapper. But love on gravel is rarely prolonged and reluctantly we laid it aside in favour of food.

18

'I have a request,' he said.

Something in his tone made me look up, a shade of the brevity of Ānando. Instinctively I moved back a little from him.

'Yes?'

'I want you to floss your teeth every day.'

'But I don't do it on principle. You know that. We've talked about it before.'

'Well, I want you to begin.'

'But it's disgusting! I can remember watching the children's father standing in the bathroom flicking food and tartar at the mirror and I vowed never to repeat it. I have never forgotten watching you flossing in public after a Dana! It's like picking your nose, something you only do in the loo if you have to do it. How can that be virtuous conduct in a monk?'

'But I want you to always be beautiful and you won't be beautiful if your teeth fall out.'

'They won't fall out! I clean them very well twice a day and if they do fall out then I'll have a mouthful of crowns!'

'That's something else I don't agree with. I've been watching how you clean your teeth and you don't do it properly. I've been meaning to talk to you about it for some days.'

'What do you mean? I went to the hygienist only a month before I came here and he said my teeth were in a very clean condition. What are you talking about?'

'I don't agree. I don't approve of your method.'

'What do you know about "method"?'

'My brother-in-law is a dentist and I've talked to him at length about it.'

'What the hell does he know about my teeth?'

'You know very well what I mean and please do not use colourful language. It offends me and degrades you.'

'No, I don't know what you mean. Yours are the only teeth I have ever seen in a human being that would look better in a horse, all worn away and flat on the top. How dare you be sitting on your "objections" to me and not saying so at the time. That is degrading, degrading to you and completely dishonest. This relationship is either straight down the line or it doesn't exist!'

'How have we managed to go from a simple request about dental hygiene to an ultimatum in a few short minutes?'

'Look at your method. Five minutes ago we were making love and then suddenly in the middle of profound passion you start talking teeth! Gregory Klein, flowers in one hand and a rock in the other! You always were the master of bad timing. I was right! If you have criticism, don't sit on it! Come on out with it and don't nit-pick! I wouldn't dream of doing that to you. You're you and I love you just as you are. Damn you!'

I exploded into tears that came cascading down my cheeks, running down my chin, completely uncontrollable. It was as though a dam of long pent up emotion had burst to flood a dark valley of shadow in my spirit. I should have been desperately splashing about in my river of tears trying to retrieve my dignity but it didn't seem to matter any more. Through the blur I saw him still sitting beside me with the cup in his hand that he had picked ready to make tea. He looked so lost. His brows knit in little lines of worry and perplexity, watching me, uncertain what to do next. He touched my cheek.

'I love you,' he said. 'I can't bear to see you cry.'

But I was locked into a convulsion of sobbing I had no control over.

'Mali? Speak to me?'

I couldn't, the words wouldn't come.

'Mali! Make the tea!'

That was Ãnando by intention and two years of conditioning moved me, broke the forced inflexibility of grief. The water in the pot shook and spilt as I picked it up.

'Mali, please believe me, I'm so sorry. I had no idea you would react so strongly. I never meant to hurt you.'

'I know you didn't.'

It was true. Neither of us had been prepared for such a storm. Tears, seeping in at the corners of my mouth, stung bitter on my tongue as I spoke. I wiped what was left of my face and washed out my mouth with the remains of the water. From somewhere I found a smile.

'I'm sorry too. It was all so sudden and so unexpected. I suppose I can't associate making love with criticism.'

'But I had no intention of criticising you. I was only trying to help you.'

'Well, maybe you did but in a different way. I wish it hadn't had to be so painful. I wasn't prepared for it. I suppose I have kept too much to myself for too long.'

'You do have beautiful eyes,' he said softly.

'Hardly, as they are now.'

'Even as they are now. Beautiful blue and wet with tears.'

'No one has ever said that to me before. Not ever.'

'I can't believe it.'

'I can't really believe you. I think you are just saying it to be nice to me. I appreciate your intention but I hate false compliments.'

'It's no false compliment. You have beautiful eyes and a beautiful face. You are a beautiful woman.'

I didn't know what to say or how to respond. This was unknown territory to me. I told myself it was just love talking, or lust. I didn't mind which but really I didn't know how to accept compliments. I never had known. I could give them endlessly and sincerely but all compliments were false when they were directed at me unless they were from the neck downwards and preferably only concerned with intelligence and efficiency levels. Anything involving face or awareness was just too personal.

'You will learn to believe me,' he said.

— ✳ —

Mont Blanc was invisible under cloud as we drove down into Chamonix to find a campsite in a field surrounded by a continual clink-clonking of sheep and bells. Being almost devoid of tourists at that time of year, there would be no queuing for showers. There was still time to shop after we had put up the tent and the Holy ones were with us. We found a pair of beautifully made, soft leather boots for Greg and two rings. Eighteen carat gold, not quite plain enough to be confused with standard wedding rings but the only two in the shop that we liked and miraculously exactly the correct sizes. Completely under the spell of Greg's smile, the assistants wrapped them side by side in their little white presentation case with paper and ribbons. With the package carefully laid in his innermost pocket, I was propelled with all speed back to the tent with only a brief stop for provisions on the way.

We didn't put the rings on immediately. He wanted to make a ceremony and we had the faint memory of pain from earlier on to alleviate and heal with our special caring tenderness, our intimate concern. Consequently we fell asleep forgetting the ceremony. That night, for the first time, he started grinding his teeth again as he slept. The sound woke me just before two o'clock. He woke seconds later to my lips and warm kisses as the best way I could think of to stop him. Then he remembered the rings and switched on the torch to find the package. Two small circles of polished gold lay side by side in the box and almost shyly he picked up the smaller one and slid it on to the ring finger of my left hand. My first real gold ring. I had had only silver and white gold before. His own went on to the third finger of his right hand.

'I will change it to the left when we have a formal ceremony of some kind. Maybe if we get married,' he said.

That was a long time away and nothing we would be pressured into. In some ways it was a relief to have the divorce standing in the way. We could not be tempted into anything too soon in the wake of passion. We had five weeks on the road in Iceland to live through yet. I knew the country, he did not, and I knew that it would be there that the test would come. At the end of it we would either say goodbye or be forever in love.

We woke to the sound of rain pattering on the fly sheet. A quick dash across the field to the toilet block revealed a morning of mist and heavy cloud. We brewed up in the tent and had breakfast in bed, wearing our Icelandic sweaters and curled into our wonderfully warm double sleeping bag. We lay listening to the rain, sipping hot chocolate and hot milk, examining our rings that were intentionally very similar but not quite the same. He held my hand out to look at it from all angles, twisting the thin band around my finger, at once proprietorial and very pleased with what he saw.

'It's just what I had in mind,' he said. 'Elegant, not too plain. I want to cover your fingers with rings and your wrists with bangles and –'

'And my neck with chains and my fingers dripping diamonds.' I couldn't resist interrupting. 'Will I be able to walk under the weight my Lord?'

21

'We may have to fix up some kind of a winch to help you along. Meantime we'll have to find a way to raise the cash to buy it all. The VA cheque might be enough to live on but it wasn't designed to accommodate a life of luxury.'

'So we'll have to write the book.'

'Oh that. I can't think that anyone would be interested in it.'

'We shall see. I'll let it float around my mind for a while and see what comes up. We have a title, that must mean something.'

'You mean you have a title.'

I reached into the back of the tent for some water to rinse the cups and then snuggled down with him into the bag.

'Gregory?'

I found I always used his full name, pronounced with a slight softening of the r's and lilting intonation, when there was something important to discuss.

'Yes?'

'Given that discipline is essential to the learning process, giving it structure and form,' I said, hesitating a little.

'Ye–es?'

'Why don't we have our own version of the Monastic Code, adapting the vinaya for our Sangha of Two? Cut out the "ye shall not lust bits" and take what is appropriate for us?'

'Why not? It's a good idea but I'm glad you said that about the lust. It would be impossible for me to live with you without making love to you.'

'I deeply appreciate that form of impossibility.'

'So what do you have in mind?' he asked, evidently interested.

'I don't really know other than an agreed list of rules which we endeavour to live by,' I replied.

'We could begin the list formally with the Five Precepts and go on from there,' he said. 'But not too many rules and they must all be negotiable.'

'That will depend on the circumstances,' I said grinning. 'So what will it be then, beloved Ajahn?'

'The precepts of course, killing nothing, stealing nothing, complete fidelity. Love and sexuality exclusive to us and no other in thought, word and deed. Complete trust, absolute loyalty. No lies, no colourful language,' he added with a sideways grin at me.

'And obviously no drink or drugs, thank goodness,' I said. 'I'm so glad we don't smoke.'

'So am I.'

'Imagine. Then we would have to floss our teeth.'

'I am forgiven?'

'You know you are. You were forgiven before you began. And so, my Lord, we were doing all those already although I obviously have a problem with language. What else?'

22

'After basic morality? Okay, no secrets, no secret action, no secret mail. Never to write anything that cannot be read by the other, never to receive letters without sharing them.'

'That's fine except what about when I want to buy presents for you? Do I ask you for some money and an hour off to go to the shops?'

'Only for that, yes.'

'That will be odd after so many years being the bank.'

'Do you mind being without money?'

'No, I haven't missed it at all so far. I'll tell you if I do. What else?'

'Fundamentally it's all down to good conduct I suppose, an awareness of grace and refinement in how we express ourselves in our relationship and to other people, mindfulness.'

'Mindfulness of relating. I like that. That's where monastic and lay training helps especially with others of the opposite sex. It's very useful to be in the habit of not making full eye contact.'

'Indeed yes. It reassures me too because jealousy is still a problem with me.'

'A lot or a little?'

'A lot more than I care to admit. The more in love I am the worse it gets. I love you so much it scares me and jealousy doesn't help. You will have to help me with it and be patient with me.'

'Well, as it all comes from intense love for me, it has to be a worthy cause. I will do my best, my Lord.'

'And do you mind if I tell you what to wear sometimes? I want you to be perfect and I would enjoy buying you clothes and perfume.'

'No problem. I would love some perfume as long as I can help choose. Let's make a deal. I'll be responsible for your appearance and you will be responsible for mine. After all as we are going to be looking at each other twenty-four hours a day, seven days a week, why not go for perfection? It is evident that I am brilliant at buying clothes for you but I hate buying them for me. It would eliminate a major problem in my life if you did it for me.'

He disconnected his left hand from my anatomy and held it out for me to shake on it, his right hand being temporarily redundant at the end of an arm that was securely wound around as much of me as it would cover. When we finally got up to shower and pack, I took a length of dental floss with me to the Ladies shower room.

Our vinaya evolved slowly over the following weeks. He looked after the day-to-day running of our lives, the money, the food, correspondence, travel arrangements. My 'witch's nose', as he put it, determined where we stayed and when we travelled. We always did everything together, consulting as we went along but his was always the last word. That evening we found sunshine and swings in a children's playground on the north-eastern shore of Lake Geneva and had one last night in Room Ten in the hotel in Gruyères before facing England again. There wasn't a lot to say as we checked in at Berne airport. Neither of us were looking forward to going. I handed him all that I had left of the English money.

'There's about five pounds and eighty pence,' I said, forgetting that, although he had lived in England for so long, he was completely unfamiliar with handling the coinage.

'Where are the bills?' he asked, bewildered.

'I'm sorry, I completely forgot. Now we have become accustomed to ruining the pockets of our jeans with a handful of coins that includes this, the newer and heavier pound coin,' I said, picking one out of his hand to demonstrate.

Our arrival was a very well-kept secret. Only Gudrun and my sister Elaine would be at Gatwick to meet us. With an hour to kill before the flight was due to be called, Greg had the assistant in the Duty Free store bring out all her perfume samples so that I could be sprayed and dipped until my arms and hands were a sickly smudge of smells that had to be well scrubbed in the Ladies room to ensure that neither of us would feel nauseous on the plane. We finally settled on a bottle of Opium as a beginning and so I arrived in England ringed, perfumed and beloved, very different from the taut apparition struggling with so much hand luggage that she almost missed the plane eight days before.

— ✖ —

Greg walked into my mother's little house grin first, guaranteeing him immediate and lasting love and sending my mother rushing to her formidably steaming collection of pots and pans on the stove, doing what she knew best when presented with the handsomest and most singular prospective son-in-law she had ever been expected to meet. Which was of course to feed him. Gillian and Mike, her husband, had left a car for us and two days later with the first of the divorce papers signed and delivered, we set off for South Wales and six days in a caravan in a field. It had been one of my quick compromise ideas when all plans had been so abruptly brought forward and I had to find some way of filling in a week before we could fly to Iceland. With some trepidation we drove west down the motorway wondering what we would find; the prospect of a caravan in South Wales had nothing of the romantic overtones of a honeymoon in the mountains in Switzerland. As it happened my random choice was well chosen and we had six delicious nights, early evenings and lingering mornings in a huge bed of pillows and quilts on the floor of a large caravan parked singly in a neatly mown and fenced little field next to a farm.

We spread ourselves out in the space, happy to be very domestic once we had set up the shrine and JBJ on a room divider and burnt some of our favourite Emerald incense to make the place ours. It was fun to lay out the nicest plates and glassware for meals, to spend an hour necking on the double seat for dessert and then to wash up in a sink with instant hot water instead of balancing a gas burner and a bowl at the back of the tent. Greg started to teach me the warm-up exercises for Tai Chi and we took long walks on the nearby beach. The sea was too cold for anything more than a quick paddle but one afternoon the sun burst through the Welsh mists long enough to inspire us to sunbathe among the rocks. Greg took off his shirt and jeans and with no one in the immediate vicinity, I was quite happy to lay out in panties and very little else until a hand came out and stopped me before I got beyond my sweater.

'You are not taking that off here,' he said.

'Why not? There's no one around.'

'There are some kids over there by that rock,' he said.

I had barely noticed them.

'They won't see me. I want to sunbathe.'

'I'm serious. You are not taking your sweater off here.'

I could feel irritation rising. Suddenly, unexpectedly, irrationally he was so much like my father.

'Why?'

'Because you're with me and no woman with me takes her clothes off in public.'

'I'm only going to sunbathe between the rocks like millions before me and millions to come after. What do you really mean? Am I never to be allowed to sunbathe?'

'You are never to take your clothes off in public.'

'How can I sunbathe then and promote this tan you are always going on about?'

'Only in absolute privacy.'

'So what will happen in Greece? Am I to be the only woman who is covered from head to foot on the beach while everyone else is practically naked? I can't see you sitting on a beach in a shirt!'

'I repeat. You will not take your clothes off in public while you are with me.'

A biting, bitter anger silenced me, compulsively twisting my hands and savagely recalling my personal vow to me about the freedom I had since abandoned so heedlessly. Ānando sat motionless beside me on the sand, becoming Greg again as swiftly as he saw the anger pass.

'You came very near, didn't you?' he said.

'Yes. You are not the only one with a temper Gregory Klein. My lower self sees you as completely unreasonable and dictatorial. At the same time my higher self tells me that your attitude is a direct result of your monastic training and your attachment to me. I'm yours, you have exclusive rights to me and my person and it is neither appropriate nor necessary for me to take my clothes off where other men may see me. Thus speaks higher self, damn it!'

'Thank you.'

'But I can't, absolutely I can't go to Greece veiled like a Muslim! I'm not a nun! Please? Please!'

I was tragic, he was laughing and gathering me up like a wailing child to be soothed and softened in his arms.

'You are definitely not a nun! We will make sure we always find secluded places where we can take our clothes off. I promise.'

'Are you really sure you really mean that?'

'I'm really sure I really do.'

Already he knew everything there was to know about me that I could think of except the one thing I had not yet found the courage to confess. I was nearly forced into it the following day when we went to the local swimming pool but he was so enthusiastically ploughing up and down length after length that he didn't take a lot of notice of the fact that I wasn't really going anywhere at my end of the pool. The truth was that he was a dolphin in water and I was scared white and witless at the idea of being out of my depth. I could float well enough but I could hardly be described as a swimmer. Earlier on during the Spring, Gillian had asked me what was I going to do about it? Had I told him?

'I'll cross that bridge when I have to,' I said, already dreading it.

I left the pool in Haverford West feebly complaining that the water was too cold compared with Icelandic pools and too chlorinated and that it was impossible to enjoy myself in a place like that. I had no admiration either for myself or my excuses but I just couldn't tell him the truth about the last great horror in my life. I had educated myself systematically over almost thirty years to come to terms with my fear of fire, riding horses had taken care of my fear of heights but despite an occasional determined bravado splashing about in the sea, I still had a major problem with water. And I had promised him that in Iceland where there was a campsite there was also a swimming pool. Clearly I was on a collision course for the 'bridge' and I felt miserably sick at the thought of it.

Chapter Three

He told me to bewitch him but I never set out to do that. I was simply myself, at last myself, free from all facade, no more acting. If he couldn't accept that there would be no relationship. I had told him how Iceland affected me and how it might affect him. I was taking him to an unstable little chunk of volcanic rock perched under the ice-cap at the top of the world, where the elements are passionately alive, every breath an inhalation of their raw intensity that in turn overwhelms every nerve and cell in the body and cuts through the psyche like a knife. There is no concession for indifference. It is impossible to travel there and leave unchanged. You either love it or you hate it.

We landed in broad daylight just after eleven in the evening, June 23rd, flying north out of the gathering darkness in England into the midnight sun. He was fascinated to see the sun still slanting in through the windows of the plane at ten thirty but the island was covered in cloud when we landed at Keflavík. Lóa was standing waiting for us in her usual place on the other side of the glass partition and it was with some amusement that I watched her face as I introduced Greg to her. Ten years older than I, we had been 'adopted sisters' since 1981 and she knew me as well as anyone knew me. It was always important to her that the girls in her family and among her friends should be with men who were 'of a good family' and that meant no drunkenness, no divorces, honest and employed; for some reason that assessment had always included me. Greg met her look equally and directly and passed the test and when she knew that he was four years older than me, he was perfect.

The sky was overcast and the wind colder than I expected as we carried our packs to the car.

'How is the weather?' I asked, always the first question in Iceland.

'It is colder than usual,' she replied. 'It has not been a good summer.'

My heart sank. The year before it had been so hot that all the population in Reykjavík had been sunbathing and imagining they were in Spain. We pulled our sweaters out of the packs and drove away from the airport towards Hafnarfjördur, following the almost empty road into a lunar landscape of ominous grey. The distant mountains cut like dark teeth against the skyline. It was all new and exciting to Greg but I could only think that we had a minimum of four consecutive weeks in a tent with this grim prospect of icy wind and rain. I couldn't trust it not to snow! But in Iceland the weather can change completely in an hour and I told myself it would be better tomorrow.

Maybe foreknowledge on the part of the weather gods kept the sun hidden in cloud, or perhaps it was compassion, so at least the elements weren't laughing too loudly as the last of my dreadful secrets came to light the next morning when we went for an early swim at the local pool. I stalled by going to the soak pots first, ostensibly needing to soak England away in the bubbling hot, slightly sulphurous water. But no one can soak forever and Greg couldn't wait to get into the large, deep, almost deserted pool. I was doing my best to make at least a show of floating when he surfaced beside me, his face all radiance and demanding I follow him down to the far end.

'I'm fine here, really I am,' I said.

'But Mali, you've hardly moved. You're not even half way down the length of the pool.'

Oh help.

'Gregory, I'm slightly nervous out of my depth.'

'But I'll be with you.'

'I'm a little bit nervous now in case the water is already too deep.'

'Of course it isn't,' he said and dived.

A fraction of a second later he grabbed both my ankles and pulled them down to touch the bottom. He was right, I was not out of my depth but the shock made me lose balance and go under, completely out of control and momentarily completely out of my mind. I fought for the surface, grabbing for anything I could lay my hands on until my fingers closed around his arm, digging in my nails in case he tried the same trick again.

'Mali! Mali baby!'

He was looking at me in amazement.

'You really are afraid aren't you? I only meant to show you where the bottom was.'

My teeth were chattering so hard I couldn't speak. He lifted me half out of the water and took me to the side rail where I clung frantically like a damp and desperate mouse.

'I had no idea you were so frightened,' he said. 'Why didn't you tell me?'

'B–because I–I didn't want to–to be such an idiot and if I–I was, I–I only wanted me to know. And that's b–bad enough!'

'You are funny. Don't you trust me?'

'Ye–es but it's difficult for me to trust anyone in this. My father's idea of teaching me to swim when I was a child was to put two fingers under my neck in the sea to support my head and then let go!'

'But you can float. Can you move in the water? Do you know the strokes?'

'No, not properly and when I do try to do them I don't seem to go anywhere unless I do backstroke. I can just about manage that. But I wish I could swim. I can't stand this misery and I feel so forlorn dripping about with the babies in the shallow bit.'

'Would it help if I took you to the deep end? If you held on to me?'

'I don't know. What would I do when I got there? The problem is that I get so frightened I forget to breathe and then I sink!'

And tears mingled with the water dripping from my hair into my eyes. I was shivering and crying and feeling utterly lost.

'Do you trust me Mali?'

'Yes. I have to, don't I? It's in the vinaya,' I sobbed.

'Come on Mali-Mali. Come on now. Let me help you. Hold on to the rail and let me see how you kick.'

I managed several half-hearted attempts and then several stronger ones and then stronger still as shame and temper got the upper hand. After a kiss and some minor adjustments to my feet and knees he left me to practise at the side of the pool. There was no mention of the deep end again.

— ✳ —

He persuaded Lóa to drive us back to Keflavík to the US Base to buy jeans and waterproof gear and, having successfully concluded his first serious foray into his military privileges, we drove over the mountains to Thingvellir where the first parliament had met beside the lake over a thousand years before. Lóa and her husband Birgir were building a summer house near to the south-western shore of the lake and we were invited to stay with them for a couple of days before we began our travelling. My worst fears were temporarily realised when we drove into a snowstorm as we crossed the mountains.

'I don't believe it! It is snowing!' said Lóa, peering over the wheel into the swirling maelstrom ahead of us.

'Gregory, I promise you faithfully, this is not usual,' I said.

But five minutes later the weather had cleared again and we saw the billowing white steam from the power station and then the lake stretching out in front of us as we came winding down the road with Lóa and me hard at it, doing our customary news exchange which was a necessary preliminary to any stay in Iceland.

'I am taking you to Elfa's summer house,' she said. 'She has given me permission to use it so that you can be guests while our own house is still building.'

I was very pleased because I knew from past experience that there was a big Jotull wood-burning stove in the middle of the house. No matter how cold it might be outside, for two days at least we would be warm. There was plenty of wood and in half an hour the house was warm and we had made a wonderful bed on the sleeping platform in the roof which made up for the lack of sunshine outside.

I had invited him to the Land of the Midnight Sun but all it had to offer us then was a generous helping of midnight cloud, sat like a sombre lid on the roof of the world, unmoved by the cold, persistent keening of the wind. Before we fell asleep a little box appeared on my pillow and a pair of sparkling earrings fresh from the Base were fastened to my ears.

— ✳ —

We made the most of the two days to acclimatise and to re-organise our packs before setting up the tent in the campsite in a village south of Mount Hekla, the cloud lifting just enough to show the black and white of the snow-streaked volcano, mercifully asleep, before the rain came down and put an end to any desire to go walking. We went swimming instead, Greg taking care to punctuate my second lesson with unceasing kisses and encouragement.

We had bus tickets designed to take us in one direction all the way around the island and the next day we began making our way south and east towards the National Park at Skaftafell. The weather improved as we went along and two days later the sun was shining as we found a place for our tent in the large camping ground under the glacier. What had threatened to be an endurance test of continuous cold suddenly brightened into exhilarating pleasure. Both born at the transcendental times when night and day are one, he exactly at the point of sunset and I exactly at the point of sunrise, neither of us thrived without the sun. When it came rising over the gleaming majesty of the vast Vatnajökull ice-cap, we were laughing and playing and breathing in great gulps of air that went to our heads like champagne.

Always in Iceland there have been times when I have felt my blood stinging into new life in my veins and he felt it too, an almost dizzily exhilarating joy at being alive and together and in love. We found Svartifoss, the black waterfall, and took pictures of each other in front of it, JBJ on a rock beside it, Greg spread-eagled behind it. Then back to the tent for a huge meal of soup and rice and bread and cheese before curling up deep in the sleeping bag. We slept smothered in sweaters to be safe from the penetrating cold that always came creeping from the glacier as the sun crawled along the northern horizon for the brief two hours designated to the night. The torch remained redundant in the top of Greg's pack. It had been hard for him to envisage the reality and the freedom of travelling in a land where the sun never completely sets.

'What is it like here in the winter?' he asked.

'It is neither as dark or as cold as you might think, although we would probably find it depressing to be here for the whole winter,' I said. 'If we ever get rich, maybe we could come here for a couple of weeks and you could teach me to ski.'

We started out early next morning to do the longest trek wearing shorts and tee-shirts, stopping to inscribe huge hearts in the snow patches that still hung in the shadows and listening in wonder at the distant booming echoing from somewhere far above us as another chunk of the glacier came crashing down towards the sea, bringing with it rain and mist and a soaking, weary afternoon before the sun gleamed again into a golden evening.

— ✳ —

It was raining in Höfn when the bus left us, with most of our fellow travellers from Skaftafell, to scramble for a place in the campsite that was appreciably smaller than the one we had just left. With barely room to walk between the tents, we left our wet gear to drip under the fly sheet and settled down to sleep wearing too many clothes and acutely aware of every breath in every tent around us. Feeling uncomfortable and exposed, I was mostly interested in sleep and silence after the swiftest and stealthiest love-making we had ever accomplished but for some reason he needed to talk. I composed myself to listen, completely unprepared for what was to come.

'I want to tell you that any doubts I had about you, about your relating to me, are completely gone,' he said.

'Thank you. I'm very glad to hear it. So you can believe me now?'

'Yes. And I can forgive you.'

'Forgive me? For what?'

'For your past, for the relationships you had before.'

Something nudged the edge of my memory. A previously unfathomable comment in that almost unbearable diary of pain labelled 'love-letters' he had sent me regularly as he walked his final pilgrimage as a monk across France and into Switzerland. So that's what he had been hanging on to all these weeks! I knew there had been something but I could hardly believe what I was hearing now that it was coming out. In tone and context he was once more the Ajahn sat before the Buddha-rupa, granting absolution to a novice who had just been seen stealing cheese. And what was my crime?

'I don't understand what you are talking about and whatever it is, I don't want to talk about it either here or now,' I said. 'Let's go to sleep. If there is anything more to be said we'll say it in the morning.'

He was quite happy with that, having found his own peace with whatever had been on his mind. It had the opposite effect on me. I fell asleep with the conversation uppermost in my mind and woke up with it screaming in the middle of my head. The bus came early, leaving no time to talk until we were standing at the bus-stop, huddled beside a wall out of the wind.

'Did I understand you correctly? You have forgiven me for my previous relationships?'

'Yes. It's a great relief to me that I have been able to do so.'

I stared at him in disbelief.

'You have forgiven me for my relatively unsensational past?'

'Yes.'

'So what about your past, so gloriously embellished with prostitutes and one-night stands? I can't begin to match it! I didn't even do drugs and I never went with a tenth as many men as you did women! You have forgiven me because I wasn't a forty-one year old virgin when I came to your bed? What use would I have been to you then, Gregory Klein? It was only my compassion and experience that helped you in those first days and you know it!'

'I agree but my jealousy can't bear to think of you having been with anyone but me.'

'I don't believe what I'm hearing! What gives you the edge on purity?'

'I think my twenty years of monastic practice may have something to do with it.'

'Twenty years of suppression! How can you be so arrogant? You never in all that time transcended your sexual energy and well you know it!'

In that moment I had to leave him. I had to get away from him. I wanted him out of my air-space and the vinaya could go to the winds. For once I didn't care if I was rude to him.

'I'm going to the Post Office with the letters. I'll be back in ten minutes.'

'But the bus will be leaving soon.'

'Not for another quarter of an hour! Make them wait for me!'

I could feel him watching me as I walked up the road. Anger and hurt fought an overwhelming misery at already being apart from him. It was ridiculous! He was just a few yards down the road and already I was missing him. I could hardly bear to admit it to myself.

As I came back, there he was standing by the bus, the packs at his feet ready for loading and with that look, those little lines of anxiety between his brows that he had unconsciously designed to melt me. I walked straight past him and into the bus, trying to hang on to something of a justifiable rage and failing entirely.

'I can only say I must really love you,' I said as he sat down beside me.

'I'm so glad you do,' he said. 'Don't ever forget or send me away. Do you forgive me?'

'How can I not?' I said, as two arms encircled me and a cheek came to rest on my shoulder.

'Sometimes, Gregory, you amaze me! You are a beast! You have such a unique capacity to be completely unreasonable!'

'But you have to admit I'm cute and that you love me. Don't you?'

'For my sins I'm realising I totally adore you and sometimes I really don't know why.'

'Don't ever stop.'

'I'll love you forever although I can't think what good it will do me.'

'It'll get you an endless supply of sugar-free gum.'

'I don't chew gum, thank you.'

The roar of the engine as the bus pulled away discouraged further conversation. The little town slipped back into the cloud that closed in all around us. Sheep ran scattering to either side of the road and for the thousandth time I wondered why so few of them were ever killed. I snuggled down against him enjoying his warmth, the smell of his skin and aware once again of being grateful, as I had been already many times before and would be again, that I had known him so well as Ānando. He had no intention of offending me. He only wanted to share what he considered to be an important insight into his relating to me, against which any pain on my part was only a passing thing.

Later I brought the subject up again as we lay snug in the tent in a blissfully deserted camp site, curled up around each other, the safest place to talk.

'There is one thing I need to understand in this forgiveness business of yours,' I said. 'Does it have anything to with the fact that you haven't yet told your mother about my two divorces?'

'No, of course not.'

'Then why do I get this feeling that you are ashamed of me?'

'Look at me Mali. Read my lips. I-am-not-ashamed-of-you, I-have-never-been-ashamed-of-you, not in the least. I wouldn't be here with you now if I was. I don't trust my mother's Catholic conditioning, that's all and that's why I haven't told her.'

'I'm beginning to dread the day when you do.'

'It'll be all right.'

'Don't you think you may have misjudged her? Things have changed a lot in twenty years.'

'You are probably right but it's me that needs to be sure. It's my problem, not yours. Don't waste time on it.'

'I've had twenty years of practice as well you know, bringing up three children and that is equally demanding. I've never had my freedom. I've never had any time to be myself and to find out who and what I am. Basically you only gave up sex. You enjoyed a greater freedom of spirit. You never truly renounced while you still wanted this, our relationship, me. You never had to worry about where the next meal was going to come from or how you would be able to afford to buy the children's winter clothes. That monastic stuff about uncertainty is purely theoretical while Thailand and Thai culture exists. Of course monks don't have to worry about money. They are surrounded by it.'

'But that support could come to an end at any time. Who knows what will happen?'

'But I know that the average family provider is more likely to lose his or her job at any time in the world we live in now. That is a far greater uncertainty. If you needed any material things you only had to get your mother to dip into your pension. So you had the vinaya but we all have a vinaya, children are a vinaya in themselves. You were following your spiritual aspirations in a totally sympathetic environment while I, like so many others, had to adapt mine around the demands and needs of three children and the frustration of living with people who didn't understand what I needed or what I was trying to do. Just giving up sex isn't practice and I know it is possible to practise in the lay life. Life is practice once you're aware of it. That was always one of Ãnando's virtues. You were never overmuch in the habit of trotting out that rubbish about having no hope of enlightenment unless you are a monastic.'

'I agree.'

'You walked out of the monastery but you haven't given up your hope of enlightenment, have you?'

'Indeed not. But can't you see the value and the importance of what I was trying to tell you? I have absolutely no more doubts about you. Don't you

33

understand? Neither of you nor your intention. I can still doubt my own worthiness of you but my mind is completely free from any doubt of you now and it is important for me to be able to tell you, to confirm it with you. In all of three and a half weeks I've made love with you, laughed with you, cried with you, played with you and I'm completely certain of you. It's no longer a question of belief, I know you are mine. Can't you see how important that is for me?'

When I thought about it more rationally, knowing where he was coming from, I could see that it was equally important for me. Mine had been a very different approach. I had set out to be certain of him without question from the beginning, not because of an excess of virtue or naiveté, rather as a practice, a commitment equal to the extremity of my conduct in helping him to leave the monastery. Likewise I was aware that a large part of this trust was built around his years as a monk and that these early weeks were critical to our commitment. If there was anything worth working on, I was determined to do my best with it. At the same time if he found our situation unworkable or fundamentally unsatisfactory I wanted us to part before the pain could become too lasting or too deep. As I told him, my 'pain-pot' had long been filled to overflowing and I couldn't take much more. But it seemed I couldn't trust myself not to over react to Ānando when he appeared. That was my conditioning and I would have to learn not to be immediately arming my guns in defence.

We continued north through the Eastern fjords, carefully budgeting our way and always just ahead of the rain but with the weather improving as we went. The bus made frequent stops to pick up people at the more remote farms, to collect the mail from the villages. We found a wonderful pool at Egillsstadir, all at one accessible depth that made no extra demands on my miseries.

'I'm fed up with being such a drip!'

'Mali, this is a drip-free zone and you are doing very well. You only cry on average once every other day now. Please be kind to yourself.'

'I've never cried so much in my life. I can't believe it! But you teach best what you most need to learn, my Lord. Remember that when your particular brand of self-disparagement threatens to interrupt our love-making.'

He smiled at that.

'I love you.'

'I adore you, horrible man!'

'Why horrible? That's very strong. Please don't call me names, Mali.'

'It's not a name, it's an observation. Because here I am in love and supposed to be on permanent honeymoon and you are making me face the worst horrors of my life. I'm beginning to think I have no self-worth at all except in your eyes.'

— ❈ —

The black laval deserts of the north always fascinated me. Mile after mile of volcanic wasteland and then past blue-grey boiling mud pools and over pink sulphur mountains to Lake Myvatn, a vast, shallow fresh-water lake teeming with fish and bird life and clouds of tiny, black midges. Fortunately their sole purpose was to feed the fish. They were curious rather than predatory with us and they showed no desire to share the tent so eating was relatively comfortable sitting just inside with the nets zipped tight.

The campsite was full of tents and tour buses but we managed to find a place a little way up the hill above the lava, pitching the tent at an angle to discourage immediate neighbours. It rained all day on Sunday July 5th. Just light rain gently pitter-pattering on the fly sheet but it was the perfect excuse to spend the day in bed, especially when we remembered rather irreverently that it was Ordination Day at Chithurst. So much had happened in such a short time.

From the comfort of our warm and established environment we saw a tour bus pull up on to the level below us and discharge its cargo of enthusiastic if mostly elderly German tourists, with a pile of tents and luggage, on to the wet grass. For half an hour we watched a frantic struggling with fly sheets and poles until a cluster of uniformly blue rectangles had sprung up around the kitchen wagon. I was glad I was neither elderly, German nor wet just then and turned my attention back to my beloved. He lay stretched out warm and naked with his hands behind his head and a light in his eyes that was only for me.

'My Lord, the horsewoman in me needs to get out the grooming kit.'

'What are you talking about?'

'Well, with every mouthful of food you are fast becoming the most beautiful man I have ever seen.'

'And with every kiss, beautiful woman.'

'But with a few extra tricks I could make you perfect.'

'How?'

'I don't need to put baby oil on your nose or polish your hooves but I think I could make a better job of your fingernails than you do. We are not in the Marines now. You are allowed to have a sliver of nail growth showing. Your hair is too short to cut yet but your rather generous American eyebrows are screaming for attention.'

'What do you want to do?'

'Even them up a little but most of all I want to pull out those few thicker, white hairs that are growing far longer and stronger than the rest.'

'I hope my problems never get any worse! Where is the mirror?'

I handed it to him.

'Won't I have gaps?'

'No. If you look carefully you will see a very respectable growth of soft, dark hair under the white hairs which will look much better.'

'Go ahead, my vanity can take it. Ow! Hey, that hurt!'

'I'm sorry, really I am,' I said, mopping up the blood. 'But already it looks much better. You have to suffer a little to be so beautiful, my Lord.'

He needed the First Aid kit by the time I had finished but he happily admitted that the final result was worth it. Once the skin had healed the operation never had to be repeated. The hair never grew back in the same way again. For an hour I massaged, trimmed, plucked, manicured, turning him this way and that as he lay quiescent, absorbed in pure sensual pleasure.

'What have I done to deserve this?' he said.

'Just had the good sense to fall in love with me,' I said. 'If humanity were categorised in the same way as horses then most men would be gelded. But not you. You would definitely have gone to stud on the strength of your legs alone. I have never seen such wonderful ankles.'

'Mali, please! Some of the things you say amaze me!'

'Gregory, has anyone in your family had cancer?'

'No, not as far as I know. Why?'

'I don't know really. I've just been noticing the glands slightly swollen under your chin and some of the little marks on your skin.'

'Oh, I've always had those. They are nothing to worry about.'

'But maybe we should take more care of them when we go to Greece.'

'I don't think it's necessary. I've never had any trouble with the sun. As you can see, I tan very easily.'

'Yes, it's disgusting. You are the only person I know who can tan in the rain in Iceland.'

I let the slightly uneasy feeling slip back into my subconscious. We had all the possibilities of such a beautiful future together. Why did something in me expect to find him lying unconscious on the floor? He said he had had no re-occurrence of the epileptic symptoms so why was I afraid? And what did I fear? Whatever it was remained nebulous, unnamed and easily forgotten under the compulsive distraction of desire.

Chapter Four

The good weather returned and followed us west. We had four hours to kill in Akureyri between buses. After a relatively weep-free swim we were looking for hot chocolate and somewhere warm to drink it.

'I have to give up eating Toblerone,' he said as we found a table in a nearby coffee shop.

'Why? You have a very satisfactory relationship with it as far as I can see.'

'Yes but it could easily be excessive and I can't tell whether it's monastic conditioning after years of cheese and chocolate or just greed.'

'Does it matter? You don't eat so much.'

'But you can't eat it and I must say I'm very glad you are allergic to sugar.'

'Whatever for? I'm not. When I think of all those wonderful cakes and pastries sitting waiting to be eaten only a few steps behind me, my mouth waters and I hardly know what to do with myself. I love Icelandic pastries! And pancakes like lace stuffed with jam and an inch of cream! Oh, oh, oh!' I was almost slobbering at the thought.

'Exactly! I could never afford you. I would be buying them for you just for the pleasure of giving them to you and then I would have to have some myself and there would be no end to it except that we would both be fat.'

'You might but not me. No matter how much I eat I never put on weight. I'd just be spotty instead.'

'Heaven forbid! But seriously I think it would be a good practice for me only to eat what you eat. You seem to do well on it.'

'Well don't start until we are in Greece. You are still not up to a reasonable weight yet and chocolate is a warming food.'

'Don't let me get fat. Promise me you'll tell me if I do.'

'You'll be able to tell for yourself, my Lord. Your jeans won't fit.'

'Please, please don't let me get that far!'

He was horrified, I was laughing. I couldn't help teasing just a little. It was so wonderful to kiss away his immediate anxiety that to my mind was based on the absurd.

'But I'm so glad you don't drink wine either,' he said.

'Why?'

'Because when I was watching Lóa filling her glass back at the summer house, I found myself thinking I could really get into that. I could almost taste it on my tongue and it would have only been one more step to dope or cocaine.'

'Are you serious?'

'Yes. I can see it in myself still after all these years.'

'Well, all the while you're with me you will never get a chance to test it out.'

'For which I am truly grateful, believe me.'

'Greg, what do you see when you look into a mirror?'

'What do I see? Sometimes I see someone who is tanned and pretty good looking, or so my beloved tells me. Other times all I can see are lines and grey hairs. Like you when you get out your make-up mirror in the morning. Your first comment is invariably "Oh God, what a mess!" But I never see you like that. If I did I would tell you. I see someone warm and wonderful who has just got up after a very satisfactory night in bed with me.'

'That is how I see you. It's interesting, isn't it, how differently we see ourselves.'

'Yes, over-critical and all based on a lack of self-worth. We have to learn to see ourselves truly as the other sees us. Quite a practice. And if I hear many more comments about being a drip when we are swimming, I shall invoke the vinaya and categorise the word "drip" as colourful language.'

'Gregory, you are not kind.'

'I don't agree. On the contrary my intention is never to be anything less than very kind as far as you are concerned.'

How could I say otherwise? He was the nicest human being I had ever had the good fortune to meet. And he loved me. How he loved me!

'Oh, my Mali, you have my heart,' he would whisper, loving me, holding me, drifting with me into sleep. At some time every day I would see him smiling to himself as he recalled the magic of the previous night, anticipating the night to come. Now I knew what it was to feel cherished despite my almost daily tears as I struggled with the swimming and struggled with my feelings over my children.

— ✳ —

In Stykkishólmur, beside a silken sea, at last he experienced the true intensity of the Midnight Sun. Golden in the evening light, it hung glowing over the distant cliffs of the West Fjords. With no wind and not a cloud in the sky we walked around the harbour and through the little fishing town, stopping to watch a football game that was in full swing near the camp site. A tractor could be seen still working the hay in a field at a distant farm.

'Mali, it's amazing! It's eleven thirty! It's supposed to be almost midnight and even the little kids are still outside. I've never seen anything like it before in my life!'

'Now you know why they advertise twenty-four hour golf.'

'Do people come here just to play golf?'

'I believe some do.'

I showed him where we would be sailing in the morning, pointing towards the outline of my favourite mountain chiselled square under the northern skyline across a sea so crowded with tiny islands that no one had ever bothered to count them, or if they had they weren't telling. Iceland is

38

very jealous of its culture and its folklore. They say that every rock and stone has a story. Every other native is a poet, a painter or a mystic when they are not singing with a bottle of Brennivín ready to hand. The image of the old Viking carousing until he collapses has not yet evolved out of the cultural consciousness and manifests to a greater or lesser degree even in the most educated and correct on feast days and public holidays.

Yet all around them the magic of the earth roars and bubbles and tumbles and whispers in the rare mystery of the summer nights, under the crystal clarity of the winter stars and the twisting green-gold luminescence, occasionally, rarely, the red, purple and white of *Aurora Borealis*. How I longed to share that with him. The wonder of the Northern lights shining over the snow. We would have to make time, sometime in all our coming winters in spite of our avowed dedication to the sun, just to experience the Arctic night.

'We have to be here for New Year some day,' I told him. 'No one celebrates New Year quite like the Icelandics and I have never seen it. They say that at midnight the whole of Reykjavík is as bright as day, there are so many fire-works.'

There were two cairns, two piles of stones, that had sat through eleven and ten winters respectively, near the top of the mountain above Hotel Flókalundur in Vatnsfjördur. We climbed steadily, following the old sheep track that led upwards through a sheltered gorge. The air was heady with the perfume of the wild thyme and the scent of the little birch trees that crawled over the rocks and crevices, stunted by the long winters under the crushing weight of deep snow. We could hear the 'Caak, caak' of the ravens hunting high on the mountain. The solitary cry of the Golden Plover, the Lóa, went up as we reached the top. Her wings dipped, she went scurrying over the moss to distract us from her nest.

I and one other had built the cairns and I slowly dismantled them and all that they represented, tumbling the heavier stones down into the gorge and throwing the others as far as I could into the sun and the wind. My Beloved sat comfortably meditating on a great cushion of grey-green-moss, naked as the day he was born to prove that it was possible to get an all over tan in Iceland. He opened his eyes in time to see me pick up the camera.

'Oh no you don't,' he said.

'Oh please? This is one of my favourite places in all the world and you look wonderful and terribly discreet. It helps to be able to sit in the full lotus position at times like this. Be brave, Gregory.'

'But no one, absolutely no one is allowed to see this picture. Do you understand? Can I have it in writing?'

'Later,' I said, pressing the shutter before he had time to change his mind.

Then it was my turn to watch while he built a cairn higher and more slender than the others, more like a stupa in Thailand, to be consecrated with kisses and chanting and then to be left to the mercy of the wind and the weather.

Traditionally Flóki, one of the first settlers in Iceland, spent his first summer fishing and enjoying himself so much in wild and beautiful Vatnsfjördur that he forgot to make hay for his sheep and they all died when the snow came in October. Now there is just the small, single storey hotel half way along the western shore, a few wooden summer houses and two farms and a church beside the quay where the fjord spills out into the sea. We had pitched the tent on a little lawn across the road from the hotel beside the river. There was only one other tent and that didn't appear to be occupied. It was too early to eat when we came down from the mountain and our surroundings too beautiful to spend any length of time in the tent. Greg took off his boots and started limbering up in the middle of the grass.

'This is a perfect place for Tai Chi,' he said. 'Come on. I'll start teaching you the form.'

No one learns Tai Chi in a day and I could feel very self-conscious as I tried to follow his fluidity and grace. But there wasn't a soul to be seen, the sun was shining, so why not? I changed into leggings and came dancing barefoot out of the tent to join him on the grass. We began the warm-up exercises but after the first three movements I was boogying a revved up imitation and humming in time to the beat.

'Come on! Are you intending to do Tai Chi or what?'

Ānando asked the question, Ānando was looking at me as I came to a halt and dropped on to my knees, putting my forehead to the ground three times in gently mocking remorse. It became one of his favourite stories, repeated more times than I can remember because behind me a young hiker had just appeared beside the river, his jaw dropping when he saw me bow and everything about his body language saying 'Where did you get a woman like that? I want one!'

There was a very inviting hot pool among the rocks beside the sea where my Lord and I lay soaking for an hour and more for each of our three mornings in the West Fjords. On our last morning the weather was wonderful and we lay watching for the strange blue light that always appeared around our bodies when the sun lit the water. We were splashing each other, making bubbles with the shampoo and then for some reason we started talking about marriage. We had been together for thirty nine days. How many hours? How many minutes? How many kisses? In this exquisite blending of energy and power the idea of marriage seemed inevitable and comfortable. After all the years a prospect of joy.

'But do I deserve you? Am I worthy of you? Do I deserve such happiness?' he said.

The old war cry coming out of that beautiful mouth that I spent hours tasting, nibbling, outlining in delicate tenderness with the tip of my tongue. I remembered that it was Leap Year. If this didn't convince him, nothing would. I floated towards him to sit directly in front of him, putting my palms together in anjali, the traditional gesture of respect.

40

'Oh my love, my Beloved,' I began, slowly, softly, as tenderly as I knew how. 'Gregory Klein, the most beautiful man I have ever known, I would be honoured if you would be my husband, if you would take me as your wife. To love you and to cherish you, to respect you and to adore you, in sickness and in health, be we disgustingly rich or horribly poor. To walk with you in all the ways of the world, my dear love, until the blue winds of spirit release us into light. Gregory, would you do me the honour of marrying me some day?'

Such a beautiful smile. The tears of happiness glistening on his cheeks said all he needed to say.

'Now you have made me cry,' he said. 'Yes Mali, I will gladly marry you. I will be honoured to have you as my wife. My wife.'

He repeated the word, closing his eyes and smiling, turning it over in his mind and savouring the possibilities, his proprietorial nature instantly satisfied. And the more I thought about it, the more I realised that at last I could be proud to be a wife to this man and proud to bear his name. I would be Mali Klein, Mrs Gregory Klein. Until then I would be just Mali with no other name except by law in Passport Control and in the grimness of the Divorce court.

We walked back to the tent very close, closer than ever if that was possible. We packed up in silence, just smiling. My beloved helped me to adjust my pack, setting the straps straight over my shoulders before I helped him with his. He wasn't happy unless his pack was huge and weighed so much I couldn't lift it. He insisted on carrying all the camping gear and all the rain gear as well as his clothes, leaving me with only my toiletries and clothes and the cheese slicer. I had adamantly refused to eat cheese without one and had insisted on buying it. Greg maintained that it was a completely unnecessary item in the baggage and on principle refused to carry it in with the pots. I made a great show of wrapping it in tissue and storing it in the top of my pack, never daring to fail to produce it at every meal.

— �֎ —

Jules Verne used Snæfellsjökull for his *Journey to the Centre of the Earth*. Dominating the extreme western tip of the Snæfellsness peninsula, at almost four and a half thousand feet high it is a perfect cone volcano capped with a glacier. In Reykjavík on a clear day the glacier can be seen across the bay shining eerily disembodied above the sea, lending credibility to the legends that appoint the mountain as one of the power centres of the earth, akin to the Pyramids of Egypt and the Americas. As such it is visited by magicians and the curious and people with penchant for snowmobiles.

I had only stood at its feet twice before. Once during driving rain and again during driving snow so I never considered I had experienced Snæfellsjökull. The mountain had always seemed intent on forcing me away until maybe the time was right or when I came back hand in hand with the right person. We camped in Ólafsvík on the northern coast determined to climb the mountain and allowing ourselves six full days until we were expected back in Hafnarfjördur, hoping for at least one cloudless day among those six. On the third day, July 18th, one of Lóa's cousins collected us at ten o'clock in the morning from the camp site to drive us in his jeep to the foot of the glacier. He warned us to keep more or less to a straight line up the eastern face to the top and not to veer too far to the south where deep and potentially dangerous crevasses had opened up in the ice in the melting heat of the summer sun.

Of course Greg had to be carrying a pack. At least it was my pack and the smaller of the two but somehow he had managed to fill it in his eternal quest to retain physical fitness. This time he had the rain gear, the cooking stove and tea bags as well as the usual bread, cheese and chocolate.

'We might be glad of a hot drink when we get to the top,' he said.

'Gregory, you're almost British! All we need now are folding chairs and a parasol and we are complete for tea at the summit.'

'I'll leave you to carry the dog,' an obliquely rude reference to JBJ who was as usual peering out of my shoulder bag.

It was a perfect day and easy going at first. Unlike the glaciers in the East, which were more like coarse, frozen tarmac to walk on and misery to fall upon, Snæfellsjökull was covered in clean, hard-packed snow. Dazzlingly white in the sunshine and impossible to look at without good sun-glasses, the aquamarine depths of the ice glistened like a great jewel when the snow was brushed aside. Half way up we were hot and we were glad to put our gloves and scarves in the pack but as we came near to the final climb to the summit, the snow became deeper and softer, not so easy to walk on and the track became much steeper. The edges of the crater at the top project like twin horns into the sky and we were making for the nearest one. As the going got harder, from out of nowhere a cloud appeared and sat exactly on the top of the mountain, enclosing us in it's silence and cold as we struggled through the snow. We stopped and put on the rain gear. For the first time I was nervous. Had Jón said there were crevasses this high? One of the many things Greg and I had in common was the concept of freezing to death on a glacier as an attractive idea but I didn't feel ready for it just then. With a final effort we came to the first of the great horns, Greg climbing gaily to the top, me following behind more warily.

'Come on Mali, we've made it!'

I peered over his shoulder and suddenly realised we were standing on a knife edge of ice that fell away steeply into nothingness under the mist. A crawling terror crept up my spine. I shook convulsively, desperate for something to hold on to.

'Greg, I need to get down from here! Please? Just a little way. Please?'

'Why? We're at the top. Come on, help me make the tea.'

'Please not here! Please, please! I can't see anything and I can't stand on this ridge.'

'What's the matter with you? What's the problem?'

42

'I told you I had vertigo once, didn't I? Well now it has just come back. Please!'

'There's no need to go down. We are perfectly safe here. Trust me.'

'Please, Gregory, please! I'm so frightened!'

'Mali, come here. Sit down beside me and help me get the tea.'

'Please! Oh please! I can't!'

I was nearly screaming.

'Mali! Make the tea!'

For the second and last time in our relationship, Ānando demanded tea and my ingrained obedience overcame the vertigo. I collapsed on to my knees and crawled over the snow to the pack. He lit the stove and set the water to boil while I wept over the bread and the chocolate.

'I hate myself for being such a drip.'

'Mali, this is a drip-free zone! Do you hear me?'

After ten minutes and a mug of hot tea, I had to admit that the glacier was not in imminent danger of collapse and that it was possible almost to relax on an ice ridge. We lit some incense and chanted our thanks to the mountain for our safe passage to the summit and in the hope of a safe return to base.

A few steps down the mountain took us back into brilliant sunshine and once we were back on to the firmer snow, Greg started running and sliding his way down, leaving me a long way behind.

'Hey! Wait for me!' I shouted.

'Come on! Run then!'

He started back towards me.

'I don't know how to! I am not used to snow! I am mostly here in the summertime!'

Why did he always make me feel so inadequate?

'Watch me,' he said and went off skimming over the snow as though he was on skis. He stopped and looked back at me.

'Come on Mali! Try it!'

I took a few steps but I felt stupid and self-critical with him watching me.

'You go on, I'll meet you at the bottom!' I shouted, waiting until he had reluctantly turned away. I tried it again, this time concentrating on every step until I could trust the impetus of movement and in five minutes I was behind him and very pleased with myself. He turned around and almost jumped in astonishment to see me so close.

'So you can do it,' he said.

'I only needed a little time to work it out for myself. That's how I learn and that's how I am approaching the swimming. If you have noticed, every day I go in just a little deeper and then make myself turn on to my back and float as soon as I feel the fear coming back.'

'Yes I have noticed and I am very proud of you, beloved you. Now come on, run with me to the bottom.'

And so we came down, laughing and shouting, skidding off the ice on to the lava, clasped in a breathless kiss.

It was two thirty and we had arranged to meet Jón and his wife for dinner at six o'clock in Árnastapi, the little village on the southern side of the mountain. We had plenty of time to make our way down the dirt road wriggling through the lava and curving away to the mountain's foot. We went slowly, stopping to examine the contorted chunks of lava that were surprisingly light to pick up and marvelling at the variety of colours. Metallic blacks and purples and blues, dull ochres, red, yellow and brown. All spewed up out of the earth, mouthful after mouthful and frozen midflow into twisted heights of pure fantasy piled higher and higher until the mountain was satisfied. Time and wind had enveloped the blackened ruin with moss and thyme and shrubby little plants with glossy green leaves that turned red in the autumn to match the berries between them.

We built another cairn beside a dry river bed in gratitude for a perfect day and made love on the moss behind a rock well out of sight of the road. It was wonderful to be naked and to feel the sharp cold of the wind on our skin, the tingling warmth of the sun and the clean tang of the sea in our nostrils. My beloved came smiling all the way down the mountain and smiled long after, remembering the light and the love, the erupting, the blending, the passion, completion.

'I'm so in love with you, my Mali,' he whispered.

— ✳ —

After four weeks on the road we began hitching back towards Reykjavík and Hafnarfjördur ready to meet Gudrun who had arrived a week after us. In Borganes we were due to pick up the last bus on our ticket to complete our circle tour. We sat in the restaurant while we waited. As usual we were drinking hot chocolate and hot milk, unashamedly our standard comfort food that Greg habitually dispensed as an antidote to tears, tiredness and cold.

'Gregory, about this book,' I said.

'What book? Oh, that book.'

I got out my notepad and pen.

'I can't help it. It has been churning around in my mind. Can I outline it for you?'

'Go ahead.'

'It's still "A Dangerous Sweetness". Don't pull faces. And it is in three sections to cover each of the different stages of your life.'

I drew out the plan as I saw it, giving each section a heading according to how I was beginning to see his life from the stories he was telling me. He sat back in the chair and closed his eyes, considering.

'Do you think it's workable?' I asked.

'How do you propose going about it?'

'Well, you say you could never write it but I have been teaching myself to write for the last four years. Maybe you could dictate it for me to write with you, correcting as we go along?'

44

'It's the only way it will ever be written. But do you think that anyone would be at all interested in it?'

'More than you think. But it doesn't have to be published. I do think it would be a useful practice for you to sit down and evaluate what you have done with your life. Whether you choose to share it with the world in the end is up to you. On the positive side it might help to clear up some of the misunderstandings that have grown up over the years.'

'Maybe. But people tend to hang on to their own conception of the truth, of what they want to be the truth and what is true for me may not be true for others. But we can try it. We will soon know if it is working or not. When shall we do it?'

'I thought we could find somewhere quiet for the winter and do it then. I don't always want to be on the move and in a tent. Don't worry, I like that idea of the world as our home but it would be nice to stay somewhere warm and away from everyone for a few months this winter. There is still the divorce to see through and a lot of dust yet to settle behind us. It would be nice if we could have a couple of years of peace to see what we are here for before we "go public".'

'A couple of years. Yes it will be interesting to see what comes up in that time. And what do you mean by going public?'

'I suppose teaching or something like that.'

'Don't remind me! How many days do we have left before we have to teach in Reykjavík?'

'Four. Come on, it will be good for you. The longer you leave it the more you will dread it. Like falling off horses, my Lord, and getting back into the saddle as soon as you can. Otherwise you never want to ride again. I will be with you, plus a ready-made sympathetic audience. It will be perfect.'

'Teaching is never perfect. I wish I enjoyed it more.'

'Maybe this time you will.'

— ❋ —

In the continual Icelandic quest for insight into the Mysteries, a North American Indian shaman had been invited to Reykjavík for several months teaching and doing sweat lodges. I had done a 'sweat' during my last visit in January, sitting in with eight others in a small, makeshift lodge around a fire pit filled with a dozen glowing volcanic stones. At the end of five rounds of chanting and inhaling the searing steam, I came out gasping and drenched all over in tears to see the Full Moon rising over the eastern mountains. The frost was already biting into the earth but after only a second's hesitation I went under the cold hose with the others. I felt torn wide open, initially exhausted and vulnerable but clean right through to my bones.

When we were told that Cloud Man was back that summer, we had to do a 'sweat' together and it was a good opportunity to find out how the sweat lodges had been used to help the Native Americans returning from the Vietnam war.

For one fleeting moment the unnameable fear returned. As I introduced Greg to the Indian, I noticed him start and – for one swift second – favour my beloved with a particularly shrewd and exacting look, at once compassionate and deeply concerned. Greg noticed nothing unusual in the look or the embrace that followed but I was instantly uneasy.

'He knows there's something wrong with him,' went through my mind but there was no chance to talk about it while so much was going on and by the time we were finished I had forgotten about it again.

I sat beside the love of my life in the sweltering darkness, growing prouder of him as each round was completed. As the first round of chanting began I felt a hand groping for mine to hold it tightly through each of the four rounds. The fourth and last was an ordeal of four long chanting sessions with all the last of the water in the bucket poured over the stones. I thought I would have no lungs left but I was determined not to be defeated. Wilfulness, stubbornness, nothing noble kept me at it. When the doorway was thrown open at the end, only Greg and I and Cloud Man were still sitting upright. The other six were lying flat out on the earth floor, gasping and groaning.

'You two sure must be fit,' observed our leader.

We found our clothes and said goodbye and an arm came round me as we were walking back to the cars.

'I was so proud of you in there,' he said.

'I was thinking exactly the same about you!'

'Did you mind me walking away and ignoring you in the beginning when we were building the fire?'

'I didn't understand why you did it but I was too involved in what was going on to take it personally. Why did you do it?'

'Can you believe I was jealous of the Indian?'

'Whatever for?'

'Because he had met you before without me. I know it's ridiculous but I can't help it. I'm sorry.'

'Do you still feel jealous now?'

'No. it's all gone. I was sitting in there listening to you chanting and thinking I'm so glad she's with me.'

'And I was sitting in there, feeling you calm and strong beside me, not moving once and I was thinking I'm so glad he's with me.'

We were tired and tender with each other all the next day, enjoying having the house to ourselves while Lóa and Birgir were working. For the first time we were together spending most of the afternoon spread out in the TV room watching one of their son Gunnar's videos. Neither of us had seen *A Prayer for the Dying* before. Woven through with a poignant story about a Catholic priest and the love of his blind, younger sister for an ex-terrorist on the run from Northern Ireland, it started violently and ended violently. We were not long into the film when I became aware of Greg trembling uncontrollably beside me. Perspiration was pouring down his face and dripping from his hands. He was watching the film intently.

46

'Shall we turn it off?' I asked.

'No, no, it's all right, it's all right. This often happens. It's all right,' he said.

More interested in him than the film, I wanted to see what did happen. I moved to hold him in my arms, cradling his head and let the video run on. It seemed to push all the 'red alert' buttons in him. The violence of war, Catholicism, the celibate priest, the terrorist who had blown up a bus-load of children but whose heart was filled with music. As the credits went up, I turned off the TV and led my beloved back into our little room. We curled up on the sofa together, holding each other tightly. I smoothed his damp hair and kissed the moisture from his forehead.

'I should take a shower. Do I stink?' he said.

'What of?'

'Fear. It usually makes the perspiration very acrid.'

I snuffled around his neck.

'No you don't. Really you don't,' I said.

'Oh, I need you Mali. Do you know how much I need you? Need this, need you holding me, helping me, loving me?'

'Yes, I do know, beloved you. It's all right.'

'I need you to be married to me,' he said.

It was the first time either of us had mentioned marriage since the hot pool in the West Fjords.

'I need you always beside me. I need you to grow old with me. I want us to be married as soon as the divorce is through and then we'll go visit my family and I can introduce them all to my wife, my beloved wife.'

'Is that it then?'

'What do you mean?'

'Have you just proposed to me then?'

He looked up from my middle where he had buried his head and smiled.

'I suppose I have. Wait a minute!'

In a single, fluid movement he was off the sofa and down on his knees on the floor in front of me. He bowed slowly three times.

'Mali – beloved Mali – will you marry me? Please?'

Putting my hands together in anjali, I answered.

'Indeed kind sir, beloved husband-to-be, I shall be delighted to marry you.'

He bowed three times more and held out both hands to me. Before I went into his arms to seal this most precious of all promises with the longest, the sweetest of kisses, I slipped the ring from his right hand on to the third finger of his left hand.

'Why did you do that?' he asked.

'It's time, don't you think?'

'Yes, I agree. It's time,' he said.

Teaching was not the torture he had thought it would be. More accessible without the Robe, even the naturally shy Icelandics were soon asking questions. He was pleased with himself and with me at the end of the day and early the next morning there was further cause for celebration when I learned to tread water and finally made it down to the deep end of the swimming pool by myself. Far more difficult was the parting with Gudrun who had a place as an au pair for the winter in Reykjavík. She and I had never been truly separated in all of her sixteen and a half years but circumstances dictated and we couldn't take her with us. I was used to crying as the plane took off from Keflavík because I didn't want to go back to England and the life I had there; now I sobbed for my daughter but this time with a sympathetic arm around me and an understanding and compassionate heart beating steadily next to mine.

Chapter Five

He always said that he learned more about Ajahn Ãnando in those first months out of the Sangha than he had known in all the years of his practice. I encouraged him to talk hour after hour about himself and his life, not only out of love and natural interest but also to begin to lay the foundation for the book that he was still reluctant to consider worth writing. Listening to his stories, there were times when he would be in full flow and I would realise that he was talking about something that had happened in the monastery while I was there or that had been discussed in my hearing. But his version was very different from how I or some of the others had remembered it. Invariably at the end of the tale I would say,

'Do you want to know what the lay people thought of that? Or the nuns? Or the junior monks?'

And he would be dumbfounded at the answer, at the general consensus of opinion, often including my own, that no one had had the temerity to challenge him with at the time.

'Did people really think I was that much of a space cadet?' he said. 'I had no idea.'

He was laughing about it with Gillian and her husband, Mike, as we sat in their garden, drinking tea and posing for photographs, during our brief thirty six hour touch-down in England. With speed and perfect precision of planning we managed to finalise the divorce petition, completely unpack and wash our Arctic gear and repack in favour of the Mediterranean, with Felix and Gabriel sat talking in the middle of it all. I was so glad to see my boys, having convinced myself that it would be impossible for the four of us to coincide in the short time we had in the country.

'What are you taking to swim in?' asked my Lord with a censorious raising of the right eye-brow.

'This!' I said, defiantly waving a brief black bikini bottom.

'And what else?'

'Nothing.'

'I can see we will have to negotiate.'

'There is nothing to negotiate. You promised we would always find private beaches,' I said, diverting his immediate attention with a kiss and pushing the article in question quickly to the bottom of my pack.

The first of the inevitable string of letters caught up with us. Nothing too bitter or accusing, mostly kind and positive. He was embarrassed but I was fascinated to read a couple of 'come up and see me sometime' letters from undefeated ladies who had evidently had more than a passing interest in Ajahn Ãnando. They went into the fire along with a difficult missive associated with the divorce, addressed to me. Again I was surprised at the almost cold-bloodedness of his reaction. He was pleased and grateful for the kindnesses but the more difficult comments he systematically put out of his mind. When I reacted more strongly he would always say,

'That is how they see it. They have every right to their opinion but it's their stuff, not yours and not mine. We are all subject to our individual conditioning. As the Buddha said "I have no quarrel with the world, it is the world that quarrels with me." You only hurt yourself by holding on to it Mali, by allowing it to have the power to affect you. Let it go.'

So easy to say, not so easy to do but I was learning.

— � —

We arrived on Limnos in the North Aegean just after midnight on August 6th after five expensive and mosquito-plagued days on Thassos. The ferry docked at the quay in Mirina just before the flood-lights around the castle went out. In the warm, inky black of the Mediterranean night it was impossible to see what kind of an island it was but I immediately decided I liked it even though all the rooms in the two or three hotels were booked and we had to put the tent up on the beach for the night. After four hours of uneasy sleep we were very tired and it was a struggle to pack up the tent and maintain a lively interest in what we were supposed to be there for. I wanted to find a cheap room to rent, I had had enough of living in the tent but there was nothing to be had until the end of the month when the tourists, mainly Greek, were gone. A surprising number spoke English with a broad Australian accent and told us that they were visiting their families for the summer, having emigrated when work became scarce on Limnos after the last War. Greg wanted to go south to another island but my 'witch's nose' prevailed and had us waiting for hours through the heat of a long, scorching morning and into the early afternoon for the only bus that would take us nine kilometres north to Kaspakas and the beach at Agios Giannis.

A large painted sign written in English read 'NO CAMPING' but with the permission of one of the residents whose family houses bordered the beach, we set up the tent ten feet from the sea, allowing for the minimal tidal increase in the Mediterranean. Our washing water came from a well in the gardens behind the sand dunes at our back door, courtesy of the kindness of the same Greek neighbours. Our drinking water came in bottles from the little taverna a mile up the beach and food could be bought in Mirina twice a week.

After a critical review of our financial situation, we decided to stay for a month to allow the September pay cheque to catch up with the Visa account. Water and food were the only outlay and that was simple enough. We lived on Rye bread and salads made up of peanuts, tomatoes, nectarines and peaches, apples and carrots and red peppers, all covered with lashings of olive oil and dried parsley and washed down with Greek mineral water. After a week I introduced several cloves of garlic into the evening salad for the maintenance of healthy bodies and we tried not to notice the taste in our mouths in the morning.

50

There were very few tourists and they were ninety-five per cent Greek. Limnos had yet to be swamped by the rest of Europe although the signs were beginning to appear in the shape of the occasional concrete skeleton of a prospective hotel or guest house. Otherwise the island was very much as most of the others probably were thirty or forty years ago. All of our neighbours had houses up the hill in Kaspakas but moved down to Agios Giannis for the summer to swim, fish and look after their vegetable gardens. We were almost embarrassed by their generosity. It was rare that we returned from a trip to the well without a bag full of tomatoes and peppers.

The Greek Islands bake in August. After three months without rain the mountains and fields are a bleached mass of shrivelled stalks and dry, spiky vegetation. The sun was so hot as soon as it cleared the mountains that we had to be out of the tent by seven thirty no matter how distracted we were inclined to be. I would prepare breakfast while Greg shook out the sheets and swept out the sand that was always a part of the night however careful we were. We didn't take a lot of notice of what else was going on on the island during that month. We didn't go to the festival in the village on August 15th. We didn't bother to explore our surroundings other than to walk to the adjoining bay, Kalogeros, content with our twice-weekly rides into Mirina and back.

Only the Meltemi wind caused me any insecurity in our surroundings. It came with alarming regularity just after the quarter moon days that month, blowing hard from the east for two full days. Passing ships anchored themselves in the bay and together we sat it out well battened down, careful not to verbalise our complaining minds when sand whirled around us and peppered our food. The wind whipped and beat relentlessly at the fly sheet on the first night, rocking the tent and straining at the pegs. I lay wide awake and terrified. The washing up bowl briefly battered on the stones before it was thrown out to sea.

'Greg, is the tent okay? Can it take wind like this?'

'Yes, it's fine.'

'How do you know? You're not just saying that, are you?'

'No. Remember I've lived in this tent since March and I've been listening very carefully to it as it moves. The pegs are all holding. Tomorrow I will go round and secure everything but it's fine for now. Go to sleep Baby.'

I tried but it was impossible with so much noise banging in my ears all night long and I found it hard being bleary and tired all the next day in a wind that would not let up. After a blustery breakfast we got down to some serious building work, shovelling quantities of sand under the ground sheet to improve our sleeping arrangements and fortifying the foundations with stones. In a couple of hours it looked as though we were camping on a primitive hill fort. Greg laid a patio outside our front door with carefully selected flat stones so that we could shake the sand from our feet before we went inside. It was a wonderful idea unless we needed something from the tent between one and four o'clock in the afternoon when the stones were guaranteed to fry our feet if we dared to walk on them.

On the third morning after breakfast was finished and our first swim completed, I brought the Buddha-rupa and the Tibetan bells out of the tent and set up the shrine on the beach.

'You did promise we could meditate together every day once you had played enough,' I said.

'Will I ever have played enough, I wonder?' he replied.

I detected a definite reluctance on his part.

'Gregory, I sat meditation every morning long before I met you and I need it. It settles me for the day. I always feel I have forgotten something if I don't do it.'

'All right then. Do we have to chant?'

'Just something short and simple because I like it and you can take the bells for the end.'

We sat facing one another with the sea on one side and the shrine on the other. My beloved facing the sun and me with my back smothered in sun cream ready for the hour of sustained passivity in an uncompromising heat. I had won my battle over beach attire on the condition that I always had a tee-shirt to hand if anything male invaded our horizon so my tan was coming along well with no fear of paler patches and white lines; I had no intention of being skewbald. On the other hand an old knee injury had always prevented me from sitting cross-legged. Now I had found a perfect opportunity to try it with an empty plastic bottle supporting my leg to encourage the long, over-tightened thigh muscles to stretch and relax. After fifteen minutes the meditation was an endurance of heat and pain but even that can be a usable focus. When the ringing chime of the bells sounded at the end of the hour, I had a sense of balance and ease that carried me through the day.

'You're right. I needed that too,' he said as we completed our three bows to the shrine. 'Thank you, beautiful woman, for reminding me,' he said.

He bowed again, three times, this time to me.

'And thank you, beloved husband to be, ' I replied, adding my three bows in turn that from then on became a established conclusion to our daily ritual as an outward symbol of our mutual respect and devotion. No matter what manifested in our learning of each other, there would never be a day when one did not feel able to bow to the other. And that regular, daily meditation, usually at ten o'clock, often at eleven o'clock on Tuesdays and Fridays after we had hitched back from Mirina with the food and post, sharpened our sense of mindfulness and gratitude for all that we had in this perfect awareness of the now.

'Don't waste a single moment of this,' my mind told me. 'Every moment is precious and perfect just as it is.'

I would feel all my senses flaring into life. The smell of the sea and the heat rising on the sand, the sparkling blue of the water and the green and white of the lily flowers growing out of the dunes. The sucking of the sea over the stones at the water's edge, the taste of the nectarine juices on my tongue and trickling down my chin, and the softness of the warm lips that put them there.

Above all I was profoundly aware of the sweetness and the intensity of the joy and the life within this man to whom I had dedicated my life. There was always a hand held out ready to mine, always toothpaste on my brush, the first spoonful of food. I was never allowed to carry anything in my shoulder bag except the dog and the passports and that would be checked every other day to make sure I was not loading myself with unnecessary weight and also to satisfy his compulsive curiosity.

He was always careful to be modest and correct in what we termed public places which in our minds excluded our stretch of beach. No matter how hot the day he always wore a tee-shirt when we went to Mirina or to the local Taverna for the drinking water. I cut the arms off his favourite red tee-shirt which made it cooler to wear but at the same time exhibited his biceps to an admirable degree.

Having mastered the confines of a swimming pool where I could be certain of the depths, the sea was another dimension but we were in a large, sheltered and relatively shallow bay where the sand dipped gently out to the deeps. My beloved was all sweetness and patience with me, swimming round and round me in circles to encourage and advise, sometimes wisely saying absolutely nothing. We had no shade and usually spent most of every afternoon in the water out of the full ferocity of the heat. When I grew tired and threatening to be out of temper with myself, he would dive and come up turned on his back, swimming round me with barely a perceptible movement, just a disembodied head moving above the water with a grin to match the Cheshire cat in Wonderland. It was so ridiculous, it always made me laugh.

'Gregory, you are like a mad terrapin,' I would say in exasperation.

'Oh, but I'm so cute. Don't you think so?'

— ❈ —

We were washing up the breakfast things and gathering the water bottles together to go to the well before morning meditation. We had been five days on Agios Giannis and already relaxing into a routine but this morning he seemed unusually irritable, not saying much, slightly withdrawn and a little short in replying to me. I watched him carefully, knowing what it was, something that had been on my mind for several days. He was tired and not pleased with his love-making. I had nothing to complain about but I knew he was not satisfying his own exacting standards and fantasies thereby sowing more seed for self-aversion. As if he didn't have enough already. Even in the best of men with the best of intention, the forty-five year old body cannot be expected to perform night after night like that of a twenty year old Marine in Hong Kong on a five day rest and recuperation break from Vietnam.

'I have another extension on the vinaya,' I announced. 'And there is no negotiation.'

Such an uncompromising statement delivered out of the air made him look up, at once interested but wary and ready to object at the slightest hint of suspected coercion.

'What is it?'

'Simply this. Henceforth in our love-making, I may have as many orgasms as you care to give me. But you may only have one orgasm in every twenty four hours.'

His brittle male ego immediately bristled in defence.

'What are you talking about? What do you mean?'

I smiled, looking at him directly, pouting a little. Just the merest hint of seduction.

'Come, indulge me, I want to experiment. We can make love as often as you like but I want to see what happens when we let the energy build without wasting it, holding it at the point of orgasm but only yielding to it once every twenty four hours. Similar to Tantric yoga.'

He thought about it, frowning, his brow clearing as he smiled back at me.

'Okay, we'll do it for a couple of days and see what happens.'

'More than a couple of days. I want this in the vinaya.'

'Isn't that rather extreme?'

'We are extreme, Beloved.' I laughed. 'There is no Middle Way!'

'In this evidently not,' he said.

His energy changed completely. Now he had to prove that he could keep to the discipline if only to prevent me from breaking any of the rules. Without the continual draining of his efficacy, he became super-alert and the orgasm when it came had all the sobbing urgency of unequivocal consummation.

We were walking up to the village early a few days later.

'You are very wise and very kind,' he said.

'Why?'

'Your version of Tantric Yoga,' he grinned. 'You knew I would never have admitted that I was getting tired.'

'I know. But it's a great improvement on yoga isn't it?'

'It is indeed.'

As our melding deepened and strengthened, our physical relationship powered us into another dimension, uniquely our own where we opened our hearts and our perception to life on our own terms, living as we wanted to live with a freedom of expression quintessential to the nature of our relationship. Whatever the day held for me, I was always aware of a continuous, breathless excitement in anticipation of the coming night. After the evening meal was cleared away we sat reading Kazantzakis' 'Last Temptation' aloud to each other, taking turns until the sun was far down in the west and the bats were swooping around our heads.

All other sounds died away except for the sound of the sea and the occasional distant rumbling of a late ferry boat appearing as an indistinct band of lights on the horizon sailing into port in Mirina. Far to the south across the bay the castle floodlights came on just as it was getting truly dark. Then, arms around each other, we laid the book aside and watched as the bloody shadows of the heat of the day faded into the shifting, myriad shimmering of the sea and the sky slowly blossomed with stars.

As the sun went down, desire flared into consciousness. We stood at the edge of the water seeing who could spit the toothpaste out the furthest between kisses. We touched each other softly in passing as we prepared for the night. Last of all I laid out the sponge and the little bowl of water sprinkled with lavender or sandalwood oil to bathe my beloved after the fire of our love-making, to send him honoured and comfortable into dreams. I loved the ritual of it all and the tenderness, befitting the man who had loved me like no other had ever done. Light was the only thing lacking. I wouldn't have a candle in the tent so we solved the problem by buying a torch and putting it in a position least likely to cast interestingly erotic shadows on the outside of the fly-sheet. The occasional fisherman sat until late further up the beach and we didn't want to distract him from his purpose.

The ritual of food preparation became intensely important to me in those first days. It was the only domestic security I had. Everything else was gone. I didn't need a home with carpets and furniture and all the mostly unnecessary appendages that went with it but the woman needed to be needed other than just in the bed. She needed to serve, to tend the fire in the hearth.

On Agios Giannis the only outward manifestation of fire was a burning, golden sun that shone relentlessly day after day, the only hearth a stretch of scorching sand and stones. Toilet facilities were the sea for Greg who could swim with confidence out to where all evidence would be borne away to disappear without trace. Unless the wind changed as it did one morning, sending his offering floating into the little harbour among the fishing boats while we giggled helplessly from a discreet distance. Half a plastic bottle to squat over beside the tent was all that could be found for me and a quick appointment with a plastic bag and a stone large enough to dig a discreet hole in the sand dunes around the sea lilies every day around dawn.

The kitchen sink was a plastic bowl and an ocean. I had a single paring knife and Greg's Swiss Army knife, two forks, two spoons, two plastic plates and two plastic mugs. It was all we needed but the ritual of laying everything out on the rice mat could assume immense proportions in my mind. Everything had to be perfect and with great care the food could be served without accompanying sand. But I enjoyed the caring and the simplicity of it all. It was a relief to be able to sit and prepare fruit and vegetables and lay aside the pain for a while.

For there was pain. Jealousy could make him temporarily utterly unreasonable. Yet he was the most reasonable, courageous, compassionate being I had ever met. Softly spoken and invariably polite, he never complained and with his example of quiet dignity before me, I would meet my spiritual and emotional crises head on. Unconsciously he was often the catalyst, triggering anxiety reactions I didn't know I had. A single word or a gesture could explode something from my subconscious, often connected with the backwash of old fear as well as the inescapable anger and resentment related to the divorce.

— ✳ —

One afternoon we had been for a walk following the dirt road to Kalogeros and up to a small deserted farm half way up the mountain where we discovered what we thought to be an old, disused threshing floor. Perfectly circular, set with large flat stones and surrounded by a broken wall. I perched on a rock and watched him as he did Tai Chi, rising to join him for a kiss and the closing movements. We walked slowly back to Agios Giannis, saying 'Yasus' to a woman rinsing her washing out at a spring beside the road. I could feel the perspiration pouring down my body even at that pace. I was glad of my tee-shirt to give my skin a respite from the sun.

'Mali, what do you mean by freedom? What does it mean to you?'

'What does it mean to me?'

I took time to consider exactly what it did mean before I answered, knowing the importance of the question.

'I think it has several meanings on several levels. Basically it means space and time unlimited to let my spirit fly, to think, to meditate and to be. Answerable to no one except a like mind. It means to live a life where "things" are not important. To be uncluttered by the host of material objects that constitute home and security these days.'

I stopped walking, turning to face him to emphasise the point. I went on.

'I used to dream of a single room that was only mine. It was a house where no one knew me and it had nothing in it except exactly what I wanted and I needed. Some books, a desk to write at, lots of space on the floor. Pictures on the wall, a single futon to sleep on, a little kitchen area to prepare food in, my own private bathroom. All neat and clean. And best of all a huge window looking out on to the sky.'

He smiled, fully in accord with the concept I was presenting.

'Oh Gregory, I have never forgotten the feeling of absolute relief I felt as I heard the door close behind me when I left the first marriage. I carried just a few books and my clothes out into the snow that day but in a matter of weeks I had to create another nest and it was so depressing. Cutlery for daily use, cutlery for guests, house plants in the window. There are only two of you in the house or five but everything comes in sixes, six glasses, six cups, six plates. Always so much to spare that might only be used three or four times a year at best. That and an ill-suited partner to deal with. You see, I never had a true companion in spirit until I met you and spiritual

56

loneliness is the greatest of all isolations. You, our relationship, the extraordinary quality of our attunement, that is a freedom to me now.'

'Yes. It never ceases to amaze me how in tune we are. I can be thinking about something and within minutes you are either talking about it or doing it.'

'Love may have something to do with it.'

'Yes, I know. But I also know that it's more than that. It is a very humbling and at times powerfully illuminating experience to love and live with a woman who is so attuned to me that there is no place to hide, even if I wanted to. It certainly keeps me very honest.'

'But isn't that also a freedom? To know that there is someone who loves and respects you for all your fears and insecurities as well as for your strengths and abilities? You can waste a lot of energy keeping up an image.'

'I agree. But what else?'

'You mean the other side of freedom?'

'What do you mean by that?'

'I suppose having my own money, a car to escape in, a plane ticket in my pocket. I tried so hard in those marriages but at every disappointment I would close another door and retreat inside into more of my own space. Until eventually I learned to co-exist in a completely unsuitable environment simply by living my own life inside myself, continually supplemented with the healing, travelling and writing. Taking every opportunity to put as much physical and emotional distance between me and the person in question.'

'The facade.'

'Yes, absolutely, but that's not freedom. It's living a lie and therefore a trap. But in relating to you it is different. You are easily my intellectual equal. Spiritually you have some advantages over me, I have others over you, according to our different experiences. When it comes down to physical and sexual attraction, I would say we are even, both curiously untouched physically by time and equally attractive to the opposite sex.'

'You're right. I can feel murderous just thinking about it.'

'Don't think about it, beloved you. When I talk to you I know I will get an answer worth considering and I know that in this relationship it is in my best interest to keep all my doors open and my windows, even if it hurts. I know that with you I can grow. So I would say to you, never to give me back my freedom. My material freedom that is. I know me. I could so easily get back into my old routine if I was hurt or disappointed in some way.'

'Can I have that in writing? What is the date?'

He looked at his watch.

'August 12th. I shall always remember you said that and I will always remind you of it when you say that I am abusing you.'

'What have I said? I can see this conversation echoing down our life together *ad infinitum*. You do abuse me sometimes.'

'Never, never by intention!'

'No, I know. But it doesn't stop it hurting.'

'Believe me, I never want to hurt you.'

During that first week on the beach, the moon had come rising and ever more rounded into the early evenings, a glowing white eye in the eastern sky staining the sea silver-green, reciprocal to Venus and more faintly Jupiter flickering briefly over the gold and rose of the western horizon. We spent one whole afternoon clearing a space beside the tent and building a pile of driftwood and cane. As the moon hung high in the sky we celebrated our Full Moon puja. Lighting the fire, we chanted in Pali, chanted Bajans, everything we could chant together, sitting in a circle of stones that had been dedicated to the welfare of all Beings. Before we sat meditation, while the fire fed by the wind was still burning hungrily into the wood, we each laid a piece of paper into the flames written before the light was gone, listing all the negative thoughts and feelings, the hurt, pain and anger still lingering in our minds. It was a symbolic gesture of a conscious effort to recognise and let go of all that was harmful to our own and to others' well-being. A full Metta meditation on Loving Kindness followed until the glowing embers of the fire had died away and our awareness had become condensed into a profound appreciation of the sweetness of the night and all that it symbolised for us then on Agios Giannis.

Chapter Six

Some people have to go to the desert at some time in their lives, for their spiritual training and hopefully for the good of all beings. Some go with a Shaman, I went with an Thervadan Ajahn. He wasn't perfect and never claimed to be. Yet it was all that he lived for and because he saw me as an extension of himself, I had to be perfect. It was almost as though in achieving my perfection he could more easily attain his own and there were times when he was ruthless. I knew his strategy came wholly from love towards me and always with the best of intention, but it was undeniably caught in the sticky strands of the web of self-hatred he wove for himself. And it could be tough.

He demanded my complete attention, that the focus of all my light and energy be himself alone. That was not so difficult. I had found my soul-mate. But I had to accept that ninety per cent of the people I had previously known were no longer to be a part of my life and he preferred that they were not discussed. I had to begin a completely new life with him. Even my clothes were vetted and any of my belongings he was remotely uncomfortable with had to be discarded. He had smiled when he saw my little bag of baby clothes left over from when the children were small, and said nothing when I put them back in our storage cupboard in my mother's house.

I had no jewellery other than the ring he had given me and a rough-cut emerald that I wore around my neck, and I was only allowed to keep that because at the same time I had bought a similar, larger stone for him, to be set as he wished when he could afford it. He needed my complete dependence on him. He needed to feel needed and to be the provider in all things. It was important to him that he was the only person in the world who could take care of me.

His jealousy was never rational. He had experienced jealousy as a monk when his self-disparagement persuaded him he was lacking in comparison to his peers. Only once as a teenager had he truly tasted the bitter intensity of jealousy in love. On Agios Giannis faced with a love that had finally broken open his heart, he had to deal with it again. It was so humbling for him and painful sometimes for us both. His jealousy and fear of inadequacy intensified equally in comparison to the reality of his love for me and caused him much searching of mind and heart. There were times when he could hardly bear himself for behaving as he did, when a single thoughtless comment would provoke an afternoon of discussion and tears.

'Mali, I'm really worried at how possessive I am of you. I shouldn't be this way, I shouldn't be like this.'

'Why are you letting it worry you?'

'Because it is so painful, it hurts me and it hurts you. I can't bear to hurt you but it seems I can't let it go.'

'But the answer is simple.'

'How?'

'Possess me then.'

Given that permission, he could let go of the guilt the emotion had aroused and consequently the natural desire to defend himself. Relieved at my compassion and understanding he came to me knowing as I knew that the symptom had only been recognised, not cured, but trusting in my love for him to see us through. Sometimes it was like walking on thin ice. I soon learned that I was allowed to talk about the difficulties and disappointments in my life and some of the funny things that happened with the children. Seemingly absurd things like the crushes I had on good-looking boys when I was in my early teens were never allowed to be mentioned. Neither were the relatively few happier aspects of my past experience of human love. He, on the other hand, felt free to talk in great detail about as many of his past girlfriends and liaisons, however brief, as he could possibly remember. It was terribly one-sided. But I had grown up alongside my father's jealousy and had made a conscious decision as an eleven year old never to let this most destructive of emotions, rooted in self-hatred, dominate either my life or that of any others in my life because of me.

In that month I went through the most intense novitiate training he could programme, designed more for a monk than a nun. He was very critical of how I sat, walked, behaved in general. Not unkindly but I seemed to be in need of a meticulous re-schooling preparatory to becoming his wife. I was ninety-nine point nine, nine per cent perfect in looks. No stretch marks from having the children, nothing sagging and no cellulite, for which I was eternally grateful because I would certainly have been sent off for surgery. The imperfection was a small blemish on my face that I had lived with for twenty-one years. I pointed out that I had asked to have it removed several years before and had been told that the resulting scar would be worse than the blemish. That was not good enough for my Lord. It had to be gone before I met his family. And one of my teeth, a worryingly cracked front crown, had to be repaired as well before we went to America. I was beginning to wonder what on earth these people could be like.

My accent was perfect, there were no complaints about that although my occasional predilection for colourful language, however mild, had to be eliminated.

'You will not say "hell" in front of my mother. You will not say "damn" in front of my mother,' he said.

His mouth folded in reproof as only Ãnando could fashion. Both words had recurred, to my lasting amusement, during his desanas and I had it on tape to prove it. But while that kind of rhetoric was beyond reproach for the Abbot in the Shrine room in the monastery, it was not to cross the Atlantic on the lips of his wife. He found some of my more ironical observations on

our working. I remembered laughing and saying that I had only to be a sorrowing widow and I would be complete, so much had been crammed into my forty years.

'So that's it, is it? My heart will break when you die on me? But please not yet. Give me five years, ten years, twenty. Maybe it won't be so bad if we are older, when we have had time together. But even then, I know it will still break my heart.'

I filed the recollection and the feeling. It had nothing to do with the now, this wonderful immediate now, choosing to lose myself in the laughter as he threw himself down on my mat and I fought for re-possession.

'Sacred space, Gregory!'

'Your space is my space and mine is yours. It's a deal, Mali-Mali! Are you feeling better now?'

'Yes.'

'Good! I'll give you a healing session when you're showered.'

'Gregory?'

'Yes?'

'You're never allowed to die on me. Do you understand?'

'Don't worry, I won't. What brought that up?'

'I was contemplating immortality.'

We took the towels and the sheets to the launderette in Mirina when they were too stiff and brown with salt and sand for comfort, laughing at how they were barely recognisable when they were laid soft and smelling of soap powder on the counter in front of us. Every week I scanned the post hoping vainly for something from one of the children, but they had always been hopeless letter writers. At the beginning of the fourth week I picked up an unexpected bonus. The official notification that the divorce had been granted and the Decree Nisi had been due to be pronounced the previous morning in England. I hardly dared to believe it could be true and walked around Mirina in a daze of relief. There was only the usual formality of the six weeks and a day before Decree Absolute. And freedom.

We went out to the taverna that night to celebrate. I wore my faded denim skirt and my turquoise top, the only formal dress I possessed, with my new bronze coloured Mary Magdalene sandals shining on my feet, feeling like a queen. We dined on delicious deep-fried courgettes and pasta with fruit and creamy yoghurt for dessert before paddling back down the beach to the tent. Under a moonless sky thick with stars we concluded the celebration in the best and only way we knew how.

The next day, sitting at ease in a fishing boat, invited by Con and Effi our neighbours, who had also offered us their house for the winter, I listened to the rhythm of the chug-chugging of the engine, trailing my hands in Homer's 'wine-dark sea'. It occurred to me that all my previous unease in boats had vanished. The boat could turn over any time and I knew I was perfectly capable of swimming unassisted to the shore. I wouldn't have to wait for anyone to save me now. It gave me a sudden exhilarating rush of a new sense of freedom to know that I was only a few steps away from managing a sail board.

Chapter Seven

Early on September 2nd we were up before dawn, packing up ready to move on to spend two abortive days in Athens, trying to arrange our wedding. The complications involved in marrying secretly in Greece far outweighed our romantic expectations. I had a beautiful green, hand woven dress but nowhere to wear it.

'Oh no, not Petersfield Register Office! Oh no!'

I wailed in despair. It had been my private nightmare throughout all my years of consent.

'What are you talking about?'

'Don't you see? Circumstances are forcing us to be married in England and the only place we can legally do it there is in our area of residence. And that happens to leave no alternative to Petersfield.'

'Are you sure?'

I looked at him.

'Gregory, with my history do you really think I don't know?'

'You're right. So what's wrong with Petersfield Register Office?'

'Nothing except that it used to be in the Town Hall and that was the most gloomy place I have ever seen.'

'Maybe it's changed.'

'That's too much to hope for.'

The question was when? Decree Absolute was due to be granted on October 6th but we wanted to stay for as much of the Greek summer as possible. At least until the third week in October. We had promised to visit Greg's mother in Virginia for a week before coming back to Greece for the winter. The house in Limnos was nice but the island was too far north and too cold to consider, except for the latter part of the Spring.

Still undecided, we booked ourselves onto a boat bound for Santorini, Crete and Rhodes but our leisurely tour of the southern islands was cut short within hours of sailing when the piece of my front crown that had been cracked for three months fell into my hand as I was cleaning my teeth. My Lord had graciously let me off having plastic surgery on my face in Athens – as if we could afford it. Seeing a dentist had become a matter of some urgency. So we stayed on the boat, watching the other islands passing tantalisingly by as only the occasional harbour light in front of a dark mass sticking out of the sea.

Twenty-four hours later we landed on Rhodes which, boasting a British Consulate, we assumed would have an English-speaking dentist somewhere in the main town as well. By the following afternoon we were settled for a very reasonable price in an ultra-modern studio on the south-east coast of the island, near enough to Lindos for shopping and buses but sufficiently far enough from the town to avoid the tourists. The nearest beach was too rocky and too messy to entice them away from their sand strips and parasols. We found a place high among the rocks, with a patch of virgin sand for our comfort that was private enough for sunbathing *au naturel*. Its only disadvantage was that it was not for the nervous. In order to swim, we were obliged to jump off a rock into thirty feet of water rapidly falling away to fifty feet and beyond. Gregory was in his element but it took all my newly-acquired courage to jump off that rock.

'Three hundred strokes, Mali,' he would say, pointing directly out to sea and off I would go with him swimming in circles around me until we were far enough out to deserve ten minutes treading water while I collected myself sufficiently to swim back.

We found a dentist who had been trained in America but retained his unmistakably Greek technique.

'You're brave, aren't you?' he said, smacking the piece of crown back into place with glue and pinching it hard enough to send shock waves from the remaining nerve, barely retained in a thin sliver of tooth, up my nose and flooding into the middle of my head. We decided in retrospect that it might be safer to have a new crown fitted in England,

An estimated two million tourists land in Rhodes every year and everything is geared up to accommodate them. 'Bus-in-ez' is thriving and while most of everything is cheaper than anywhere else in Europe, the natives keep a careful eye on the drachma, encouraging their visitors to spend as much as possible during the seven-month season to justify the comparative lack of activity during the winter on the island. 'Spec-ial price' appears everywhere, even when the rest of the notice is in Greek and completely incomprehensible to ninety-nine per cent of their clients, who like to think they have found a bargain whether they have or not. Whereas it was starting to cool in the mornings and evenings on Limnos, two hundred miles to the south on Rhodes it was as hot as ever, guaranteeing sunbathing and swimming every day unless we were in Rhodes Town or Lindos trying to arrange our wedding. Gillian was obligingly negotiating for us but it took a nightmare of phone calls, once or twice a week all through September, before everything was arranged to everyone's satisfaction for October 29th in Petersfield Register Office, thankfully no longer in the Town Hall.

It didn't help that every call took at least three-quarters of an hour to connect through the antiquated and overloaded Rhodian telephone system and if the central OTE telephone office was closed, which it usually was in Lindos, we had no alternative but to use the telephone in a street kiosk or a travel agent's office, which cost three times as much. Greg's careful budgeting system was severely strained as the drachma mounted in their thousands in the telephone column. The only time I ever heard him swear was after he had been trying unsuccessfully for an hour to arrange our flight to America and was cut off as soon as the call finally connected.

'Son of a bitch!' shook the thin wooden panelling of the telephone booth and the travel agent, who prided himself on his ability to provide everything on demand, looked up in some alarm as the receiver crashed back onto the phone and Greg came bursting out into the office. I was laughing so hard I had to be helped into the street, not daring to mention anything about the vinaya and colourful language.

There was no alternative to the telephone. The entire Greek postal system was on a six-week strike and all the mail was at a standstill. When we heard that some had arrived in the main Post Office in Rhodes Town, we caught the seven o'clock bus from Lindos and joined the early morning queue that stretched from the counter to the steps outside overlooking the harbour, unaware that we would be standing there for three hours in a building growing progressively hotter and stuffier, the air conditioning being strike-bound as well. Native Greeks don't have the ability to wait in line quietly. There was a lot of scuffling and raised voices. Elderly ladies used their elbows and glared around at anyone likely to object while we waited for the single employee available to sort herself out. After two hours, when even Greg's formidable patience was wearing thin, a large young man pushed directly in front of us on the convenient pretext of knowing one of the phalanx of Greek matrons who were our immediate neighbours. Greg leaned forward and tapped him on the shoulder.

'Excuse me. This is a queue,' he said quietly.

Something in his tone made me take a lot of notice.

'It's okay, I knowa, I knowa. I'm in a hurry, please,' said our intruder, patting Greg placatingly on the arm.

'This is a queue. It begins outside the door,' he replied in that same very quiet voice. I noticed with alarm that my ex-monk was standing too finely balanced on his toes with his hands dropped to his sides. In a flash I could see the Marine Corps all over again. I leaned over and whispered in his ear.

'Greg! Twenty years of practice!'

'It's okay, just relax,' he said, putting me to one side but it broke the tension and we consented to step demurely back one place in the line. When our turn came at the window there was nothing in the slot labelled K.

'Gregory, I would not like you to hit me. Promise me you'll never hit me.'

'There's no need to promise, it will never happen.'

'You don't know how grateful I am to hear that.'

'What's the problem?'

'I would crumple like tin foil, that's what's the problem. Were you going to hit that guy in there?'

'No, of course not.'

'Well, I'm not convinced.'

'Mali, you must curb this tendency to exaggerate.'

'This time I don't think it's me that's exaggerating.'

— ✻ —

Sometimes we talked about how it might have been if we had met when we were young, when he first came to London in 1970. And then I would remember that we were already forty-five and forty-one. Time was precious, every moment had to be savoured. I loved watching him. Walking down the street, in airports, always in charge, arranging passports, tickets, putting up the tent, in every movement so quick and efficient and completely in command of himself and of me. My heart was full of him. There in the moment, loved and being loved, the joy and the delight of our contract of bliss. I would lean over him while we were lying together in bed or on the sand, just to look at him. Simply for the pleasure of looking at him.

'Gregory, it's almost obscene how good-looking you are! You are so delicious, just delicious!'

He smiled up at me, pleased and shy all at once.

'I'm so glad you think so.'

'So am I. I could just pick you up and eat you, just bury myself in you and devour you, but then there would be nothing left for tomorrow.'

He pulled me down beside him and held me tightly to him, breathing into my hair.

'I love how you love me, how demonstrative you are with me. It gives me so much confidence,' he whispered.

The early mornings were beautiful as we made for our sand patch among the rocks for morning meditation. Invariably the sun came rising out of a blue-silver sea into a cloudless sky as we picked our way through the scrubby vegetation, past the farm and its free-range cows, between the rock pools. A natural indentation in a huge boulder conveniently facing east made a perfect position for the Buddha-rupa. We chanted and sat for an hour until hunger drove us back to the studio for breakfast at eight o'clock. I usually prepared the food and Greg did the washing up afterwards but only by his choice, not mine. I still enjoyed serving him at meals. My respect for the monk had easily transferred to respect for the man.

'You're definitely not a feminist. I hate admitting it but I'm very glad,' he said.

'Why worry about admitting it? I don't feel the need to have to campaign for my rights, I was given them by being educated. I think men are the ones who are in crisis now, not women.'

'Why do you say that?'

'Because their role has been taken away from them. They can still strut and be peacocks but essentially they are no longer needed as providers. Women can have careers and children if they want to without having to be dependent. They don't even need husbands. They can choose to get pregnant and then discard the mate spider-style. Or they can be artificially inseminated. Men are in crisis.'

'Don't say that in California.'

'I hardly think I will ever be expected to.'

'We may go there some time.'

70

'I hope not. I don't really want to go to America.'

'Why not? My family are there. You can hardly avoid going to meet them.'

'I know but for years I've known that something awful is going to happen there. Whether on a large scale or a small scale I'm not sure. I am afraid to go there. It's as simple as that. It could be nonsense, my witch's nose playing overtime. I don't think I want to live there.'

'I've never wanted to live there but it might be different now I have you.'

'Then it would have to be somewhere dramatic and wonderful. A little house like this studio but by itself in the mountains or the desert. That might be all right.'

'In that case I would probably have to teach you to shoot. I doubt that we could live in a place like that in America without a gun.'

'That settles it then. We are not living in America.'

The divorce wasn't easily laid aside. Anger disturbed my dreams, forcing me into painful wakefulness. So many times, sensing my misery, my beloved would pull himself out of sleep to sit up beside me and chant one of the healing suttas over me until I fell back into unconsciousness.

'I must really love this woman,' he said, more than once to the darkened room.

On the day Decree Absolute was declared, we dined in style in Lindos in a restaurant with a roof garden and early enough for it to be dark but not too noisy in the bars. I was still amazed that the British judiciary system could accommodate a divorce in just over three and a half months and in three and a half weeks I would be Mrs Klein. Neither of us doubted that we were 'doing the right thing' but we admitted to each other that privately we had both looked very carefully at the step we were about to take during the previous month, using the opportunity to make sure that it was what we really wanted to do.

'I feel a love and sense of commitment towards you that I have never felt towards anyone before,' he said, covering my hand with his own as we sat at the table. 'Our physical and spiritual attunement seem to make marriage a worthwhile reality, a perfect opportunity to find out what we are here for together. And I want to get rid of that other name!'

He grinned shamefacedly.

'Gregory, when we have some money, not a lot, please, please could I have an engagement ring? A real one? I've never had one, you see. Not huge clumps of diamonds but maybe one little emerald that I could wear stacked on top of my wedding rings like other women?'

'Mali, I promise I will buy you one as soon as I can. Do we have enough money now do you think?'

'You're the banker but I doubt it after all the air tickets we have bought.'

He handed me the folded restaurant bill.

'Do you have a pen? Work it out on this and see if we agree,' he said.

According to my estimation we had exactly enough to cover our return flights between England and Rhodes, going on to Virginia by way of Iceland to see Gudrun, as well as the wedding expenses which would be very little considering we had invited maximum of six guests. The only problem was that even with the November cheque we would not have enough to pay our full four months' rent in advance and in cash when we came back to Rhodes. We had been offered a little studio in an olive grove a few miles south of where we were staying, just outside Lardos. Greg frowned a little.

'What shall we do about it? Do you have any suggestions?' he said.

'There's the Life Assurance you have. Do you need that? I have no ambitions to become rich on your death. You're not allowed to die on me, ever, and I'm not staying around here if you do. You've taught me not only to live with you but that I can't live without you. It will be a quick bottle of pills and here I come Gregory.'

'Are you sure?'

'Yes, I have no desire to be a wealthy widow.'

'How much do you think we would get?'

'I don't know. Not less than you put in. I cashed one in once and I was surprised at how much I got back.'

'Then we might have as much as six thousand pounds or even ten,' he said.

'That would certainly pay the rent,' I said.

'It would indeed. We'll see about it when we're in England.'

'There's one more thing,' I said. 'I've always wanted to get to a silver wedding anniversary. Twenty-five years with one person always seemed like an important achievement to me and it always grieved me that I was unlikely to make it as things were.'

He raised his glass.

'Mali, I will happily promise you twenty-five years,' he said.

I wasn't so happy a few days later. My monthly period had coincided with a telephone call to England that left a residue of more of the unpleasantness that was circulating in our absence. I had always said I had never regretted anything in my life, seeing it all as a part of the learning process, but I spent most of October 11th and into October 12th regretting I had ever allowed myself to stay for so long in that second marriage. During the morning Greg began complaining of a headache and stomach upset, which was so unusual for him that I began seriously to wonder if my miseries weren't affecting his health. In the depths of remorse added to despair, I walked with him into Lindos to try to find some medicine in the Pharmacy. Before we could get there he was clutching at his stomach saying he must find a toilet fast. I was so worried.

'Shall we go to one of the bars?' I asked.

'No, I'll go. You go to the shop and buy the food we need. Here's the money and the list. I'll meet you there. Go!'

He disappeared into the crowded street, leaving me even more worried and upset. He had never allowed us to be parted before. I had never been told to go shopping by myself. He had never had a stomach upset before.

Miserably I walked back to our usual shop, so wrapped up in anxiety that I had walked past it and was almost out of the town before I realised what I had done.

I had filled three bags and was in the process of filling the fourth, keeping a watchful eye on the door, when suddenly there he was, leaping down the steps into the shop, wearing a grin that literally split his face from ear to ear. He was looking very happy and remarkably well.

'Are you better?' I asked, rather unnecessarily.

'Yes, I'm fine. I didn't go to the Pharmacy. I was well after I had been to the toilet.'

My conscience clearing, we hitched back to the studio in time for our afternoon swim.

'Let's take a nap first,' he said.

'Why? The weather's wonderful and I need to soak away these last few hours. I was really frightened about you this morning.'

'I know, I'm sorry. But I'm better now and I'd be better still if we had a nap.'

I didn't want to go to sleep at all and it wasn't with a terribly good grace that I helped him put down the bed. Still wearing that radiant smile he dived under the sheet and held it up for me to follow, not in the least perturbed by my obvious lack of enthusiasm. I put my head down on something hard. A red box, four inches square. 'Alexis, Jewellers, Lindos' I read as I turned it over.

'Well go on, open it.' he said.

A gold bracelet and a ring lay gleaming together on white satin.

'What have you done?' I said.

'Oh, not "how wonderful you are" but "what have you done?",' he repeated. 'Mali, you're engaged! Aren't you pleased?'

'But how did you get the money? Have you mugged an old lady or something?'

'I don't believe this! No, all the old ladies in Lindos are intact as far as I know. Come on, put them on.'

He clipped the bracelet onto my left wrist and slid the engagement ring onto my finger above the ring from France. It fitted perfectly, an emerald set in eighteen carat gold between two tiny diamonds. I didn't know what to say, I was so happy. All the darkness evaporated from my mind and heart while he told me how he had raced around Lindos, making telephone calls and plotting with the jeweller. It hadn't been an on-the-spot decision. He had made tentative plans with Alex a few days before, when we had been in the shop looking for something for Gudrun, but out of my hearing and on the condition that I wasn't to be told.

'And you may have a thousand drachma to spend entirely on a telephone call to Gillian to tell her you're engaged,' he said.

The wedding rings were on order from Athens and I had some beautiful bronze earrings to wear to match my sandals. He was always holding my hand, raising my fingers to his lips, examining my rings. He was so proud of himself and of me. His hair was growing quickly, a curly brown that had bleached out in the sun to understate the silver at the sides and on the top, very easy to cut and shape. There was a large mirror in the bathroom and I was just out of the shower, standing beside him as usual in the morning while he shaved, unable to resist touching him lightly down his spine or on his arms, knowing that in an instant he would be shivering and covered in goose-bumps in reaction to my touch.

'Gregory, why don't we have our lady photographer take a wedding picture of us like this?' I said, moving behind him to stand with my chin on his right shoulder, my hands discreetly placed over his anatomy. He gave up shaving and grinned back at me in the mirror.

'Only if you stand exactly behind me and nothing shows below the waist.'

'But you're perfectly decent like this. What's wrong with my right breast?'

'Nothing, as long as it's not in the picture.'

'Beast! I think we look wonderful.'

'So do I but I couldn't trust you not to show the picture around.'

'What would your mother think?'

'Don't ask.'

We wanted more than just a civil wedding so we wrote our own wedding vows, prepared on the day to cut out all references to anything spiritual to appease the civic system. As usual I was the secretary, sitting at the table with my pen poised.

'How shall we begin?'

'Your proposal to me in the hot pot comes most immediately to mind,' he said. 'Something on those lines.'

I began to write.

'I bow to you Greg/Mali as my lawful wedded husband/wife,

In true devotion of spirit,

To love you and to cherish you,

To honour you and –?'

'I quite like the idea of you obeying me,' he said.

'Don't I already?'

'Yes, but I'd like it in writing.'

'So that I have to declare it before all witnesses?'

'Yes.'

'You are a beast! Then you'll have to swear to protect me,' I said.

'That's all right.'

I continued writing.

'To honour you and to obey/protect you,

In truth, reverence and fidelity,

In whatever circumstances the Holy Ones ordain for our life together.

In joy let it be, beloved husband/wife

beyond the blue wind of spirit
releasing your soul into light.
With these rings I offer you freely and without limit
the flame in my heart.
Let my freedom be for ever your love.
Sadhu.'
'How does that sound?' I asked.
'Sadhu,' he said.

— ✳ —

We spent our last few days of summer on Symi, one of the islands north of Rhodes. We wanted it to be wonderful because we had been invited to stay in a house there, but my witch's nose was twitching even before we got off the boat and our six days and nights were haunted by an indefinable shadow that seemed to hang over the island. Nothing diabolical, only sad, generating a heaviness and oppression that grew with every passing day. In this psychically charged atmosphere we swam and made love and talked about our wedding, usually in bed where it felt safest. One afternoon my beloved was leaning over me to kiss me when for no particular reason I said,

'I'm the one you were waiting for all those years,' meaning during his years as a monk. But I was not prepared for the extremity of his instant reaction to me. He looked hard at me for a fraction of a second and then jumped backwards as though he had been shot.

'What's the matter?' I said.

'You're right! You're absolutely right! Mali, I've seen this before, you, me, us here like this. What did you look like ten years ago? Tell me! It's important!'

'Obviously younger. My hair was longer, slightly darker, not as sun bleached, my skin not anything like as tanned as it is now. Why?'

'That's it! That's it! You're the woman in the dream I had the year my father died. You're her! It was true! It was after that dream that I accepted what I had always known would happen, that one day I would leave with a woman. I had been terrified by the idea until then but the dream took away the fear and the guilt. Once I accepted it, it didn't matter any more. It was you, it was you! I was right!'

So many years, both of us with a dream, both of us waiting, but I hadn't been prepared to find my beloved in a monastery.

— ✳ —

There were no newspaper reporters from one of the seediest rags in England waiting to jump out of the crowd with a camera when we met Gillian at Heathrow on October 24th. They were as unimaginative as I said they would be and missed us completely. The kind person who had tipped them off had done himself no lasting favours.

'What have you done with him?' she asked as we went to the car. Greg was loading a trolley with luggage and ploughing through the crowd in front of us.

'What do you mean?'

'He looks wonderful, quite apart from the tan. At least ten years younger and a good two inches taller!'

'Only loved him. What else could I do?' I said.

My mother didn't recognise her son-in-law to be when he went running into the house for a kiss, convinced for one horrible moment that the reporters had finally come to lay siege to the house. Fortunately she didn't have time to get out the buckets of cold water she was prepared to throw at them.

Five days later, contrary to all tradition, we arrived together and early at the Register Office. Greg and Mali Klein were legally bound by special licence at nine thirty on a clear and perfect autumn morning, with Felix and Gillian as witnesses. It was a happy little wedding. It meant so much to him to be married, to have me as his wife.

'My wife, my wife,' he would say over and over again, stroking my hair, confident of an instant and glowing response. I had fallen in love with Greg Klein but I knew that I had married Ānando as well and all that went with him. The wisdom and the pain and the aftermath of the image he had created. We posed for studio photographs and then went on to Mike and Gillian's house for our wedding lunch. Later she took my bouquet of white lilies to lay at the feet of the Buddha in the garden at the monastery.

So we formally entered our contract of bliss, on a beautiful day that ended in a smart hotel in London on a specially reduced rate for our two-day honeymoon. We saw *Don Giovanni*, changed my passport according to my newly-married status, made love, ate expensive breakfasts, cheaper dinners. We were back to Gillian's to celebrate Greg's forty-sixth birthday and then on to Iceland the day after to spend two days with Gudrun. She hardly recognised us, tanned and happy as we were; we hardly recognised her, pale and quiet as she was. It was obvious that she wasn't thriving and we had another week before we saw her again on our way back from America to decide what should be done for her.

— ✳ —

I shook uncontrollably for the entire six hour flight to Baltimore. My years of dread of going to America, together with the fact that my new family still didn't know the truth about my previous status, combined to turn me into a shivering wreck. How was I going to keep up such a pretence for a week? I had already had a mother-in-law who had taken care to teach me what it was to be flawed by divorce and she had been an atheist. Now I was to be presented to a convinced Catholic, reputedly of the most conservative order. I was terrified. I was still adamantly refusing to lie so silence would have to serve and if anything awkward came up, Greg would have to deal with it himself. He had totally forbidden me in advance from having any private conversations with his family so effectively my hands, or more accurately my tongue, was resolutely tied.

'Our private life is our own affair, Mali. I have always been far more reticent than you in sharing all. My family don't know everything there is to know about me and I want you to respect that while we are visiting.'

'Yes Sir!'

'And don't go into any great detail about how you brought up your children.'

'Why? My children have survived remarkably well. They're not ashamed of me.'

'Mali, once again I repeat I am not ashamed of you but your rather liberal method may appear unorthodox to my mother.'

'They never lacked discipline.'

'You know what I mean.'

Did I know what he meant?

'Yes Sir!' I said, nevertheless.

'Don't be upset with me, Mali-Mali. It's only for one week.'

'And the sooner it's over the better for me it seems.'

'Don't worry, Baby.'

'The things I do for love. Will you always be getting me into trouble?'

'Mali, it's very simple. If they're not prepared to accept you, they won't see me. You're my wife, the most important person in my life and they have to understand that too.'

'But look how you're making us begin.'

'It'll be all right,' he said.

His eternal answer to everything. Meanwhile I had to make sure that it was all right by doing nothing to excite the situation still further. I was taken to bed that first night by an eager husband with an ear-to-ear grin who, if it was possible, was more ardent than usual in his love-making. Before everything became too distracting for words, I stopped him for several seconds.

'Gregory, do I detect an element of male victory here?'

He laughed.

'So tell me,' he said.

'That for the first time in your life you can make love to a woman under your mother's roof and there's nothing she can do or say about it at all?'

'You're absolutely right,' he said.

I survived the week, enjoying the warmer weather and the colours of the Fall but I was continually surprised at how differently his family saw him and reacted to him. But then they had never really known Ānando.

'You don't know me,' he said to his mother one day.

'You're right, I don't,' she replied.

And it seemed to be true. My husband, who kept careful daily accounts of our finances and was a master of neatness and economy of movement, appeared to be careless with money and clumsy in the house in Virginia. He managed to negotiate a full driving licence in four days, saying nothing about epilepsy and passing the sight tests, which amazed me. But money, our perennial problem, raised its head almost immediately over misunderstandings in communication between Greece and America and we left with it unresolved. It became even more important to cash in the Life Assurance policy. As the plane lifted off, heading back for Baltimore, my husband held me tight and smiled.

'That wasn't so bad, was it?' he said.

'No, except that every night I had progressively less sleep. Apart from tension everything was fine.'

Any irony was lost on him at that moment.

'How did you like my mother?'

'Well, I can love her but I couldn't live with her. We have very different cultural backgrounds and values. Do you know that she seriously asked me if I had considered having you tested before I married you?'

'I don't believe it! Why?'

'Because of your colourful past, my dear,' I said, laughing.

'How did you respond?'

'I told her that, as it has been twenty years and you didn't seem to be showing signs of anything untoward, I thought it was worth the risk.'

'Oh dear, isn't she funny? She still hasn't forgiven me. Mali, I promise you will never have to live with her. I've spent years just visiting. Nothing's going to change.'

'I'm glad because I think I understand now what you meant when you said once that you thought America brought out the worst in you.'

'Why? What do you mean?'

'Because your energy is so strange here, very restless and odd. It might even be difficult for me to like you all of the time if we lived here permanently.'

'Don't worry, I have no desire to spend the rest of my life in America. We won't live anywhere that you're not completely at ease with. I have learned to have great respect for your witch's nose and if you're okay, I'm okay. Like everything else, it's as simple as that.'

Chapter Eight

We had nearly four and a half months of peace and tranquillity in our little house in the olive grove on Rhodes. Even though I ruptured several ligaments in my left foot in the middle of January, effectively crippling myself until March. Lardos was only twenty minutes' walk away for shopping and bread and the post, and large cans of cheap dog food when we found ourselves feeding two howling cats who naturally assumed they were a scheduled part of our tenancy. Ten minutes away in the opposite direction, the beach was beautiful. A large expanse of white sand with great cliffs at the southern end and a sea frothing white waves when the wind came roaring from the east and the north, milky calm on cool, winter days when the wind blew gently from the south.

It was much too cold for swimming; we lasted less than thirty seconds and came out screaming after our first attempt. My husband was determined to buy us wet suits. I wanted to save the money for a weekend in Cairo at Christmas but healthy bodies took precedence over healthy minds and I found myself being zipped into a 'shortie' wet suit ordered from a diving shop in Rhodes Town. It looked professional but symbolised duty rather than pleasure for me when it failed to prevent that first freezing rush of water getting in under the collar and running down my back.

The weather was decidedly colder than we had expected. We had only fourteen days of rain all winter. For most of December and into the first week in January, it was not unusual to see frost glistening under the olive trees and rimed on blackened bushes by the side of the road early in the mornings, as we shivered and ran up and down to stay warm until we got a lift into the town. On clear days we could see the snow in the mountains to the east in Turkey. On January 8th, snowflakes came drifting down for over half an hour while everyone came running out of the shops to look.

Nearly all the buses were cancelled until April 1st. The early bus that apparently came through Lardos remained elusive to us all the time we were there so we always had to be at the roadside by seven o'clock to be sure of hitching a ride. Greeks smoke ceaselessly, taking some pride in being the world's second largest tobacco consumers after Cuba. So quite apart from taking our lives in our hands when we put ourselves at the mercy of the national driving technique, we got into passive smoking in a really big way that winter.

Our little house was one of two adjacent studios in a converted cow house with walls eighteen inches thick. The main room was charming with three shuttered windows looking out at the olive trees, rugs on the floor, a large, unusable fireplace in one corner which housed the shrine, and an open beam and bamboo ceiling. The little kitchen and bathroom had been built onto the back when the building had been converted. Solar heating panels had been installed on the roof to heat the water, which worked wonderfully provided we had a regular daily three hours of sunshine. When Ra turned his attentions elsewhere for the day, we got up to cold showers before meditation the following morning. The house hadn't been built with winter tenants in mind. The thicker walls became increasingly damp and the newer single brick walls let the cold come streaming through and went obligingly mouldy in February. We huddled over our single-bar electric fire and wrapped up in blankets and Icelandic sweaters to work at the computer.

Our landlord was a garrulous, elderly Don Quixote character for whom normal conversation appeared to be a series of imprecations rasped through the noticeable gaps between his time-stained teeth. With a greasy black cap jammed down hard on his spiky grey head, he toured his territory on an ancient motorcycle hung all over with plastic bags filled with tools. We arrived at the house to find him absorbed in the olive harvest, muttering and cursing as he beat at the branches and shouting orders to his wife and her relatives, who were sat with bags at intervals under the trees picking up the fruit. As the day wore on and his enthusiasm waned, he would come back to the tool bags ever more frequently to refresh himself from the bottle of wine hung on the handlebars until it was empty and the sun was disappearing over the mountains behind the village.

When the harvest was done, he spent the rest of the winter pruning the trees with great vigour, sawing madly at the largest branches and piling them into several heaps in the middle of the field, each as large again as one of the trees. Nothing was spared. We found one tree that we had been admiring in front of the house completely gone one morning when we came back from Lardos. His wife was shaking her head and making scissor motions with her fingers.

'Cut, cut, cut,' she said sadly.

The orange and lemon trees fared better and he was always leaving piles of the fruit on our doorstep, many more than we could eat. We found ourselves stockpiling until Gabriel came for a visit in February and could take a bag full back to my mother to make marmalade.

Christmas as such has no place in the Buddhist calendar but our first Christmas together was magical. It was a case of either allowing myself to be overwhelmed by a sense of loss at not being able to contact the children as I wanted to, or making the effort to appreciate exactly what was going on for me right there and then. The effort was the wiser choice, helped by a well-timed sneaky phone call we had made to the boys a week before and made fun by hiring a car for the three days of the holiday. We decorated the house and made a tree out of a pine branch covered in lametta and propped in the fireplace over the Buddha-rupa. We made tangerine balls stuck all over with cloves and hung them on the tree and piled up the parcels we had collected for each other ready for Christmas Eve.

Greg could hardly wait until our Christmas bean stew was over to give me my presents. Another gold bracelet went around my wrist and a new chain was hung round my neck. A hot water bottle was laid at my feet with in-bred American scorn until he realised how nice it was and then I was forced to share. I gave him more music tapes, a warm sweater, fresh ground coffee and chocolate, both luxuries in our life now. Our passionate gratitude for each other lost us some of the time we had paid for on the car but we managed to tour the island completely, surprised at how beautiful it was, especially to the south and the west. We climbed spectacular Tsambika to the little shrine at the top, taking care not to pray for babies as we lit our candles. We visited monasteries and ruined castles and drove through the two thousand acres of silent, blackened forest razed by fire the previous autumn. Another gold ring appeared to begin the formal decoration of my right hand for my birthday at the beginning of January.

It was often warmer to be outside rather than in the house but it was always warm in bed. We made sure we exercised every day, walking either to Lardos or to the beach. Sometimes we made a vain attempt to swim. Most of our time was taken up with Greg dictating the story of his life to me, usually in the afternoons so that I could type it into the computer the next morning. After breakfast, he 'did the dishes and the washing' with the tape deck playing continually to make up for his twenty years out of contact with music. Opera, baroque and Mozart flooded our little house with sound, changing to rock when my concentration at the computer was no longer a major priority and we would go boogying out of the door onto the little concrete patio and on under the olive trees to Bryan Adams and Bruce Springsteen. He was as shy dancing after so long as I was doing Tai Chi but he had a wonderful natural rhythm; we vowed never to let the other dance with anyone else. We found ourselves much too attractive weaving around each other in time to the music, always ending with a lingering kiss at the fading of the final beats. Every so often one of us would slip the *Unchained Melody* into the machine and we would be singing and dancing so slowly, so close, in sweet nostalgia. In the evening as soon as dinner was cleared away we made a huge bed up on the floor with blankets and quilts, snuggling into it usually by eight o'clock ready for me to read aloud to my husband, beginning with Mary Stewart's 'Merlin' Trilogy and followed by all six books of 'Dune'.

— ✳ —

By January 10th the weather had turned unexpectedly warm. We sunbathed every afternoon during dictation before adjourning to the beach for increasingly competitive ball games. The public toilet block wall served as a make-shift squash court until everything came to a halt when I wrecked my ankle. After my experience with the dentist, I refused either to see a Greek doctor or to go to the hospital. Not even to have an X-ray. Careful examination decided that no bones were broken but that one or more of the ligaments were badly damaged.

I treated it initially as I had treated the horses, cold-hosing the swelling for twenty minutes every day or alternatively sitting on a rock and dangling it in the sea while my Lord jogged along the beach. The bruising gradually spread from my toes to midway up my calf, uncomfortably reminding me of my father's legs turning black with gangrene as he died. Greg worked on the ankle every day for weeks, using hot and cold compresses and the healing technique, and the ligaments eventually healed very well. Although it was five weeks before I could put any weight on the foot and another two before we could return the crutches we had been loaned by an old man in the village. I crawled on all fours everywhere indoors. Twice every week pushing me balanced on the bicycle that came with the house, Greg took us into Lardos, carrying me in and out of the shops and the Post Office when we got there.

With nothing else to do but write I felt oddly disempowered as even cooking the dinner fell to my husband's hands. He had always made breakfast, a delicious concoction of bread, olive oil and full cream milk flavoured with a generous pinch of nutmeg. It sat on the back of the stove while we were meditating and came steaming to our improvised table on the floor at eight o'clock while the newscaster on VOA Europe gave us the American version of what was going on in the rest of the world. Now Greg was back in the kitchen at five o'clock, chopping vegetables and frying onions and garlic.

'Mali!' he sang from the steam cloud that came drifting past the blanket that doubled as a door. 'Mali! How do I make bean stew?'

We got to know many of the local people in Lardos but we didn't socialise, preferring to spend all of our time together. Enjoying 'this delightful dance' as my husband loved to call it. Making the most of the time and space to allow our relationship to unfold and develop. We always got into bed to solve a problem. No matter what time of day he would be taking off my clothes, slipping out of his and pulling me under the quilt to talk it through. I cried so many tears on that beautiful chest until the hairs were matted together and wet. He made me feel safe and welcome to cry.

Ours was so complete an emotional, physical, psychic and spiritual merging. We hardly needed to talk but we never stopped talking. Even in silence we were still communicating. I loved the little lines on his face, his beautiful eyes, the contours of his neck and throat, his beautiful mouth, even the silvery tinges to his hair. Kissing an ear and tracing the line down his neck, across his throat and into the little hollow where the clavicles met, nuzzling into the softness of the brown hair of his armpit, his chest, his forearms. Outlining the smooth hardness of the muscles and veins of his arms, feeling the smoothness of his nipples shrivel and harden between my teeth. And his hands, small, well-shaped and expressive, and so tender with me, stroking my hair, my cheek.

'Beautiful eyes,' he murmured, so many times in so many days.

How many times a day did we say 'I love you', and at night waking up just enough to murmur the words again and fall back into sleep? The last words on our lips as we closed our eyes, the first as the morning came to wake us up. I always lay at his right side in bed, his arm around me, my cheek pillowed on his chest, feeling his heart beating strong and steady, his breathing soft and slow. He never snored or twitched as he slept. In his sleeping he was as neat and elegant as he was in everything else he did. Never sloppy, always meticulous, cleaning his teeth carefully and flossing regularly after our evening meal.

He insisted on exercising every morning before meditation, doing press-ups and head stands. He even perspired elegantly. He didn't think so but he always smelt fresh and clean and so essentially male. I could spend hours snuffling him all over in sensual appreciation with an accompaniment of the little noises of love and pleasure that came naturally to me and that he loved. We were always tender with each other, passionate, easily aroused, eager for the night. When my hormonal cycle brought me down, I would say,

'Tonight you have to just lay there and take it while I make love to you. I need to be active to take my mind off my uterus!'

'Great! Shall we start now?'

And he would be getting out the bed and running the shower, appearing clean and cologned and ready for anything.

— �֍ —

He wasn't pleased when anyone wrote to Ãnando rather than Greg. He took it as non-acceptance, as a lack of recognition. His name was Greg and he was learning to know and to accept Greg Klein for the first time in his life. He was not happy when the few refused to recognise him as such. He was both Greg and Ãnando now and wanted to make the most of his newly-found freedom to discover and explore the possibilities of the duality finally recognisable as one.

As Metta Master he supervised my flashbacks from the divorce every morning as a regular part of our meditation practice. I was very resistant at first. I had no great desire to wish Loving Kindness towards a situation that symbolised such anguish. But I had no choice. As the sitting neared its end, he would begin.

'Bring to mind someone you hurt and using their name say please forgive me.

Bring to mind someone who hurt you and using their name say I forgive you.

Using your own name say I forgive you.

Using your own name say you are forgiven.

Using your own name say I love you.'

For weeks I would watch irritation rising and feel my jaw tighten. Nevertheless I did it, if only so that I could honestly say that I had joined in the formal practice when asked. It took a full three months before it didn't matter any more and the memories could rise in my mind and pass on without arousing so much of the old anger and resentment.

My mind became very finely tuned as time went on. Living and meditating in that quiet place day after day, I became acutely aware of the sound of silence as we sat in the pre-dawn serenity, the candle flickering before the Buddha, the sensuous smoke of our favourite incense wafting into the room. My husband sat directly in front of me. Our knees touching, holding both my hands, often using the heart centre as the focus for our practice. Occasionally I felt a kiss brush my lips, sending my mind immediately into delightfully inappropriate distraction.

'Gregory! Don't kiss me when I'm meditating!'

'Sorry! For a moment I couldn't help myself.'

'Really!'

Meditation began with chanting and ended with a blessing. We made the traditional three bows to Buddha, Dhamma, Sangha and then turned to make three bows to each other, always with a prolonged kiss and giggling midway through the final bow. We did an absent healing service every Monday evening and at every Full Moon we did all our favourite chanting either in the house or in the church at a local Orthodox Monastery. No one ever came in to object to Pali chanting and we were always very respectful, lighting our candles and leaving our drachma in the collection box. When the chanting was finished we repeated our wedding vows as a gesture of the continuation of our mutual love and respect and formally asked forgiveness of each other for any thought, word or deed that had caused misunderstanding or pain.

'My meditation practice seems to be focused mainly on samadhi these days,' said my husband.

'Mine's getting there,' I said.

'And the metta practice?'

'It's coming along. What about you? Have you noticed any of the old anger coming up from last year?'

'No, not any more. It was time I left. It was the right thing to do. I know it hasn't been so easy for you with the divorce but for me it's been like one long, delightful holiday since I left the monastery.'

'When can we go back to the Sangha Gregory?'

'In about five years when I feel I've done enough to prove that I can survive in the lay life.'

'Why so long? I miss the nuns.'

'Because I know monks. They can be very critical and very condescending. Don't forget I've been there.'

'Don't you miss it at all?'

'No, I can't say that I do. Or indeed ever have done. I have never regretted leaving the monastery and I know that a lot of that has to be because I had the wisdom to leave with you, my Mali-Mali. The four M's in my life,' he said smiling.

'What do you mean?'

'My mother, the Marines, the monastery and Mali. Beautiful woman, you saved my spirit. But I have never felt my time as a monk was wasted.'

84

'Absolutely not. It's made you into a wonderfully sensitive husband.'

He bowed.

'Thank you. Any anger I had towards Ajahn Sumedho is long gone. I've done a great deal of forgiveness meditation towards him. I never doubted his intentions towards me. As I said in my last letter to him, I see my anger as a result of my own lack of wisdom. But if he had come on heavy to me as he once did to one of the other monks, there is a very good chance that I would have lost it completely, hit him and put a book, preferably from the Pali Canon, through the window as I left. And that is something I may have regretted for the rest of my life. US Marine Corps conditioning dies hard and unfortunately Scorpions don't easily forget. We would have parted with a great wall of pain between us which for my part is not there.'

'There are many paths to enlightenment. It is a delusion to think or to say otherwise.'

'I agree. So what about your own enlightenment Mali? Do you think you can achieve it during this lifetime?'

'I don't know. Probably not. When I think of all the situations and people I have had to leave half-settled, I should think I shall have to be coming back several times more to sort it all out.'

'But that's only in your own mind. It doesn't have to be that way.'

'But women have too much to divert them, especially when they have children. It's more possible for a man to get enlightened than a woman,' I said.

'Why? How can you say that?'

'Because of the very nature of masculine energy as opposed to the feminine.'

'How do you mean?'

'Because in ninety-nine per cent of cases women are continually diverted in a host of subtle ways. By the womb, the need to nurture and to nest. All their energy is pulled into nurturing the child so that even when the child grows up and the mother hopes she is free, there is still a deeply-rooted conditioning that takes a lot of wisdom to fully comprehend and to let go of. Whereas men are capable of a very single-pointed energy, especially once they can transcend and redirect the inevitable early morning erection which will appear however resolutely they have gone to bed.'

'Even that was rare with me during the last years.'

'Is that why you were so terribly nervous when you decided to fall in love with me?'

'Of course, I was terrified.'

'Now that that particular nightmare has been laid to rest, do you think you still have the chance of enlightenment this time?'

'I would hope so. Certainly by the end of my time in the Sangha and maybe for some time before that, I didn't think I would attain it by remaining a monk. I have never felt that I renounced all hope of enlightenment by leaving. Like you, I am inclined to think that there is more than one path. But when you use the word "enlightenment", what do you mean? What does it mean to you?'

'I believe–' I began.

'No. It has nothing to do with belief,' said Ānando, immediately irritated. 'I'm interested only in what you know to be true.'

'Sorry, wrong speech. Okay. I know it's the same as at-one-ment. To be at one with the light, the great whatever, nameless and beyond the limitations of a god-head. Notice the use of the word, very different in concept and meaning from the traditional Christian viewpoint. "The Lord thy God is a jealous God". I have always thought that a truly terrifying idea. They say God made man in his own image, don't you think man made God to suit himself? There is no room in my Universe for dark and vengeful gods.'

Ānando sat motionless, assimilating the desana. Greg looked up as I paused. Eye contact. Silence. Encouraging me to investigate further.

'Then what is God? To me, it is not an entity. It just is. Like the power behind the Great Cosmic Breath pervading all worlds, all dimensions. Here and now, past, future and present, all rolled into one. Enlightenment? Greg, I know it's only a breath away. I can hold out my hands and it's there, just one breath away. It's all around us continually. As you say, only our minds create the barriers. We effectively blind ourselves to the simple reality.'

'Then why do you think it is so difficult to realise?'

'I suppose because we are so complicated, we expect our ultimate truth to be complicated. We would probably be disappointed if it was not. We romance about simplicity but we remain caught up in our complicated world where true simplicity has no place. How simple was your life as a monk?'

'In the beginning I should say it was pretty simple but not so in the end. Especially in a position of leadership in a western Sangha. My standard of living has certainly dropped since I left!'

He laughed.

'Exactly. Because now you have to pay the bills. There are no adoring lay people offering you the best of the best as the Ajahn. And you have to admit that you did have quite a lot of material possessions for a homeless alms mendicant.'

'I suppose I did. I never really thought of it at the time. One thing certainly does surprise me. I am amazed at how quiet my mind can be now. Much more so that it ever was at Chithurst.'

'Why do you think that is?'

'Because my life is much simpler now. I don't have to be anything for anyone, only you and you know me as well as I know me. Probably better. I don't have to prove anything to you. Well, only to myself concerning you I suppose. We are so fortunate in that we don't have to work and that we have been given this time to be together with no other obligation than to learn each other, to be here for one another.'

'Yes, I am truly grateful for the VA and the pay cheque but I wish it could have been earned in some other way than your being shot in the head. A part of me would almost rather have us grubbing in some boring job and only being together evenings and weekends like other people, rather than having you with part of your skull missing.'

'Yes, I often wonder what will come of it. I have been extraordinarily lucky so far but for how much longer I wonder?'

'Why? Do you feel ill at all? Are your eyes okay?'

'I'm fine. But I know me. One day I'm going to be so sick that you will have to do absolutely everything for me. You are my wife and I will expect nothing less. So don't worry about me having to look after you now. Besides I enjoy it. But this life seems almost too perfect somehow. It's like a beautiful bubble, huge and shining with a rainbow of colours that could burst at any moment.'

'Why do you say such things? It's almost as though you are willing it to happen.'

'I'm not. Not at all. It's just that I don't know what I've done to deserve you.'

'The monastic doubting mind! Why shouldn't you be good enough for all this? By whose standards are you judging? Why shouldn't you deserve it?'

'I don't know. I just never feel worthy. I never feel good enough.'

'Well, take it from me that you are. We've loved each other for centuries of lifetimes and we'll go on for centuries more. We're not restricted to one life and one time. Why don't you just shut up and relax and enjoy what we have now?'

'You're right! You're absolutely right!'

The Lord of the Rings became the perfect evening antidote to afternoons of intense dictation as we wrote the Vietnam section of the book. The 'sex, drugs and rock 'n' roll' parts sometimes embarrassed him but Vietnam was particularly painful to resurrect as he resurfaced memories he thought were lost. He was so terribly unforgiving of himself and intensely self-critical. We got into bed for the worst bits. It was easier for him to talk with his head against my breast while I scribbled on the pad with my free hand.

'Have you no compassion for natural youth and ignorance?' I asked him more than once after a particularly difficult transcription.

'Yes there is that, but I always expected more of myself and I didn't see myself in the same way as others chose to see me. No one ever knew me and I didn't know myself. You are the only person I have ever fully opened up to. We have to go to Vietnam. I need to go back.'

'I think I know why, but tell me.'

'Because I want to say I'm sorry. I need to ask forgiveness for everything we did and didn't do.'

'Do you realise that this could offend some people?' I said, indicating the printed screen in front of me.

'Why?'

'Because it crashes through the illusion, the myth.'

'Well, that is entirely their problem, not mine. Everyone believes their own version of the truth and what was true for the others was not necessarily true for me.'

'So what was true for you, Gregory?'

He paced up and down the room, absorbed in memory. Moments became minutes, became time passing, an afternoon fading fast. I leaned over the little table to turn on the lamp. The leaping shadows filling the opposite side of the room narrowed as the pacing paused; he stood poised as though on the brink of the abyss.

'Yes indeed,' he murmured. 'What was true for me?'

And so we lived through that winter, absorbed in each other and in the writing, ever conscious of every moment. Driven on by a sense of urgency that offered neither respite nor definition.

Part Two

Charles

Chapter Nine

March 1st 1993
'Once I knew Ānando –
I know him still and better now,
in all his sweetness,
his dangerous sweetness,
my husband and lover,
my wonderful lover;
"Are you mine?" he asked me –
I always have been
and always will be,
Beloved Ānando,
Beloved husband,
Mine.'

I gave him the poem with a sprig of almond blossom cut from the tree that held up one end of the washing line. He read it, saying nothing, his eyes misting over as he remembered.

'That had to be the happiest day of my life, the day you said you were mine,' he said finally, smiling down at me.

'Not our wedding day or the day you left Kandersteg?'

'They were happy but not the happiest. After that evening in the lane everything was all right.'

Cold and rain in February had combined their efforts to turn the ceilings in the kitchen and bathroom black, concentrating a lingering odour of damp and mildew that threatened to choke us before it was warm enough outside to open the windows in the morning. On the first dry day Greg put on a large plastic coat, rubber gloves and, with a bag advertising Lardos Supermarket tied on his head, he threw everything movable out of the house and attacked the mould with bleach. I was perched on a chair on the patio with my leg on a stool watching the progress of the plastic and rubber tornado as he powered around our desecrated living space. It reminded me of all the years I had spent buying houses and ripping them apart to make them habitable.

'I'm glad we don't own this house or any other house,' I said.

'So am I. I've never wanted to own anything like a house although it might be fun to build one on that plot of land my mother bought for me in Florida.'

'And then sell it?'

'Yes, probably. Or rent it out.'

'I made a vow to myself the day I left the first marriage that I would never own a house again and never commit all my hard-earned money into maintaining a building. House-owning never made me feel secure. Just the opposite in fact. There was always something that needed doing and never any time or money left to have fun.'

'Yes, I can understand that. There's a far greater security in owning nothing than too much, but not a lot of people would understand that.'

Money was an everlasting problem. Cashing in the Life Assurance brought nothing like the dividend we hoped for but it did pay our winter's rent and then kept us in funds until the money from America could be sorted out. Greg was always so careful with our budget, diligently revising the lists of our economies as soon as we came back from shopping. But it was like walking in the inky black of the Labyrinth without a torch until our account had been properly opened in America and statements began to appear every month. Even so it was February before that happened and March before the National Bank of Greece worked out how to liaise successfully with a bank in America.

We had been married for over three months before it occurred to us that we might be due an increase on the pay cheque to cater for a dependent wife.

'I wonder how much the VA thinks you're worth?' said my Lord, lost in speculation.

'Well, maybe by the time they have decided, the bank here will have worked out how to convert dollar cheques into drachma. We are the poorest people I know who technically have enough to live on.'

'We only have a cash flow problem, that's all,' he said.

We were nearly climbing the walls in exasperation one morning when we had made a special trip into the town for an early appointment with the bank manager only to find ourselves locked out and staring at notices that clearly announced a national strike. Even storming the place behind an employee only resulted in the usual Mediterranean shrug.

'We can do no-thing. Come back tomorrow. Tomorrow is okaya.'

On the day when the drachma finally appeared on the computer system we made a celebratory tour of Rhodes Town, buying a radio cassette player to take to Limnos as the other one belonged to the house, and eating huge pizzas in a restaurant in the Old Town. When the last delicious crumb had vanished from the plates, my husband took me to meet a jeweller who had become one of his secret associates since Christmas, to buy us matching gold chains to commemorate our first delicious year of love.

Coming home from the town with our parcels, laughing and talking, pointing out the wild flowers that were coming up everywhere in the surprising warmth of the Spring sunshine, we were in sight of the house when he suddenly lost control of his bladder. He was very distressed and confused.

'I don't know what's happening,' he said.

'Come on. It happens to everyone at some time or another,' I said, handing him a clean pair of jeans with a kiss. The others were washed and out on the line in five minutes.

'I'm so grateful for your attitude towards me in this,' he said. 'I know it means nothing but I couldn't bear to be incontinent when I'm old. I remember wetting the bed once in a hotel when I was a child and my parents having to pay for a new mattress before we left. They didn't make anything of it but I was so ashamed.'

'Gregory, I've done six and a half years of continuous nappy-changing with the babies and I've nursed. One pair of jeans is nothing in comparison. Forget it, beloved you. It's not a problem,' I said.

It didn't happen again and we made no reference to it. But I was worried too. There was something more going on in him that I couldn't understand and couldn't find a reason for. Since mid-February as we were finishing the Vietnam section of the book, I had been noticing his face beginning to change. Sometimes I saw a look in his eyes that had never been there before. A hollow weariness and an almost grey bloom to his skin, if that could be possible in someone so tanned. His breathing had also changed. Whereas I had always been able to time my breathing with his to go to sleep, now he was breathing considerably faster and more shallowly than I when he lay down to rest. In the mornings when he lay holding me and talking to me before we got up for meditation, the vein in the middle of his forehead would be noticeably prominent. It disappeared as soon as he got up.

I didn't make anything of it. He never complained of any pain. Nevertheless there were so many times when I found myself thinking, 'What's making pressure in your head?' At least once every week I asked him,

'Gregory, are your eyes okay? Can you still see as well?'

'Yes, I'm fine. What's worrying you?'

'Nothing, I don't think. I just want to be sure, that's all.'

He would never willingly discuss his health. He was always 'very well' to all queries. Ill health was a weakness he preferred not to think about. At the same time he always added 'keep us healthy' as a regular addition to grace before meals, and future plans for travelling would often have 'if we stay healthy' as a codicillary clause.

A golden Labrador dog had been added to our menagerie after a herd of goats ate their way through the orchard one night towards the end of February.

'You see? You see?' howled our landlord, dancing up and down with rage. 'Colour? What colour?'

It was almost impossible to explain that we weren't able to identify the culprits by starlight at two in the morning but he decided who in the village would have to pay. He came back followed by two trucks and several goat owners. The dog was in the back of one of the trucks as an offer of appeasement and she was tied on a long run that stretched across the length of the tree plantation. Her new owner gave her water once a day and a quarter of a dry loaf every one or two days. By the fourth day she was eating a bowlful of dogmeat with a worming pill, along with the cats.

She was bred to be a working dog and was quite mad from continually being tied up. Our comings and goings were always serenaded by wild yelpings and howlings from across the garden. On our last afternoon after the old man had gone, having spent the day packing and cleaning the house, we decided to take her with us for a final walk on the beach. She had a wonderful time running round and round us, rushing off into the groves of bamboo hot on the scent of tantalising smells. She was surprisingly obedient to a whistle.

It was March 31st and already the first tourists were appearing on the island. Lindos, having been a ghost town all winter, was due to open the following day and the Rhodians had been painting hotels for the past three weeks. We were not sorry to be leaving. It had been a wonderful winter but we found ourselves unwilling to share our space with the enthusiasm of the first pale plane loads on holiday. We were looking forward to seeing Limnos again.

Greg whistled up the dog and we walked slowly back to the house to find the old man returned and stood scratching his head under his cap. He held the untied end of the dog's rope in his hand. He said nothing as she slunk up to him and crouched down while he wrapped it through her collar in several complicated knots. We left her silent and looking wistfully after the taxi that took us away up the road early next morning; she knew.

— ✳ —

All the almond trees were covered in blossom as we came down through the valley below Kaspakas to Agios Giannis. The mountains were green and covered in flowers. April on Limnos was appreciably colder than March on Rhodes and the sun shone through clouds that hung grey-blue over the sea with the coming rain.

Our house, although larger than our studio in the olive grove, was in many ways more primitive. Our first priority was to establish a large supply of fresh drinking water, as I had been diagnosed as possibly having kidney stones in the hospital the day before we left Rhodes. It seemed to be a fairly common complaint in the Greek Islands, probably not helped by the decided alkalinity of the water. I was under orders to drink at least four and a half litres of water each day. The water on Agios Giannis was supplied from wells in the gardens of each house; ours was conveyed by means of two separate pumps, first to a holding tank and from there into the house. It was brackish and undrinkable and both pumps blew out during our first week. Once they had been replaced and a large stack of boxes of mineral water had been delivered from the village, we began to feel comfortable. With our bedroom cleared of unwanted beds and the shrine set up, my first duty in every new house, we were home again.

Greg was always pleased with how I arranged the shrine. Surrounded by our wedding photographs and flowers, the Buddha-rupa sat on a flat stone specially selected for the purpose from the edge of the sea. The candle in the

94

bronze dish and the incense smoking in the carved wooden holder completed the ritual requirements. More gradually, we added a selection of coloured stones and shells that we picked up as we took our daily walks on the beach.

For a few days it was a nuisance to have to remember to turn on the electric heater for the shower and then to try to have enough hot water left to take to the kitchen in a bowl for the washing up, but we were always easily adaptable and soon thought nothing of it. The kitchen table and chairs were so rickety that we immediately banished them to the spare bedroom. On Rhodes we had found what looked like a wooden well-cover which made a perfect round table for meals, as we always preferred to sit monastic fashion on the floor to eat. A thorough search of the outhouse and the garden on Limnos produced nothing similar until, equipped with a rusty saw and several rusty nails, in half an hour my husband had converted two old shutters into a larger, rectangular replica. It only needed a red cotton tablecloth from Mirina to be complete. It was so nice to be married to someone who just got on and did things without waiting either to be asked or to be told what to do. If we had a problem he always immediately set about solving it. The insignificant was never given time to become significant. It was the cold that troubled us most until our neighbour lent us an oil-filled radiator and we had bought an enormous gold and pink fluffy blanket for our bed.

A day of thirteen hours of unceasing rain kept us indoors and watching our minds. We had been spoilt on Rhodes and now the unrelenting beating on the streaming windows made the house seem small and intensely claustrophobic. The sea was only two hundred yards away across a field of young corn but on that day it was grey and uninviting, with white waves whipped into a frenzy by the wind to come crashing onto the shore, sucking up the sand and stones and piling up sodden brown drifts of weed that dried to look like heaps of dun-coloured shredded paper on the beach.

Limnos and Agios Giannis were as near to a home for us as anywhere we had ever been. It was a quiet and uncomplicated agrarian community. The land was still worked and well tended, the animals well looked after. Every morning the men rode down from the village on their donkeys, horses or mules to go trotting past our house up to their land around Kalogeros, working the farms that had probably been in their families for generations. On calm days, mostly at weekends, we heard the chugging of the little boats putting out from the harbour to fish through the evening and into the night, their lights twinkling far out to the horizon all around the bay.

There were fields all around the house. Some mornings our meditation was punctuated by muttering and the occasional yell as two cows, or more rarely two horses, yoked together were being guided in front of a primitive wooden plough. When we walked to the village, everyone was kind to us, calling out 'Kalimera' or 'Yasus', asking how we were, asking about the pain in my back. In Kaspakas only one person needed to be told something for it to become common knowledge. There was always someone willing to give us a lift into Mirina. We couldn't walk down the main street without hearing 'Hey, Gregorio! Kalimera!' from the shop doorways or one of the cafés. They could never say my name but one served for both.

Olive trees, bent and windburned in the bitter winter months, never thrived on Limnos but fig trees and almond trees were in abundance and our garden was a meadow in miniature, luxurious with wild flowers. I was adamant that it would not be grazed by the donkey next door. All the houses dotted along the length of the dirt road were still closed up for the winter and our few neighbours only appeared at weekends to begin planting their summer vegetables. The house next door was always closed except for the Orthodox Feast Days and public holidays. Then the entire family would appear for the day to roast a whole sheep's carcass directly opposite our door. We calculated correctly that they needed a minimum of four hours for the entire rite so on those days we packed our lunch and went out walking all day, regardless of the weather.

Once we climbed up to the little hill shrine above Kalogeros that looked out west across the sea to holy Agios Ouros, the centre for the Orthodox Church. The mountain appeared only on clearer, cooler days. We found the door left open and oil and donkey droppings on the floor. A layer of dust blurred the holy pictures. Everything was long neglected and dirty.

'We must come up here again and clean this before we leave,' I said.

Several times as we were walking, we met wild tortoises crawling purposefully on the path in front of us. Immediately memories of our menagerie left behind on Rhodes came to mind.

'Oh Gregory, I miss the cats,' I said. 'Can't we have a tortoise in the garden?'

'Must we? What makes you think it would stay?'

'It might.'

'And how would you persuade it to go there in the first place?'

'Well, maybe you could carry it there for me in a bag. Couldn't you?'

As it happened, every time we found one neither of us had a suitable bag and I made a point of not noticing that my husband's relief was almost too obvious.

Another neighbour introduced us to Therma, the local hot spring nine kilometres away, north-east of Mirina. The water was clean and pure, not yellow and sulphurous like the ones we were used to in Iceland. Greg was anxious that we should have a regular supply of it to supplement our drinking water and found a container in the shed that would hold twenty-two and a half litres. It was just the right size to fit into the big pack. Only he would elect to carry such a weight for eighteen kilometres. But carry it he did once every week until we left at the beginning of June.

There was a strong military presence on the island as a reminder of the close proximity of Turkey, the ancient enemy. Every time we passed the barracks on our way to Therma, Greg would point out to me all the World

War Two and Vietnam era equipment still in use in the Greek Army. Even the aircraft that came occasionally, flying fast and low over Agios Giannis, brought back the memories, and the odd burst of gunfire would have him starting up from whatever he was doing to check it out.

We had several offers to teach but in places where he had taught previously as a monk. It seemed that it was expected that we would have something very similar to offer as lay teachers.

'But why should we?' I asked.

'Because that's what they expect of me,' he said.

'That's what they expect of Ãnando. Why did you leave the monastery?'

'Because I had something more to do.'

'So teach that. There are plenty of ex-monastic lay teachers on the circuit. It doesn't need any more.'

'But that's all I know!' He was becoming almost aggressive in defence.

'What have you learnt since you left?'

'A lot.'

'Isn't that worth teaching? The practicalities of relating as a practice, how to apply the practice within an intimate human relationship. There are plenty of couples who would be very interested to hear what we have to say about that. How many people are aware that it is their own self-hatred and self-doubt that often destroys a relationship?'

'But the established retreat centres are geared up to the standard teaching.'

'So we won't go there.'

'But where else is there to teach?'

'Where we're needed. Something will turn up. We don't have to teach in order to live.'

'For which I am truly grateful,' he said. 'You're right. We'll leave it and see what comes up. I will happily go on as we are. Do you realise, Mali, we have been together continually for twenty-four hours a day for almost a year now? We blend like milk and honey, a continual melding and it never ceases to amaze me how the feeling grows, deepens, expands; it never lessens. If I can only do something about your pain, everything will be perfect.'

The hot water bottle spent most of its active life on my back. Kidney stones are painful but mine were unusual in that the pain went on for so long and seemed to spread out all over my upper back. Nothing stopped us making love, we were masters of improvisation but the pain, however dulled with pain-killer and anti-spasmodic drugs, was almost continual and had to be allowed for all through April. I was mortified when it became impossible for me even to carry my shoulder bag and JBJ became resigned to a life guarding the shrine. Greg practised healing on me, kinesiology, massage, everything we could think of, using every skill we possessed.

By May 1st we had to admit that a visit to the hospital in Mirina might be a good idea. A man operating an ultra-sound scanner in a half-constructed building in the middle of the town confirmed my right kidney clear but showed us evidence of stones apparent in my left kidney. More water, more anti-spasm pills and for almost two weeks I was better. Already tanned from eating our lunch and writing every day on the beach between clouds, on the night of May 12th we celebrated my returning health with a glorious, crazy abandonment, free of all constrained improvisation. The most exquisite and intimate of all sharing, falling into deep and blissful sleep at the end of it, curled all around each other content.

I was dreaming. A knife was being stabbed into my back repeatedly, punching through my skin and tearing out again. In, out, in, out. I could hear myself screaming.

'Mali! Mali Baby! Speak to me! Speak to me!'

Greg was shaking me, forcing me out of sleep. The pain was still there.

'What's the matter? What's happening?' I murmured. 'Oh my back hurts.'

'Mali, you were groaning aloud in your sleep. Were you dreaming?'

'I thought someone was stabbing me. It feels as though they still are.'

'That settles it. We are going to the hospital in the morning and there is no negotiation. When my wife is in pain even in her dreams, something has got to be done.'

'But I'm not going back to England. I don't want to leave here until we have to.'

'Don't worry. We'll get something sorted out here even if we have to go down to the Base on Crete.'

The hospital staff were beginning to get to know us. A kidney X-ray was arranged for the following week for which Greg was instructed to prepare me with doses of laxative and an enema. Before that, summer came to Limnos on May 15th. It was as though someone had pulled a switch. The sky cleared completely, the sea was silken smooth and our lunch-time dictation sessions on the beach prolonged into the afternoon.

The incense, burning on the shrine, curled through shafts of golden sunlight during morning meditation but another source of concern manifested to keep us on our toes. As my beloved got out of bed one morning to make his customary three bows to the shrine, he suddenly put both hands to his head.

'Oh! I have a headache!' he said.

A second later it had passed. When it recurred at the same time the next morning he immediately did a head stand against the wall.

'This always works,' he said.

And apparently it did although he was perhaps a little more dizzy than usual when he stood upright. He showed no other symptoms of anything unusual. The following morning he was fine. The grey look that had became habitual to his face during the last six weeks could so easily be put down to his continual worry and concern about me.

'I'm so frightened I'm going to lose you,' he said.

'You're not going to lose me. Why should you?'

'This pain in your back worries me. You're so precious to me. I couldn't bear anything to happen to you.'

'Nothing's going to happen to me. Whatever is wrong will be sorted out and then hopefully I can convalesce in America.'

He wouldn't let me out of his sight for one moment, not even to go to the Post Office while he was making boring telephone calls about the computer.

'Mali, we have the vinaya,' he said, 'You did promise to obey me.'

'But it's only around the corner. I'll be five minutes.'

'Mali! Please!' said Ānando.

It was ridiculous. I stamped up the steps into the Telephone Exchange building, slamming through the doors and flinging myself down in a chair outside the telephone booth. I could hear him laughing quietly as he came behind me. Ānando, as always, had had the last word but I felt I had made my point. We were laughing about it together when we came out.

'I'm sorry Mali. It's just my paranoia,' he said.

'But I was only going to the Post Office.'

'I know but I'm so worried about you.'

'I was hardly going to die just walking to the next street.'

'I know but you must understand.'

I did understand. How deeply I appreciated his love and concern. How he cared for me. He was still doing all the cooking and the cleaning, still going to great lengths to keep up with the washing as he had done since January.

We found a radiologist, a pathologist and two doctors muttering over my X-rays which were still illuminated on the wall when we were called back into the consulting room. The left kidney looked like all the kidneys I had ever seen in diagrams. The right kidney, although normal in shape and size, had something very strange in the tube, distorting it all the way to the bladder.

'What's that?' I asked, pointing it out.

'We don't know. You must go to a big hospital in Athens. We cannot do anything for you here.'

So we left with the X-rays in an envelope. The radiologist's report was carefully written in Greek. Greg held my hand very tightly as we walked into the town.

'Mali, what do you think it is?'

'I haven't the faintest idea. It looks like a growth of some kind but the tube isn't blocked so I don't feel inclined to panic. At the worst they obviously think it's cancer but I don't think so. It could be something similar to a fibroid, a benign growth.'

'Are you worried about it?'

'No, oddly enough I'm not. Obviously I'll have to go to a hospital in England and have it checked out and I'm not looking forward to that. I may have to lose the kidney but I don't think it's fatal if that's what you mean.'

'If it is, shall we buy a big bike and drive it off a cliff someplace?'

'Messy. Tough on whoever has to identify us. Pills are easier.'

'A bike's got more style.'

'You mean a sort of Bonnie and Clyde without the guns?'

'If you like. What shall we tell Gillian when she comes tonight?'

'We mustn't spoil her holiday by worrying her so we won't show her the X-rays until she's just about to take them back to England. Then we'll give her a covering letter for the doctor in Liss so that he can get me an appointment with a specialist as soon as we get back.'

All discussions pertinent to my health were kept to a minimum during the week of Gillian's stay. Except that it was impossible to hide the results of the back spasms that ripped through me every time I tried to swim. On her last day we hired a jeep in Mirina to take her on a grand tour of the island. We were sat bolt upright in hard, narrow seats that conspired with unmade-up dirt tracks to send my back painfully into spasm once more. I said nothing until Greg started gunning the jeep round and round in a tight circle, for no obvious reason and without warning, on an open salt flat, smashing us from side to side in our seats.

'Greg! You're hurting me! Please stop! Please!'

I screamed at him. All I got in return was a sideways look as he put his foot down harder on the accelerator. It was so strange after all the months of care and attention. I carried on screaming until he came to a stop.

'But I have to play, Mali,' he said.

'But it's too much for my back! I can't stand it!' I said.

Gillian stayed silent sitting behind us.

We stopped for lunch and everything was fine. Gillian took some crazy photographs of us necking over the front of the jeep before we piled back into it and drove for another hour to the south of the island. Then, again for no apparent reason, he put his foot down hard on the accelerator and immediately jammed on the brakes to crash us hard back into our seats. This time I screamed in fury and threw the cup I was holding out of the window.

'I'm not sitting here any longer!' I shouted, getting out and slamming the door. The jeep pulled up beside me.

'Mali, get back in please,' he said.

I was too hurt and angry to answer. It was not so far to walk to Mirina and then only two hours back to the house. The jeep kept abreast of me as I walked along the road. Only a few steps and the fury evaporated. It didn't matter any more. Whatever was going on I knew he wasn't being deliberately cruel and I would have been heartbroken if he had driven off and left me. I loved him too much to stay angry for long.

Gillian left the next day and we were booked to follow in five days on Monday, June 1st. The next morning Greg had a slight flash of head pain again as soon as he got up. It vanished almost immediately. Just a single spasm, nothing more. Reluctantly we started packing.

'I wonder if we will be coming back in August,' he said.

'I've been wondering that too,' I said.

'We'll leave all the things we don't have to take with us now anyhow.'

100

'As a kind of insurance you mean?'

'Something like that. Let's hire a sail board when we come back.'

'As long as I can use it too. I won't be left high and dry on the beach squinting into the sun trying to make out the little black dot and the triangle on the horizon.'

'Maybe we'll hire two then.'

— �֎ —

I wanted the days to be longer, the nights never to end. I couldn't bear the thought of leaving our paradise of peace and sea and profound intimacy. On the Saturday morning I woke up early just after first light.

'Gregory! Beloved and wonderful husband, wake up!'

He came out of sleep immediately concerned.

'What's up? Do you have any pain?'

'No, I've been dreaming about the little church on the hill. We have to go and clean it.'

'What now?'

'As soon as we've finished breakfast after meditation.'

'Will you be all right climbing all the way up there?'

'Yes. I'll take pain-killers before we go. My sense of urgency says we have to do it.'

He never argued with that.

There is something very beautiful in the ritual act of cleansing a holy place. In silence we opened the door and all the windows, filling the little sanctuary with sunlight and sweet air. Greg found an old broom and began sweeping all the litter off the floor. I mopped up the residue of dust and oil that was spilt down one wall and onto the floor. The icons and paintings grew colour and form again with careful cleaning and I searched outside on the mountain for some of the little purple flowers that dried intact to lay on the altar. We found a supply of candles and incense in one of the cupboards and after cleaning the dust and cobwebs from the candle stands, we stood our candles upright in the sand, one for every group of people we could think of. Before we lit them I started the charcoal fizzling and spluttering and dropped two large chunks of incense into the burner in front of the altar. As I stepped back my head knocked against something that swung forward and poured a cool, sticky liquid all over my head. It ran among the roots of my hair down my neck and onto my clothes. I went rigid.

'Greg! What is it? What's happened?'

'You've only walked into one of the hanging lamps. I had no idea they still had oil in them,' he said, taking a tissue to me to clean off what he could. In doing so he knocked into one of the other lamps and the same thing happened to him although not quite as copiously as before. Both well anointed, we lit the candles and more incense and chanted all the chants we knew for the good of ourselves and all beings. Greg closed the door and bolted it carefully as we left.

'I wonder when it will be cleaned again?' he said.

The path down the mountain was a narrow sheep track, very steep and treacherous with loose shingle, and we were only a little way down when I slipped and fell forward, impaling my right hand on one of the thorn bushes that grew among the stones. I counted eighteen unbelievably painful splinters in my palm and fingers, all of them stinging so badly I could hardly catch my breath.

'I have the perfect remedy,' said my ex-monk, ex-Marine unbuttoning his Levi's. After all we shared all other body fluids so why not urine? Bathed in instant blood-hot disinfectant cum anaesthetic, the stinging disappeared. Not one of the puncture wounds infected after we had dug out the thorns. He had the grace not to say 'I told you so' after all our months of debating the liberating qualities of human urine.

We spent all of our last Sunday sunbathing and swimming and trying not to think about England and my kidneys. In the evening we walked to Kalogeros to watch the sunbathing the sea in golden light as it set over distant Agios Ouros.

'We will come back even if it has to be after August 10th,' I said. 'We will come back, Beloved.'

'I hope so,' he said. 'There's just this feeling –'

There was no need to elaborate.

'I know but I don't know why. Logic tells me that even if I have to have an operation it will be done very quickly.'

'What does your witch's nose say about it?'

'Ambivalent. Neither one way or the other.'

'Well, at least it doesn't say never again,' he said.

'No. It doesn't say that. But although I don't have to worry so much about your family now, the witch is still not happy about America.'

My 'confession' to my mother-in-law about my two divorces had been written in March.

'It will be all right, you'll see.'

'You always say that and it always gets me into trouble. And I can't see next winter. There's a kind of blank darkness over it which bothers me. It's odd.'

I had one last photograph to take to finish off the film in the camera.

'Come on, Gregory, take off that tee-shirt. I want something beautiful in the foreground while I take a picture of the moon over your head.'

He was still a little bit self-conscious posing semi-naked for photographs. He had held out successfully all winter against the ex-art student covering him in oil and posing him discreetly lit while she crouched over the camera taking tasteful art shots.

As the light was fading from the sky and the night shadows came gathering in the valley under the mountain we went home and to bed, to enjoy the last remaining night of peace and unbroken sleep I would know in this life with my beloved again.

Wedding,
Petersfield, England
October 29th 1992

Greg as a
samanera/novice,
Thailand
October 29th 1972

Mali and JBJ in Gruyères, Switzerland   June 13th 1992

Skaftafell National Park, Iceland   June 28th 1992

Agios Giannis, Limnos   August 22nd 1992

Wedding, Greg, Mali and JBJ, Petersfield, England   October 29th 1992

Greg and cats, Rhodes   January 12th 1993

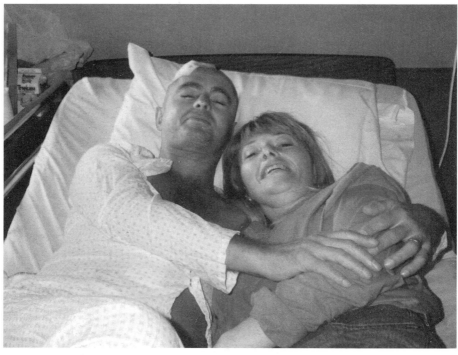

Veterans' Administration Hospital, Richmond   July 13th 1993
106

At the pyramids, Egypt   November 2nd 1993

Gudrun, Greg and Mali, Lacoste   March 25th 1994

Gudrun, Greg and Mali, Lacoste   May 3rd 1994

Greg and Mali, Lacoste   April 12th 1994

Chapter Ten

Gillian met us at the airport with a bottle of super-strength pain-killers and an appointment for me with the doctor for the following morning. In just over twenty-four hours I was in hospital in Guildford undergoing tests.

The first night was terrible. I was missing Greg so much I was sick, vomiting all over the floor before I could get to the bathroom.

'Have you had headaches like this as well as the back pain?' asked the nurse.

'No.'

'You're just missing your husband, aren't you?' she said.

'Yes. We've never been separated before now.'

'He's coming back tomorrow?'

'Oh yes, early. And you won't be able to throw him out. He's an ex-US Marine Vietnam Veteran and he won't take no for an answer.'

Even earlier next morning I was moved to a private room and my Vietnam Veteran, who came walking in the door behind a huge bouquet of flowers and very amused by his desperado status, stayed all day until eight in the evening. I was X-rayed and scanned, a camera on a tube took intimate pictures of my duodenum and every drop of urine was measured and tested until I was discharged late in the afternoon the next day, still slightly stoned from anaesthetic. My kidneys were officially certified undamaged. The overly dignified British consultant would not lower himself to give a name to the 'thing' that was distorting my tube but I was obviously not about to die of kidney cancer. I had a small duodenal ulcer, probably as a result of the drugs I had been taking for my ankle over the past few months and that was healing. The consultant strongly recommended that I book myself a series of appointments to treat the inward curvature of my spine which looked attractive but did nothing for my currently painful muscular-skeletal condition.

I was exhausted, Greg was relieved.

'Never mind,' he said. 'It's fundamentally good news and we'll get you fixed up in no time. You can take it easy in America. I'm so glad it was nothing more serious. I was worried.'

'Yes. It would have been a waste of a good bike, wouldn't it?'

'It would indeed.'

We had six weeks in America but we decided against the West-East trek we had originally planned. Instead we would go away for a week, maybe to the Blue Ridge mountains, and then go on to Buffalo so that Greg could show me Niagara Falls. We would pick up Gabriel on our way back south, visit Parris Island in North Carolina and then drive on down to Florida to take a look at Greg's land. He was still enthusiastic about the idea of building a house there one winter. I couldn't see us living there. It sounded too humid and too flat after a winter in the Greek Islands.

Gudrun had left Iceland before Christmas and we took her and Felix and Gabriel out to dinner to celebrate the first anniversary of our being together. Dinner in an English pub was not as dramatic as the events of June 6th one year ago but Greg always enjoyed the few times when he could say 'have whatever you want' when the menu came round. My back was slowly improving as the treatment got under way.

We drove to the US Base near Cambridge to investigate the possibilities of being able to fly for free to America with the military. The answer was affirmative as long as I had a current visa, which meant a trip to London and the Embassy. Everything seemed to be going well. My physical pain was diminishing daily but my general feelings of unease had not lessened. We were swimming at the local pool every morning after meditation as part of my therapy, and Greg got back into Tai Chi which he had seriously neglected for the past few months since my illness. I stood watching him from the window as he practised on the lawn outside my mother's house, only missing a move once. He was still as graceful as ever if not quite so perfectly balanced on the full turn. Gillian had lent us her car while I was having treatment and for the first time I was nervous when he was driving. Not all the time but he seemed to be having trouble judging distance to the left of his field of vision and more than once we came perilously close to the inside edge of the road on corners. Added to that, there had been a couple of incidents when he had been unusually aggressive when meeting new people, particularly women. Enough for me to talk to him about it in the privacy of the car later. He couldn't understand it.

'It must be my American conditioning coming out again. They have always been socially more forceful than the British,' he said, with a wry smile.

I wasn't so inclined to agree but I couldn't think of a better answer. His wayward behaviour transposed itself to watching TV. He was getting too involved with whatever he was seeing and unable to shake off the emotions it aroused for a considerable time afterwards. I wondered if the epilepsy was about to recur. I didn't feel happy about how the screen flickering seemed to be affecting him. So much so that I invoked the vinaya and called a ban on evening viewing in favour of late walks around the woods and the lanes to exercise my back before bed.

For some reason I have never forgotten that it was on the evening of June 16th when he first admitted that he was getting worried about himself.

'Why? In what way?' I asked.

'I don't know. Except that I feel spacey.'

'How do you mean?'

'Not quite in my body, not quite connected. And I can't walk in a straight line. Look!'

110

He tried walking down the central line on the deserted road to demonstrate, stumbling continually to the left in his effort to concentrate. I was very concerned.

'Can you see well enough?'

'Yes, I think so. But sunlight is beginning to bother me. I'm getting tired if it's too bright.'

'But you are a confirmed sun-worshipper. Gregory, what do you think is the matter? You know you – and you've had plenty of experience of head wounds. What do you think?'

'I don't feel that it's anything badly wrong. It's not a constant feeling and I am quite well for the rest of the time.'

'Could it be anything to do with stress from having to look after me for so long?'

'Not unlikely. Maybe I'm just tired and needing a holiday.'

He grinned.

'Do you think you should see a doctor?'

'No, no! I'm not that bad.'

Five months of almost continuous physical pain in one way or another had left me too tired to insist otherwise. I had to trust that he knew himself well enough to know when to ask for professional advice. Early the next morning he had a few flash pains in his head as we got up but nothing more and we went to London as we had planned. The 'powers' decided I couldn't have my visa unless I applied for a residence visa which would take several hundred dollars and several more months to be negotiated. Exasperated we gave up on the Embassy and our free flight and went to visit Sophie instead.

She had been one of the senior nuns at the monastery until she had disrobed the previous October. She was currently living in London with her parents, helping to nurse her mother who was dying of cancer. Sasha was much weakened by her illness but still very positive and bright when we went to her room to say hello. In the course of conversation the subject of where we were planning to spend the next winter came up.

'There's the house in the south of France,' she said. 'Go there. We won't be needing it then. Just pay enough to cover the bills.'

It was a very kind offer but one winter in the Mediterranean had already convinced us that a whole season without being able to swim did not conform to my husband's fitness programme. We thanked her and said we would bear it in mind. She died less than a week later.

Too much of our carefully saved money went on two return tickets to Washington DC for June 23rd to August 4th, giving us just five days in England before we flew back to Limnos. Greg spent all of Sunday, June 20th in bed asleep but he was well and happy enough when he got up in the early evening. Of course nothing stopped our love-making.

'Gregory, I do believe that if an earthquake occurred while we were making love, we would simply think it was the cosmos concurring with our ecstasy. We would carry on regardless even if the house was falling down around our ears!'

'Mali, did you feel the earth move just then?'

Friends invited us out for dinner on our last evening in England. One of our fellow guests practised as a medium and was enthusing about a new healing technique he was using. He grabbed Greg, who was never unwilling in these matters, to demonstrate. While he was working on his head, I pointed to the place where I had seen the green mass and mouthed 'What is that?' to him. Greg had his eyes closed and had no idea of the silent conversation going on behind him.

'What do you mean?'

'What is in his head?'

He shrugged.

'I can't see anything.'

Once again I hoped it was nothing but my imagination. Then what is imagination if not the key to magic?

—✻—

We landed in Washington DC with barely an hour to spare before our connecting flight to Norfolk and the suffocating humidity of the Virginian summer. Greg was fine all through the flight, insisting on carrying all the hand luggage and absorbed in the in-flight movies for most of the seven hours in the air from London. Next morning he woke up with sharp pains in his head that continued intermittently throughout the day, sending him almost to his knees as the spasms gripped their iron fingers into his brain.

'Oh Mali, I don't know what's going on. Hold me, help me Baby,' he said, staggering forward, trying to hold his head and hold on to me at the same time.

On Saturday, June 26th, using me as a support because he could no longer walk steadily alone, we paid our first visit to the VA hospital in Hampton.

'Do you qualify?' the receptionist asked us.

'Yes, I'm rated one hundred per cent disabled,' he said quietly.

He always hated admitting it.

'Do you have your card?'

'What card?'

'You should have a purple card.'

'I don't have any card. I live abroad.'

'That doesn't stop you having a card. Give me your name and social security number and I'll check it out.'

She ran the computer.

'Yes, you're a hundred per cent. We'll get you a card. Sit down until you hear your name called and a doctor will see you.'

The importance of the card still lost on us, we waited for another two hours. Greg spent most of the time lying on the floor with his head in my lap. His mother was not pleased that we should have to wait for so long but the whole situation was just too awful for either of us to feel like complaining. It was better not to think. Just to be with the situation and see what came up. The practice, always the practice and what better time to remember it than now?

The doctor told us that there were sixty reasons why Greg should be having head pains and gave us some pain-killers.

'Come back in a couple of days if you're no better,' he said.

As soon as we returned to the house Greg took the pills and went straight to bed; he was asleep almost as soon as his head touched the pillow.

Unfamiliar with the house and hardly knowing his family, I felt uneasy and intensely alone. What was going on? What was happening to us? With the beginnings of fear gnawing at the edge of my consciousness, I diverted myself into making us some soup in case he should wake up hungry. But he slept on and eventually I had to eat it all myself. When I got into bed beside him and cuddled up in my usual place, he was hardly aware of me. For the first time I went to sleep without a kiss.

We were back in the VA on Monday morning and again on Wednesday all day until a neurologist could be found to authorise a CAT scan. This scan clearly showed an accumulation of fluid in the brain. The cause could not be accounted for.

'Can you drive to Richmond right now? You need an MRI scan and you'll have to be admitted to have it,' said the doctor.

It was four thirty in the afternoon and we hadn't eaten all day.

'Is there time for us to eat and pack some things?' I asked.

'Yes, I should think so. What time do you think you'll be leaving?'

'Around six thirty, seven o'clock.'

'Okay. I'll notify Admissions that you'll be there around nine, nine thirty.'

It took two hours to drive to Richmond. We took his mother's car. I had my first experience of driving on American highways. Greg was still not convinced that he was about to become an in-patient and insisted on finding a room for the night in a motel before we went to the hospital. He didn't want us to be driving around Richmond with nowhere to go at midnight. He paid the bill in advance and inspected the room, in case I should have to come back alone. I couldn't help but be proud of him. He was so careful of me even though by now it was obvious he was very ill.

When I left him just after midnight in Ward 2C, he was wearing a pair of VA issue pyjamas, still not sure what was really going on but very conscious of the wheelchair parked beside his bed.

The Hunter Holmes Maguire Veterans' Hospital was a big modern hospital in the suburbs of Richmond, Virginia, accommodating almost every facility currently available in America. Unlike the British, the American veterans have always been militant and have set up a fairly comprehensive support system for all veterans and their dependants. Without a National Healthcare network, I didn't know what the rest of America did when they were sick but no one was more grateful than I for the VA then. Maybe like all institutions it has its critics but I wasn't one of them. As a one hundred per cent rated veteran, Greg was entitled to everything he needed and we wouldn't have find a single dollar to pay for it.

A huge flag saying 'America is # 1 thanks to her Veterans', hanging over everyone who went through the revolving doors into the main hall way, declared an undoubted belief policy. For the first time in my life I was to encounter a society where war was not something to be forgotten or not mentioned over much. Both my grandfathers served in France in World War One. My father volunteered for the Royal Air Force in 1940. My mother's hearing was permanently damaged after surviving months of the German bombing campaign on the south coast that finally destroyed her home and her parents' business assets in one spectacular night raid. I suppose because the entire country had been directly affected by the last war, the British, wearing the imperishable stiff upper lip, buy poppies once a year for Remembrance Sunday, which only falls on November 11th once every six years, watch the ceremony at the Cenotaph on TV and take notice only of the Veterans that one really couldn't avoid. How can you pay a whole nation compensation for the trauma of war?

Hearing Greg and my mother talking together one lunch time about the bombing and the sound of gunfire, their reactions and the panic attacks that lasted long after, I had realised that they were speaking the same language. About different times and different places but the same war. By contrast, the citizens of America were never bombed. The idea of spending night after night in an air raid shelter or a subway is beyond their national comprehension. Strict rationing and interminable food queues have no place in the 'Land of the Free'. In America the Veterans are a minority group but they are acutely aware of their rights and they see to it that they get them.

'There's nothing they don't owe you,' one told me.

The scenes I had watched on TV last Veterans' Day in Hampton were real. The World Wars, Korea, Vietnam were not forgotten and never could be until the last surviving member of a family directly affected by whatever war was dead.

That night, alone in the early hours of July 1st, I sobbed my way out of the hospital, feeling very much abandoned in a big American city. And terrified. Greg had given me all of our money to look after and I hardly knew what to do with it. It felt so alien. I felt so alien and so lost. I didn't want to think about the morning. I had to concentrate on surviving the night.

The motel was standard American issue, slightly seedy and just off a huge boulevard covered in billboards and lights. Greg was on the phone minutes after I had locked myself into the room. When I had sobbed myself to a standstill, I fell into an uneasy two hours of sleep, waking up at four thirty with still an hour and a half to lose before I could decently go back to the hospital.

I lay on the edge of the huge double bed that smelt of countless strangers, trying to plan for the worst so that I could be pleasantly relieved when I found myself driving him back to Hampton in a few days' time. Eating was going to be the major problem. Almost everything in America has sugar in it. Even the bread was sweet and I have never thrived on fast food. I had a packet of cereal with me, the only one we had found with no added sugar, so with luck I could live on that mixed with milk from the cafeteria. I had the car for transport and if I could find a bank that would cash the travellers' cheques that Greg had already signed for we would be okay for money. I was back beside him by six thirty, eating my cereal and waiting to see what the day would bring.

'Ma'am, do you know about the Hospitality House?' said the ward secretary as I was walking past the nurses' station.

'No. What is it?'

'It's run by the Veterans for the wives to stay in while their husbands are in the hospital. It's about five minutes' drive around the perimeter and costs five dollars a night. Do you want me to find out if they have a vacancy for you?'

It was like a gift from heaven.

'Yes! Yes, please! Please do!' I said.

'I'll let you know,' she said.

I wheeled my beloved to the MRI scanner midmorning and by lunch time I had met Jim who allocated me a bed in the Hospitality House and somewhere safe to store my bag.

'Just one more thing, Ma'am,' he said as he was leaving. 'Always tell the officer on duty when you are about to leave the hospital late at night and he will see you to your car. Drive straight to the house and keep the car doors locked. Don't attempt to walk it, even in daylight. Can't be too sure Ma'am.'

My heart sank. What kind of a place was this?

—⁂—

Greg had been put into a private room and we were curled up on the bed together asleep when the doctor came to tell us the result of the MRI scan.

'You gotta brain tumour. If we don't operate, you're gonna die. When we do operate, you got four possibilities. Blindness, paralysis, coma or death.'

Poor Doctor John. He was only two days into his final year of residency in Neurosurgery, probably the last people he needed to meet right then was us. We sat very still, saying nothing, both of us looking at him steadily. Somewhere in the depths of my psyche a silent scream formed a single word.

'No-o-o-o-o-o-o-o-o!'

Like bees buzzing among the flowers on a hot June day or the cicadas in Greece on a hot August night, that sound became consistent within my state of being. Henceforth whatever I was doing would be always against the background of this muted, agonised scream. In a matter of fractions of seconds I watched fear flooding through me and in its wake, practice.

Be with it, watch it, don't give in to it. You know nothing beyond this moment. There are endless possibilities. Not all brain tumours are fatal.

'So what happens next?' I heard myself asking.

Neither of us had moved a muscle. Blindness, paralysis, coma or death. Not a lot to choose from. One thing I knew for sure. He was not going to die on me without an almighty fight. We had too much going for us. No matter what happened we would fight it all the way. There had to be some meaning to all this, there had to be a good reason why this was happening to us right here, right now.

How do people take a death sentence? We didn't cry, not then. It was hard to grasp the reality of it all. What do you do when a stranger walks into your life and tells you you're going to die? When all your bright dreams fall misbegotten into a nameless void?

'You'll be scheduled for surgery next week, probably Tuesday, so that we can take a look and see what kind of a tumour you got there. Until we know that we can't say for sure what we're gonna do with it. We'll get another scan to see how much of a vascular system it has set up.'

'Why?'

Greg stayed silent. I became spokeswoman.

'Because the more blood it has in it, the more chance of cerebral haemorrhage when we cut into it.'

'Where is it?'

'On the cerebellum at the back.'

'Beside the gunshot wound?'

'Yes.'

'Will you shave off all his hair?'

'Usually we do.'

'Oh no!' That was too much for Greg.

'Please, he had his head shaved for twenty years. Couldn't you just shave off the bits you need and leave the rest?'

'We can try. I'll be in again in a couple of days with the consent forms for you to sign and it might be a good idea if you think about making a Living Will so that it's clear what you want if things get tough in surgery.'

So that was it. He left us looking at each other. Just looking at each other.

'Well,' said my husband.

'Yes,' I said.

'A brain tumour. Funny, I never thought it would happen to me.'

'It has to be called Charles.'

'Why?'

'Why not?'

'Then Charles it is.'

'He's not going to beat us. I refuse to let him beat us. I'm not living without you. I can't!'

My husband held me, closely, quietly. The nurse came in with his first steroid medication. Practise, don't give in to the fear, you have each other right now. Trust. You know what to do.

'You had better make some phone calls,' he said eventually.

116

'Yes.'

'Use the AT&T card. It's in my wallet. Tell my mother I'm okay. She doesn't have to come immediately. I want to get this all sorted out while there's just the two of us. I don't want them to be worried.'

'Shall I telephone Chithurst?'

'If you want to.'

'I want to.'

'Go ahead then.'

England was already five hours into the evening. The monks would still be in the Shrine room for evening meditation. I left a message on the answer machine.

'Hello, this is Mali Klein calling from America. Greg is in hospital. He has a brain tumour. Please, chant for us, pray for us.'

What on earth was I going to do about Gabriel? He was due to join us from England in a few days. I couldn't bear to disappoint him.

'Gregory, what shall we do about Gabriel? Shall I tell him not to come?'

'No, no, not at all! I'll be better by then. I want him to come. Please don't put him off.'

I went out to find Doctor John.

'Is there any possibility that everything could be all right and we'll be walking out of here in a couple of weeks?' I asked.

'Difficult to say until we know what type of tumour it is.'

'Do you have any idea?'

'No.'

'How long has it been there?'

'Maybe three to four years, maybe longer.'

That explained a lot of things.

'But even if you can take it away there's going to be a long convalescence.'

'Yes, I should think so.'

I could tell by the expression on his face that he hardly knew how to look at me. I had to tell Gabriel, I couldn't have him landing in the middle of all this. There was nowhere else he could go, nowhere else he could stay. It was one of the hardest phone calls I have ever made. I didn't tell Greg what I had done. Not then.

At four o'clock the staff for the evening rota came on duty. Tom came in and introduced himself as the head nurse until midnight. A little over an hour later he was back. In retrospect I suppose he had read the MRI report and he had seen beings like Charles before. He spoke to us quietly in his soft, Southern accent.

'I want to tell you that I have spoken to the night superintendent and recommended that your husband's condition is much improved by your being here Mrs Klein. It means you can stay all night but –' he brought his face closer to mine, 'you have to ask my permission first.'

I laughed.

'I'm asking,' I said. 'Please can I stay?'

'Sure thing. Go right on down to the Reception desk in Emergency where you first came in and sign on.'

I couldn't get there fast enough. I made up an improvised bed for myself on two chairs beside Greg but no one noticed if I wasn't in it when they came in.

'They're doing this because we're young and they think he's going to die,' I thought. 'Please don't die, Beloved. Please don't die.'

The phone started ringing the next day. Everybody was worried. It was so nice to be able to talk to the monks again after more than a year of silence. We paid another visit to the scanner sometime in the afternoon. Bill the social worker took us under his wing and Greg made a Living Will, negating all life support systems, leaving it up to me to make the final decision.

'I'd rather be dead than a vegetable, my Mali. I don't want to do that either to you or to me,' he said.

'I know. I know what to do.'

'Yes. I know you do.'

'Got a history of it after my father, haven't I?'

'I know you'll do what's best for me.'

'Even if it breaks my heart. Isn't that so, Gregory Klein?'

'Oh I love you,' he said, stroking my hair.

'I love you too. Damn it, you're my husband! You can't die on me! you can't! I've only had you for a year! We've only been married eight months! If you die, I'll have nothing. Absolutely nothing! Please!'

The dam burst. Mercifully we were alone. Sobbing, shaking, both our faces wet, it had to happen some time. It was the only time we really let go until much later. There was no place to scream on Ward 2C. There's too much going on in a Neurosurgery unit.

Tacitly I knew that part of the deal that was allowing me to stay in the hospital meant that I had to behave myself. No hysterics, stay calm, stay cool, be useful. Practice, don't give in to the fear.

'I want to go some place quiet just with you when this is all over and then either get completely well or die in peace,' he said. 'I know you will be able to look after me.'

'I've never nursed a brain tumour alone.'

'It will be all right. You're my wife and I only want you helping me, no one else. Remember I've been a monk for twenty years and used to my privacy,' he added.

And so I became exclusively Greg's personal nurse with an hour off between six and seven every morning to go to the hospitality house for a shower and to talk to the other 'girls' who were staying there. All my nursing-auxiliary experience came back. I became super-practical, organised, the perfect diversion for the hell that was going on inside me. If it were possible we became more intensely reliant on each other, putting on a brave public face and doing our best to be co-operative. But no one else spoke the same language. Everyone was so kind to us, doing everything they

118

could to make things as easy for us as possible but we had been set down in an intensely Christian part of the world. Culturally and in terms of religious practice we found ourselves in a vacuum.

Greg still retained some ethnic familiarity but I was a stranger in a strange land, in a culture and society that was the most alien I had ever encountered. Essentially on the most subtle levels there is not yet a common language between the Old World and the New and I was too deeply in shock to be able to help myself with the social difficulties that inevitably arose. I had been used to tease my beloved about his accent and his American terminology. Now I realised exactly how his years away had remoulded him into a European both in character and outlook. His 'Up-State New York' slang had been carefully laid aside when he went to Thailand, to vanish almost completely as he assimilated his odd mixture of English and Thai acculturation.

I began to call America the 'Land of the Five Star Lie, French fried with a choice of toppings'. Amid the affluence and the ever-present flaunting of the dollar, I had never seen such poverty. A drive through the poor, black areas of the city dropped the jaw of the country child from the south of England. I saw people living in houses where the windows and doors were falling out, the roofs falling in. The old Greek farmers with their donkeys and their sheep were far better off than many of these people. I had spent the winter listening to American propaganda on VOA Europe, hearing how Uncle Sam was sending millions of dollars to Somalia and Russia, but what about his own back yard?

It seemed that without the VA, many of the Veterans would be sick and on the street. Not so many had wives and families to visit them in the hospital. Late at night when I went to sign on, the police would be bringing in the drunks from the street to sober up. The Pharmacy was permanently barricaded behind several inches of bullet-proof glass. The Vietnam veterans were unmistakable, a lost generation of middle-aged men with that haunted, hollow look in their faces, that poignant body language. Others with an air of hopelessness that was devastatingly unfamiliar, further compounding the intensity of the trauma as I tried to assimilate the reality of what was happening to my husband. It was like having a raw nerve operated on without anaesthetic.

'Semper Fi!' shouted a young Marine in an elevator who knew Greg had been one of the Leathernecks. 'Keep the Faith!'

I almost saluted.

The staff in the hospital were predominantly black and so friendly. Who could be sweeter than Nurse Effi? Some of the nurses had wonderful names and I was continually fascinated by their variety of hair styles, so much more exotic and imaginative than their paler sisters. Even with my fading Greek tan I felt like a limp washout by comparison.

'Hey Baby, I love that smile!' as I walked past the wheelchairs gathered around an early cigarette outside the main entrance.

'Good morning,' I said.

'Hey, you gotta accent!'

'No, you've got the accent!' I countered.

In that atmosphere, in the heat and humidity and driving past the Philip Morris Tobacco factory that was more like another city just down the road from the hospital, it wasn't so hard to imagine what it must have been like in Virginia in the old days on the plantations.

I always enjoyed my hour in the Hospitality house every morning when I went back for my shower. The 'girls' would be all up and sat around the kitchen table drinking coffee when I came in.

'Hello Mali. How are you doing?'

'I'm fine. How are you?'

They each had their tragedy. Robbie was waiting to see if her husband was going to be permanently paralysed. Ruby's husband was scheduled for open heart surgery. Mary had all her money stolen as she slept in the corridor outside the operating room, waiting for her husband to come out of surgery. Diane's first husband had beaten her and crippled her and she was now officially bankrupt because her medical insurance hadn't been sufficient to cover the cost of the surgery necessary to repair her knees. She was forty-six years old and only able to have the much needed medication to treat her high blood pressure while her doctor was able to keep her in free samples. I met few people in Virginia who weren't actively practising one form of Christianity or another but hadn't Jesus preached compassion for all the poor, the meek, the sick? Or was the Saviour more selective in America?

On the morning of the fourth of July I wheeled my husband out of the almost too cool air-conditioned atmosphere of the hospital building into the heat and humidity of the day. We found the perfect place for our final puja before surgery, in the shade of an enormous tree. I gave him a blanket to sit on while I set up the Buddha-rupa and lit the incense. He had no pain and was enjoying the high that comes at the beginning of the steroid treatment. As we began the chanting the tears began to fall. Piquant memories of all that we had and all we could soon lose danced between us. What were we doing here? Why did it have to be this way?

'Why Gregory?' I said aloud. 'Why a brain tumour?'

'Obviously I needed it and therefore you needed it too,' he said.

'I didn't need it. I don't need it. I need you.'

'I need you too. Don't ever leave me.'

'How could I possibly? You're my husband.'

'But I might become permanently disabled from the operation. I don't want to tie you to anything you can't handle. It would be kinder to divorce you.'

'How can you say that? Don't you remember? "My lawful wedded husband, in truth, reverence and fidelity, in whatever circumstances the Holy Ones ordain for our life together." And that includes brain tumours. You can't just put me aside like shrugging off an old coat. What would you do without me?'

120

'Die. I couldn't bear it.'

'Neither could I. Do you want my suicide on your conscience through countless lives?'

'No, indeed I do not. Don't look so worried. Like you say this is our brain tumour. But I hope that whatever happens won't be too hard on you.'

Greg's mother and Joyce, his younger sister, came that afternoon just after we had signed the remaining formalities. His old buddies Rick and Sam and Danny, from the early days in Buffalo, were driving down to Richmond the next day. Each of us with our own reasons for sitting the eight and a half hours that it would take outside the operating room. We all went out together to eat at the nearest Spaghetti Warehouse on the last evening, acutely cheerful as the disciples must have been during the Last Supper. Inevitably the conversation turned to religion. Greg and Jean had amicably argued dogma over dinner for years as families do but I never found it palatable. When my children were little and sitting down for a meal I had always said,

'One thing at a time. When you eat, only eat. When you talk, only talk.'

It didn't always work out in practice but it was a nice idea.

Of the seven of us at table that evening, five were technically lapsed Catholics. Greg was content to sit back this time and let Rick take the field with Jean until at one point when the exchange became particularly heated.

'You'll all go to Hell,' she said, quite sincerely. 'But I'll pray for you.'

To a practising and deeply convinced Catholic to whom the reality of Hell is an indispensable part of life, it was a perfectly normal statement to make. It was like a red rag to a bull to us with Greg's possible demise only hours away. I felt all the old anger rush through him and quickly jammed my hand down on his leg as he made to stand up. When the surgeons had finished with him the next day, his most recent memory was in tatters but that was one thing he never forgot. It took all my powers of persuasion during all of our time in America to prevent him from telephoning the local priest and demanding to know the reasoning behind what he considered to be the rubbish that had been fed to his mother in her daily contact with her Church.

Chapter Eleven

We signed back into the hospital at ten o'clock. Tom came in with the medication as I was helping Greg get back into bed.

'No one is coming into this room again until after midnight,' he said, significantly.

I shut the door behind him and jammed a chair under the handle, just to be sure. My husband was waiting for me with a smile and our favourite cologne sprayed over his chest.

Afterwards we lay together talking, making the most of our wakefulness, knowing there would be no more time in the morning. He was due in surgery by seven. I had a blank tape in the Walkman and he made me a tape to listen to in case he should never be able to talk to me in that way again. It began as a talk about love that became a conversation as we became absorbed enough to forget that the machine was still running.

'To my beloved wife, my Mali Klein. To talk about love I have to talk in very personal terms of course, in terms that relate to you. Because you're my only real experience of love. It has so much to do with the small things, the little things. A look, the warmth of your kiss, the softness of your lips, the way you hold me. The way you talk to me, the way you support me. Your caring and the way that you affect the opening of my heart/mind in direct opposition to the things which keep it closed. My fear, doubt, hesitation.

'I love you so much. I surrender to you. I've no choice. Your gentle persistence, your intelligent reasoning and undying effort in the face of these doubts, fears, bleakness and self-disparagement keep my heart open and the sense of love, of gracious energy and of thankfulness towards you flowing in such joy. Such joy. It is a spark of the eternal and it is a joy to be able to understand that this can be applied to all Beings everywhere so that when everyone needs and seeks after the same thing it becomes truly universal, the panacea by which we can say that we reach our true human potential.

'It is not lessened by being brought to a more personal level. Rather it becomes very intensified so that our experiences can be made to be brought out into our society to teach us to communicate to all Beings with that same lovingness.

'The focus of my life right now is you and I find it so instructive to almost instinctively put your welfare and wishes before mine. As you were saying last night, that you wish we had had a child, I wish that also, just to taste the sweet bitterness of that experience. The intensity of the love and attachment and also the other side, the frustration and disappointment. I can speculate about it but it's not the same as the real experience.

'When I think of our time together, our moments together and the blending of our energies, it's such a mysterious sweetness. The complete loss of self as a separate entity into a merging of something that is more than just the two of us. To be able to stay there, which to my mind can be reached using the physical almost as a catharsis to push us into another realm of experience, giving rise to a sense of just visiting this place called Earth but not being overly pre-occupied with it. In some ways I've felt that is the case with us. We've played some of the games, the worldly games but not very seriously or too determinedly, so it stays light and not deeply involved. If I'm blessed with more time with you I think that this lightness will just continue and that what people have seen in us, sense in us will grow and develop, heighten and become more profound.'

'You've taught me so much, Beloved.'

'Have I?'

'Oh yes you have. You've taught me about Metta but it's only in the last two or three months that I've finally understood what it is. Like now. When tomorrow is just a few hours away and I've seen such fear in moments. I want to be crying but instead I am lying here with you and I want to give the whole situation into Metta, you know, approach the operation with Metta, with joy, with Loving Kindness. Somehow I feel we have learnt so much and now is the time to put it into practice.'

'I think that's quite wise.'

'How do you see tomorrow?'

'I'm still quite ambivalent about it. It's interesting. I haven't really dwelt on the significance of it to any great extent. It's just there as a potential. I suppose that my intuition says that it will be fine and so I'm going to be all right. I don't know if that's blindness or the real thing. My mind hasn't gone very much into the murky realms of possibility. It's quite a precise demarcation point in life, major surgery, when the odds are what they are. I can still wonder why it's so hard for me to be kind to me when I've done lots of nice things over the years. It's interesting how prevalent this self-disparagement is in me.'

'Well, maybe tomorrow they will cut that old monster out as well as Charles.'

'That would be nice wouldn't it? And then you can send a fax to all the monasteries if the operation is a success saying Greg Klein gave birth to a tumour called Charles by caesarean and he's doing well.'

'I'll do my best to put it as appropriately as possible.'

'Well, that's pretty succinct isn't it?'

'It is but surely even you cannot forget what you've done as Ānando, can you?'

'Well yes I can. I don't view my time as a monk in quite the august ways that other people have. I think it's just the problems of self-criticism. Like someone once referring to me as the grandfather of the Sanghapala project. To my mind I played an almost insignificant role but obviously not from his point of view. I remember being around there but always either in the shadow of Ajahn Sumedho or in just a very secondary position. I know personally I inspired him pretty much so maybe he's right. I understand where he's coming from because maybe it was through his connection with me that he got interested in getting something started on the West coast. But it's so easy for me to forget it, to dismiss it, to overlook it and instead to remember and to cling to the shortcomings or the perceived failings. This is something I have harped on about for years almost *ad nauseam*. It still seems to be quite a strong conditioning in me.'

'But it's not so difficult to think back about the good things that you did as Ānando, is it? You have some idea. It's not a wholly dark area to you.'

'No it's not, not at all. I do know to some extent.'

'And not one second of it was wasted?'

A slight hesitation –

'No, but that would depend on how you looked at it. What is time and time wasted from an ultimately critical point of view? Any unmindful moment is a wasted moment. That is very hard-line but then all of that which is done under the umbrella of good intention could be seen as something that is worthwhile. Whether or not one is actually continually mindful, as long as there is the intention to be and to live a virtuous life, harmlessly and so on, then it's fine. It's all right.'

'And wasn't that your intention?'

'Yes, always. And renewed very frequently.'

'You've had such a special life and that's why you're irreplaceable Greg Klein. I'm so proud to be your wife, to be in your heart and to have you in mine. Because my heart was only partly open until I met you. Until you took me by the neck and showed me how to love you.

'I remember all that learning to let go of things when we were first together. You teaching me that my home really was in your heart so that wherever we are together is home. Now more than anywhere it works, it's working. We are here in this place in Richmond, in a hospital, not the kind of place we would ever think of as home but here we are laying together –'

'With the nurse's agreement, even tacit encouragement.'

'Deliberately told more correctly. We have the Buddha-rupa on the shrine on the windowsill and with our few bits and pieces, suddenly even this hospital room is home. But you are my refuge, beloved husband, and I don't think it's such a bad thing.'

'Neither do I.'

'And I know that refuge exists beyond the physical body. You're not going to die on me tomorrow but I know that if you did, the refuge wouldn't change. The heart is greater than the mind. Love is the one thing that is constant, surviving death, trauma, growing greater each time. We are the product of lifetimes. Greg and Mali Klein.'

'Yes, indeed we are.'

124

'And so in theory tomorrow's waiting for you outside the operating theatre will be less than a breath in time.'

'Yes. The waiting bit. I think that is the more difficult part. I hope it won't be too bad for you.'

'Oh, it'll be agony! The longest hours ever! But I won't give in to the fear. I'll be with you all the time. All the time. Only you could go and do things like this to me. Did you think you hadn't taught me enough?'

'I don't know.'

We slept deeply until the alarm clock woke us at five fifteen. An hour later the others came from their hotels while we waited for the nurses and the stretcher to come.

I can see it all now, in and out of focus in my memory. The pink shirt he bought me on Limnos. His hair curly and damp after the shower. Holding my hand as he was pushed along the corridor. Rick taking photos. The double doors of the operating unit.

'You can't come any further Mrs Klein.'

'Be cool, Beloved, be Ānando. Remember the practice, be cool. I love you, I love you, I love you!'

The last shouted as the doors closed between us.

Staring out of a window. The scream strangling itself in my throat.

'No-o-o-o-o-o-o-o!'

The six of us sat together all morning and into the afternoon. Brought up by Ānando, it would have been easier for me to sit it out alone. Things weren't that way in America. I thought of all the candles on all the shrines burning all around the world as everyone who cared for him kept the vigil too. Just after two o'clock, John emerged from the operating room. I ran to him.

'Is he okay? What's happened?'

'He's okay.'

'Could you take away the tumour?'

'No, only a little bit from the centre. We'll know in three or four days what it is.'

'When can I see him?'

'I'll tell them to come and get you when he's in the recovery room.'

'Just one more thing. You have your training, I have mine. That's the love of my life you have in there. You're doing your best to help him but if anything goes wrong, now or at any time, I have the right as his wife to do anything I can in the way I've been trained to save him. Make sure you call me. I'll never forgive you if you don't.'

'I'll call you, don't worry.'

I hadn't expected them to be able to part Charles from his host. I was so relieved that my husband was still alive. But how was he? Could he still talk? Would he still remember me? How would I take it if he did not? When John took Jean and me to the recovery room most of my fears evaporated as the man in the green gown linked by tubes and cables to the machines surrounding his bed whispered,

'I love you, I love you, I love you,' smiling up at me through tears and slightly swollen eyes, doing his best to kiss my hand through the oxygen mask and rumpling his other hand through my hair.

We had six days in Intensive Care. I camped in the waiting room waging a silent running battle with the cleaners who turned on the TV as a matter of course as they came by. I climbed on a chair and turned it off as soon as they were gone.

'As Mr Klein appears to perform better with his wife at his side', I was called in as often as possible while Greg hovered between life and death during those first thirty-six hours. Not daring to flinch, I was with him when the tube was pulled out of the back of his head. When the catheter was removed, my face was a frozen mask. Hour after hour John would come in.

'Greg! What day is it? What month is it? What year is it?'

With persuasion the inert form on the bed would rouse himself enough to answer with a variety of random guesses that had nothing to do with July 7th 1993. The day would be the nineteenth or the twenty-third, the month was continually September. The year went backwards from 1992 to 1973, stabilising for several hours on 1967 which I thought was significant. When it got to September 1942 it was absurd.

'Gregory, you weren't even born then,' I said.

'Wasn't I?'

'Okay Greg, tell me again. I want to know what day it is, what month it is, what year it is,' said John.

'Right here, right now.'

John looked at me.

'What's that supposed to mean?'

'It's a skilful use of Buddhist jargon meaning that he doesn't know, he doesn't care and basically he's pissed off with you for continually asking him.'

Greg was grinning but John was not amused.

'Well, he's got to get it right soon,' he said grimly.

'Maybe you're asking the wrong questions,' I said.

As soon as he was gone I leaned over my beloved, who lay serenely unperturbed by the ceaseless ticking and whining of the machinery.

'Gregory! Wake up! You're not doing so well in your exams. You can't get the date right, let alone the essay.'

'That's okay.'

'Not to Doctor John it isn't. Tell me, what colour was my dress when we got married?'

'Green.'

'Where did we buy it?'

'Athens.'

'And what colour were my shoes?'

'Sort of gold.'

'Where did we buy them?'

'Limnos.'

'And what colour was your shirt?'

'It was – let me see. It was blue and green and purple.'

'Where did we buy it?'

'Marks and Spencer's.'

'Chant me two blessings.'

'Two?'

'Yes and loud enough so that I can hear every word!'

He was word perfect and at last I knew for sure that my husband was not going to die on me right then.

I had to get him to start functioning again, eating, defecating, everything associated with the process of recovery. I had to find something to stimulate him back into life. Initially it had to be something simple and basic that he would do instinctively for himself. He went back to sleep while I searched through the packages on the trolley and came up with the perfect answer. Lemon flavoured glycerine swabs on sticks that could double as tooth brushes. Putting one in his right hand and holding it up to his mouth, I shouted in his ear,

'Gregory! Clean your teeth! Now!'

He twisted the stick between his fingers and slowly put the swab into his mouth.

'Go on! Clean your teeth!' I said.

Very slowly he moved the swab backwards and forwards over his front teeth and then opened his mouth to clean the ones at the back. I was so proud of him.

— ✳ —

When the Path lab report came back, John came to tell me that Charles was a *glioblastoma multiforme*, the most malignant of all brain tumours and the most impossible to treat. Radiation might put it into a few months of remission at best. Greg's case was unusual in that this type of tumour was mostly found at the front of the brain and only rarely on the cerebellum.

'What's the prognosis?' I asked finally.

'It's hard to say in that position,' he said.

'So you don't know then. Prognosis unknown. One thing I do know is that my husband is a very unusual man, he has lived a very unusual life and you can be certain that he won't do a brain tumour in anything less than an unusual way. I'll tell him what you have said if you don't mind.'

I did my best to tell him as simply and concisely as I knew how but he was too tired and weak to take the full implications on board. As far as he was concerned, he was alive, I was with him, he was going to get well and we would be going back to Greece as we planned after radiation. He squeezed my hand.

'Mali, here I am feeling like death, looking like death and probably smelling like it too and I look up and all I see are two big, blue eyes looking down at me, so full of love. I'm going to be okay, Baby, I promise you I'm going to be okay,' he said.

Jean and Joyce went back to Hampton and Bob and Donna and Karen took over. It was odd to meet the rest of my in-laws in front of the electric doors leading to Intensive Care. They stayed with me during the second operation. Only a four and a half hour wait this time while Greg had a shunt fitted into his head. He had remained completely dependent on a machine to drain the fluid from his brain during all of the six days after the first operation and it was obvious that he would not be able to live without some supplementary assistance.

We were back in Ward 2C later that afternoon and when the anaesthetic had worn off sufficiently to allow him to sit propped up, I found my scissors and cut off all his remaining hair. I was prepared to see Ānando again but surprised to see the Marine instead. Ten days of steroid medication had begun very slightly to puff up his face, not so that it was obvious but so that many of the fine lines on his face had disappeared. With the hint of swelling still under his eyes he looked exactly like the young Marine pictured on the front page of the *Buffalo Evening Post* in June 1967.

At that time it was difficult to tell how much the surgery would affect him long term except that almost imperceptibly his voice had changed in tone. But he had no pain. A CAT scan showed that the shunt was in place and draining the fluid through a tube that followed a straight line under the skin across the right hand side of his head, down his neck, over his chest and into his stomach. We began discussing where we would go when we left the hospital while he underwent six weeks of radiotherapy. The other three were going back to Hampton and I asked them to find out if it was possible to rent a house there while Greg was convalescent. I had seen one standing empty several doors down from his mother's house and thought maybe that might be suitable. It would be far enough away for us to maintain some degree of normality in our life but near enough for her to visit and for the loan of her car during radiation.

In a determined effort to grasp at anything resembling health and rationality, on the third morning after the shunt was fitted Greg insisted that I leave him sat up, so that he could try to read while I went for my shower. He was still reading when I came back an hour later but I was uneasy about him and his strangely aggressive demeanour. Although he had eaten all his breakfast and checked out well when the nurses came in at nine o'clock to monitor 'vital signs'. As his eyes were not focusing properly and it was difficult for him to concentrate for any length of time, he preferred to have me read to him. I was arranging myself at the bottom of the bed with the book in my hand when he suddenly sat bolt upright, watching something that was going on over my head.

'Oh! The colours!' he said.

'Greg! What are you talking about? What can you see?'

'The colours. It's amazing!'

I jumped off the bed and ran to the nurses' station.

'Come quickly! He's hallucinating!' I said.

Three of them dropped whatever they were doing and followed me back into the room. He was still sitting up but his eyes were flickering rapidly and he was no longer conscious of us standing beside the bed. As we watched his head turned hard to the right and with a half-strangled scream that imprinted itself forever on my consciousness, he fell back onto the pillows in a full tonic clonic seizure. John came in and pumped a shot of Valium into his arm and we stood by helplessly as his body convulsed in repeated epileptic spasms, his face green-grey, the foam bubbling out of his mouth and running down his neck.

'This shouldn't be happening. It shouldn't be happening! The tumour's in the wrong place for epilepsy!' John shouted.

'Why are you so surprised?' I said. 'This happened after Vietnam. I'm not surprised.'

Greg came round as John and I were taking him for an immediate CAT scan. He raised my hand to his lips as he came fully back into consciousness. The scan showed that the shunt had moved a little and he was scheduled for surgery again the following Monday to have it repositioned. A twice-daily dose of Dilantin was added on to his medication schedule. He was not pleased.

'That stuff makes your teeth fall out,' he growled.

'You have to be on it for some years before that is likely to happen,' said the nurse.

He was depressed at the recurrence of the epilepsy and at the prospect of another week in the hospital. It was a depression that was contagious and I could feel it beginning to nibble at the edges of my own brittle facade. After two weeks on diet based mainly on breakfast cereal, added to sleepless nights and overwhelming fear, I was as good a candidate for gloom as he was. I went shopping in the Mall in the central hall of the hospital and came back to the room with a large pad of lined paper and a folder.

'Gregory, I have another idea,' I said.

'What is it this time?'

'If we sit here just looking at each other we will go crazy. I have some paper and a pen so why don't you carry on dictating the book to me?'

'I don't think I can.'

'Try it. Tell me about Thailand, when you first went there. When you first met Ajahn Sumedho and Ajahn Chah.'

Once again my intuitive guess was the correct one. His recent memory was terribly disjointed, especially since we had been in the hospital. He couldn't remember one day from the next but his far memory was intact. When John came in to check on him again he found me sitting cross-legged on the bed and scribbling as fast as I could. I already knew most of the stories from our walks in Greece but there had never been time to write them down while we were still working on the first half of the book. Day after day he lay for hours with his eyes closed, recalling his early years as a monk in Thailand, while I filled up one pad and started another.

'This is very good for me you know,' he said. 'It stimulates me and reminds me that I still have a brain, not only a tumour.'

The hospital staff were getting used to seeing me pushing a bed or a stretcher trolley around the corridors with my husband giving orders as we went along. There was always someone ready to help with the doors or the elevator.

The Oncology unit was a completely different experience from the rest of the hospital as we knew it. The doors opened on to a quiet world of softly muted pink with pictures on the walls and a smiling, extra-caring receptionist. If we hadn't considered the full implications of cancer already, this tastefully sweetened atmosphere brought it home with a bang. We were there to talk radiation and the possibility of a short, intensive course of stereotactic treatment at the end of the standard six weeks of radiotherapy. As we would be based in Hampton, it was decided that the treatment would be arranged from there and we would come back to Richmond towards the end of that six weeks to apply for the rest of the treatment.

We held hands tightly all the way back to the ward, the stretcher weaving erratically through the corridors as the full horror of the reality of our situation began piercing even Greg's armour-plated optimism. I had been carefully hoarding our holiday money, hoping against hope that we would still be able to spend it on something wonderful but a hundred dollars went that afternoon on a bargain CD/tape player that had been wrongly priced in the Base Exchange in the Mall. His face lit up when he saw it and the two tapes I had bought. Choice had been very limited but I had found a 'Best of Motown' tape that had some of the good old songs from the sixties that I thought he might like. Our fragile enthusiasm turned to tears at the first line of the first song.

'Baby, I need your lovin', got to have all your lovin',' sang The Four Tops while we held each other and wept. All the brightness, the essence of Greg and Mali Klein, would it ever come back?

— ❊ —

The nightmare had only just begun. News came from Hampton about the house. We couldn't rent it, we had to buy it. Our worst imagining.

'Oh no!' said Greg.

'We can't afford to buy a house. Why can't we rent one? There must be some others. I can't believe there aren't.' I was not convinced.

But apparently not and we didn't need any extra money if we used Greg's GI loan from the VA that neither of us had ever heard of. When we wanted to leave the loan would just pass on to another GI. It sounded all too easy to me. The deal was already negotiated. All I had to do was to give our consent and Jean and Karen could go into the house and start cleaning.

What could we do? We were stuck in the hospital many miles away from Hampton and the Real Estate Agent, with no one else to discuss it with. I knew all about buying houses in England but nothing about the formalities of purchase in America. From my recent, if limited, experience of American litigation, I knew it had to be very different. With a third operation facing us in as many weeks there was no time to do anything about it myself and I was too exhausted to know where to begin. I knew I had to get Greg out of the hospital at the earliest possible opportunity if he was going to survive. Which left us no option other than very reluctantly to give our consent.

All the flags outside the hospital were torn down and burned in my mind's eye during the three and a half hours that Greg was in surgery. I was sat mentally pouring petrol in silent fury when one of the Baptist pastors came along and cheerfully listened as I told her exactly what I was thinking about. We had met several of the Baptist ministers in the hospital. All of them were black and warm and friendly, very strongly committed to their faith but never attempting either to impose it on us or to convert us. She didn't mind me in the slightest.

'You have to understand,' I said. 'We don't want to buy a bloody house! I can't let any emotion out here and I can't tell Greg how angry I am. It takes all the energy he has left just to stay alive. Mentally burning flags is the safest way I can be furious.'

'It's okay, you go ahead and burn them. I understand,' she said.

When I could, I stamped. Buying a house was an absolute betrayal of our principles and personal values. It went against everything we were about. And in America! My husband had spent all of his adult life leaving America. What were we doing coming back now?

He came out of the anaesthetic hearing two nurses and me discussing the colour and splendour of his legs as we put him on a stretcher for an MRI scan.

'Women!' he groaned.

He wasn't so well after this operation, complaining of increasing head pain. By the second morning he was moaning aloud and holding his head. A worried Doctor John came into the room.

'What's happening to him, John?' I asked.

'I don't know. The MRI was okay.'

'What could be happening?'

'It could be the tumour. They get angry when they're cut. I'll get him a big dose of steroid and see if we can get another CAT scan right away.'

For the second time in seven days I helped load him into the scanner, holding onto the bags that were dripping a steroid and saline solution into his arm so fast that it was burning his vein. John came and sat with me while the scanner was in operation.

'What could be happening to the tumour?' I said.

'It could be getting away from us,' he replied.

'So how long would we have then?'

'Two weeks.'

We were supposed to be going back to Hampton the next day.

'I'm not ready for this,' I thought.

'And if the steroid works?' I asked.

'It will reduce the inflammation and the pressure and he will be okay.'

'What else does steroid do?'

'It swells up the face, gives a voracious appetite and puts unnecessary weight on the torso. It wastes the muscles of the arms and legs, causes stomach ulcers and rots the pancreas. High doses can also account for behavioural problems and it's addictive. Reduce it too quickly and he could experience withdrawal symptoms.'

My poor, beloved fitness fanatic. The solution was everything he had always dreaded.

'The next few months are going to be tough on you, Mali,' he added.

'I can take it. I'm his wife. That's what I'm here for,' I said, wearing my best brave face. 'With a tumour like this, how long have we got do you think?'

'Maybe a year with radiation. If you're lucky,' he said.

He went in to check the scan. I sat on the corner of the arm of the chair repeating over and over to myself,

'Please let the steroid work, please let the steroid work, please let the steroid work.'

The telephone was ringing in the corridor as we got back to the ward. I picked it up and spoke to Gillian, our self-appointed news-relay to the Sangha. I told her what had happened.

'When will you know if the steroid is working?' she said.

'I don't know. Maybe later today. He's having two large intravenous doses now and then he's on forty milligrams a day instead of eight.'

'You will let me know, won't you?'

'Yes.'

John was being generous in his estimation. The nurses were more inclined to give us six months. The word 'hospice' floated into the conversation more than once rather than 'home' when moving him was being considered. A word that meant sanctuary to so many people ignited the silent scream into an instant, white hot rage within me.

'No-o-o-o-o-o-o-o!'

Hospices are the answer for ninety per cent of people but for some they are not. My husband was one of that ten per cent. He had travelled all his life and nothing would make him die more quickly than shutting him up somewhere, no matter how beautiful the place was. Our hospice was the world and he wasn't going to be shut away anywhere to die. I wouldn't let him.

'John, how soon can we get out of here?' I said.

'You can go the day after tomorrow if he stabilises.'

'Can you arrange it then? He's going to die anyway if we stay here. I can look after him.'

'I'll see what I can do.'

By the afternoon we had our miracle. The pain was gone and he was sitting up and talking.

'Gregory Klein, do you realise what you have done today?' I said.

'No, tell me.'

'You have frightened us all out of our wits again. That's what you have done. And what's more, you have almost succeeded in personally cancelling the ordination at Chithurst.'

'What do you mean?'

'Ajahn Sumedho was so concerned that you might die before he had a chance to see you that he was prepared to drop everything to come straight over here, which would have effectively put paid to the ordination next Sunday.'

'He was prepared to do that?'

'Yes, of course he was. Everyone is so worried about you in the monastery. They have been chanting themselves silly for you. Don't you realise?'

'Maybe I'd better talk to him.'

'Maybe you should. How are you feeling now?'

'Fine.'

'Well enough to sit in a wheelchair?'

'Yes, I think so.'

'Okay, I will go and call Amaravati. If they hear your voice they will know for sure that you are still alive.'

John arranged for us to travel to Hampton VA hospital by ambulance on Friday, July 23rd and Joyce's telephone campaign got us booked into Riverside Cancer Unit for the radiation, only twenty minutes' drive from the house. We left the hospital with a bag bulging with medication and a new wheelchair as a mobile contribution to the furniture in this new home we were still dreading moving into. John came to see us as the paramedics were lifting Greg onto the stretcher.

'Mali, can he walk?' he asked.

'Of course he can,' I said, knowing perfectly well that he could not. I was determined to drag him by main force into the car at Hampton if I had to. We couldn't stay in Richmond one minute longer.

Chapter Twelve

The house smelled of carpet shampoo and cleaner overlaying the faint, stale tar odour of too many cigarettes that no amount of goodwill and chemical can get rid of. Neither Jean or Karen had ever lived with us but they had interpreted our needs wisely, moving in the minimum furniture, laying a big bed out on the floor and loaning us just enough linen and kitchenware. Nothing in excess. I was immediately nervous of the cane rocking chair that Jean told us was a family heirloom. I hoped very much that Greg wouldn't fall on it while he was still so unsteady on his feet.

Between us, Karen and I half-lifted, half-dragged him out of the car and up the steps into the kitchen. Completely exhausted, he went straight to bed while I set up the shrine, always the first task wherever we stayed. I made a thorough inspection of all the cupboards, the bathroom, the windows, finding out how everything worked and where everything was. Gone were the days when I unpacked under direction and the heaviest thing I had to lift was a plate. Looking at the house and its situation, it was nothing I would have chosen for a living space but it seemed that the luxury of choice was no longer ours for the asking. Greg had to live and we had to be here while the question of his living or dying still hung in the balance. All I could do was to swallow my feelings and personal preferences and make the best of it.

Among the cards and letters waiting for us was a packet of the incense that had almost always been used at Chithurst while we were there. With absolute relief I carried the burning sticks around the house bringing the familiar peace of the Shrine room into the bewildering chaos of our latest home.

'Mali! Where are you? I need to go to the bathroom!'

I walked into the bedroom to lay the last stick of incense on the shrine.

'Hello, my lamb. Did you sleep well? Do you like the shrine?' I said.

'Yes, it's fine. Will you help me please?'

'It would be easier for you to use the urinal for the first few days until you can walk.'

'No, I want to go the bathroom.'

'Gregory, I'm not going to attempt to stand you up on my own so you will have to crawl. Do you remember all those lectures you gave me on Rhodes last winter about right brain, left brain co-ordination when I hurt my ankle?'

'No.'

As I was talking I was manoeuvring him to the edge of the bed and rolling him on to his side ready for the lift.

'Well here's your chance to practise what you preach even if you don't remember it. It's the only way I can think of moving you until you are stronger on your legs.'

I heaved him up onto his knees. As long as I went in front with my hands on his shoulders to steady him it worked out very well. With one hand on me and the other on the bath he was able to pull himself upright to manoeuvre on to the toilet. It disturbed him that he was still not completely in control of his bladder but as it didn't disturb me he was content to believe that the condition would improve. As it did over the coming weeks.

'I don't want my family to see I'm like this,' he said.

'But it's only your mother and your sisters,' I said.

'It doesn't matter, I don't want them to see this. You're my wife. I don't mind you helping me but no one else.'

'I must never be ill,' I thought. 'I must never leave him, even to go shopping, unless he is comfortable and in bed. I must be better organised than ever before.'

At the same time all the old feelings of self-disgust at always being so damned efficient came up to drain my fragile emotional reserves. Was it paradox or a perfect example of the Great Cosmic Joke that had dictated that I spend twenty-two years in relationships where I had been continually criticised for my ability to think and articulate until I met the love of my life who, among other things, had fallen in love with me for precisely that? But the old scars were still tender and it was with very little self-respect that I pushed myself into my super-efficient, all-sewn-up role.

It was only after we had left the hospital that I realised fully how much we had lost. They had given me back the pieces of my husband. All the refinement of body, speech and mind was gone. Even his lips were no longer so sensitive. He complained that he couldn't respond so intimately to a kiss. The back of his head was distorted by a long central scar that ended in a hard lump of traumatised muscular tissue at the base of his neck and I had to be careful how I cuddled up to him to sleep as the tube from the shunt lay directly under the skin on his chest where I had always lain my head.

It took almost all of his available energy simply to function. The little that was left manifested as a mixture of innocence and aggression, the child and the man. More of the child presented itself to his family, the pseudo-dependence and the sweetness. I got some of the sweetness but mostly the man. Afraid, enraged at the possibility of the loss of his strength, his vitality, his manhood. Dependent only because he had to be. When the contrast in his behaviour became so extreme that I couldn't bear it any longer and pointed it out to him, down would come his fist, smashing repeatedly into whatever was nearest, his face with those slightly swollen, desperate eyes jammed into mine.

'I'm ill! I'm ill! I'm ill!' he screamed, his frantic mouth twisted in bitterness.

He insisted on making love to me twice during our first night in the house and afterwards I lay almost crushed beneath the weight he could no longer support for himself, feeling all the muscles in his body twitching in their unaccustomed weakness. With difficulty I swallowed the sobbing that stuck in my throat. Instead the tears poured silently into my ears, spilling out onto my neck and onto the pillow. Drowsy and unaware of my crying, he made no sound as I kissed him gently and eased him over onto his side of the bed. For me the grieving process had already begun.

I knew I had to give him back as much of himself as I could. Greg and Ānando. It was up to me to stimulate every particle of all that was left. To that end and to ensure the continuing possibility of my sanity, our days always began with morning meditation. Except that now I lit the candles and the incense and led the chanting while Greg lay in bed, hands held in anjali and doing his best to stay awake for at least the first ten minutes of the sitting. No matter how early we had to be up for a hospital appointment I made sure that we had completed our devotional hour before we left the house. The last twenty minutes were given over to a full healing session. I worked on him as he dozed, invoking the Medicine Buddha, the Holy Ones, all Wise and Kindly Beings and doing all that I could to clear the shock and the deeper wounding from his body, mind and heart. We were both encouraged when after a week he could pull himself upright to walk with me supporting him and he could sit at the table for meals. It was tempting to continue feeding him but as that only helped me, I put all his food in big bowls on a tray to minimise spillage. Once he began to totter around the house by himself, with all my senses straining to catch the slightest hesitation, I kept resolutely to whatever I was doing while at the same time firmly willing myself not to interfere unless I had to.

We had led a preciously secluded, private life in Greece, enjoying a unique exchange on all levels conscious and unconscious, but now as well as a brain tumour we had a telephone to deal with. It was only natural for people to want to be in contact with Greg if only to be reassured by the sound of his voice. But he desperately needed to rest and I wasn't strong enough in myself to see the ringing as anything less than an intrusion while we were both so weak and tired. Consequently I found myself pulling the plug out of the wall for more than half the day and obstinately refused to buy an answering machine.

Cancer is not content unless it rules your life and Charles was a powerful and demanding parasite with an energy that almost bled us dry in those early days, while we were doing our best both to recover from the trauma of the hospital and to adjust to the demands of our new and all too public existence. My husband had always been so insistent that a large percentage of our life be kept entirely to ourselves and criticised me quite severely if he considered that I had talked too freely about what we were doing or were about to do. Undeniably, after a year of such rigorous schooling it was very difficult for me to hear him relating almost everything we did to his mother over the phone. It emphasised how completely our world had been turned upside-down.

136

Continuing on forty milligrams of steroid a day, he was beginning to exhibit some of the side effects that John had predicted. My beloved would always be beautiful. When you've got the basics even steroid can't totally obliterate it, but his face was beginning to show signs of the infamous 'moon' face as it filled out around the eyes and the cheeks. His arms and legs had already lost shape and muscle tone, his chest had lost its breadth and despite medication to counteract it, he rarely ate a meal without some discomfort in his stomach.

At the same time he was always hungry. He left the hospital craving salads and two days later nothing would satisfy him except pizza and French fries. This became a major source of conflict which we tried to keep within the relative privacy of our own domain. Not so easy when your mother-in-law lives a few doors down the road and you can't be sure how much the neighbours can overhear through thin, wooden walls. When the day came when he could look critically at himself in the mirror, I didn't want him to see an overweight, ugly parody of what he had been staring back at him. Accordingly I banned all junk food and sugar and held out doggedly against his demands and his wheedling. His higher self respected my intention without hesitation when I related in detail exactly what the steroid could do but, like all parasites, the tumour was determined to bring out the worst in him until we were strong enough to fight back.

His capacity for telling people only what they wanted to hear increased dramatically. He could never be trusted to report fully to the doctors or to repeat all that they had really said and he became extraordinarily sly, playing the poor, hard-done-by invalid to his mother, deprived of the foods he needed most so that she would make them for him instead. He wasn't unaware of the vagaries of his behaviour but he was powerless to do much about it and at times like that there was very little reasoning with him. I would have to scream louder than he could to get his attention.

'I know you're ill, but I'm only trying to help you! I want you back, I want you well! That's why I make you walk every day. That's why I'm trying to make you think! Before you forget!'

But at the same time he had not lost his sense of humour nor the ability to laugh at himself. Many times he related with delight how he had stopped with his mouth watering in front of a cookie stall in the Mall one afternoon while we were shopping.

'Mali, can I have a cookie?' he asked, indicating a giant chocolate chip cookie.

'No Gregory. Have an apple,' I said.

'Mali! Please!'

'You're not going to turn into a fat slob. I'm sorry Gregory,' I replied, pushing the wheelchair firmly on.

'You're merciless!'

'I love you.'

And so I did. I never once felt any lessening of the love I had for my husband. Neither did I lose my desire. I was careful not to encourage him to make love to me more than two or three times each week, which was all that he could happily and comfortably manage, but it meant that the quality of our accustomed intimacy was gone. There could be no more 'getting into bed to solve problems'. I fought my personal battles mostly alone, not helped by sexual frustration which only served to amplify my loneliness and despair. I missed him so.

— ❈ —

The house was a problem from Day One. The real estate agent gave us the first weekend to ourselves before he moved in with the mountain of paperwork.

'Have you both read everything I left you, Mali?' he asked.

'Don't be ridiculous! Of course not. When would we have had the time?' I said, indicating Greg, who was not much more than semi-conscious and sitting on the floor propped up with pillows against the wall because I couldn't trust him not to fall out of a chair.

'We don't want to buy this house, we don't want a house but we are told that circumstances leave us no other option,' I continued.

'Well, you have agreed to purchase,' he said.

'We did not agree to purchase,' I said with the emphasis on 'we'.

Greg opened his eyes.

'It is something I have avoided all my life,' he said.

'Look, we're not intending to give you a hard time,' I said. 'Our situation is not your fault. We have to stay somewhere so we had better get on with it. As long as we can get rid of it just as easily when we want to move on.'

'That shouldn't be a problem,' he said.

But he wouldn't make eye contact with me and something in his look and his tone made me very nervous. There was something going on that we hadn't been told about and my witch's nose began twitching overtime as we signed all the papers. Greg had to have the pen put into his hand and guided along the line and I added my signature feeling that I had allowed us to be betrayed into the nether world.

I took to prowling round and round the house, beating myself up, trying to put my finger on what was wrong, wishing I knew the whole story behind the purchase agreement. Greg thought I was overreacting.

'Take it easy, Mali. It will be all right,' he said.

'No it's not all right. We haven't been told everything, I know we haven't. I have bought and sold houses before, remember. I tell you there's something going on here.'

But no one was prepared to enlighten me. We had agreed at the beginning that the realtor should work both for us and the vendor but it soon became obvious that the arrangement was not to our advantage. He made it clear that he intended to take care of the vendor first and then mop up as best as he could for us afterwards.

Then the cheque-signing process began and far from costing nothing, by the end of the first week all of our carefully saved money had been spent for us in placating the American realty system. With nothing else to do but to make the best of it, I arranged to borrow one thousand, six hundred dollars to buy a refrigerator, a cooker and a washing machine, which had not been included in the purchase, and to pay it back over the next three months. Karen and I went shopping and in twenty-four hours the kitchen looked a lot better and I had the means to deal with Greg's occasional incontinence without having to carry the tell-tale laundry down the road to his mother's house.

My mind ran on, trying to relate to all the positive possibilities in our situation. Norfolk Air Base was only a few miles down the road, which meant that if I sorted out a visa for myself we could fly for free from there to Iceland for New Year and the Caribbean in February. We would still be able to travel. Then if the time came when he had to die, he could do it here with his family around him if that's what he wanted.

But when would we see the children again? We would have to buy a car. The house badly needed decorating. There would never be enough money left over to send them tickets. I could feel the steel jaws of the trap closing over us. My head ached continually. Three hours of unbroken sleep each night was a luxury and there weren't many days when I didn't get up feeling sick.

Hampton represented home and security to some several thousands of people but not to us. It would have been easier on Greg's family and friends if he had married an American girl. As it was, my accent and very different ways, coupled with our continuation of the meditation practice, served as a constant reminder that his roots, if he had any at all, lay elsewhere and in a wider world than Virginia USA. Born and brought up near Chithurst in Green Belt Southern England, I was not designed to thrive in a suburb, least of all an American suburb. After more than twenty years abroad, neither was my husband.

The houses were all detached, single-storeyed, primarily wooden structures tucked in among huge trees that should have been beautiful except that they cut out most of the light. It could be argued that they cut out most of the heat as well but we were veterans of sun-parched Mediterranean summers where trees and air-conditioning played no part at all. Every night I looked out at the patch of sky above the street, claustrophobic and desperate to see the stars or the moon. In Hampton the universe was a pale ghost of what had been so familiar in Europe, dimmed into insignificance by the neon city lights. There were no stones in the garden and no rocks by the sea ten minutes' drive away. The beach was a continuous stretch of swept, sterile sand. The soil around the house powdered away between my fingers. There was not a single pretty pebble to be found to decorate the shrine.

There was nowhere to walk other than around the streets. There were no woods, no fields, no mountains. There were no trains, few buses. We found ourselves non-starters without a car in America. Spiritually we were as far from like minds as we had ever been. Our neighbours were all very kind. Even those who didn't know Jean personally and weren't members of her church always said hello when they saw us. Everyone of them seemed to belong to one of the wealth of Pentecostal, Baptist and Catholic churches that appeared on every other street corner, all well equipped with congregation and cash and each vying with the other to do good in the community.

— ✳ —

But the humidity was immediately the hardest of all to bear, and the eternal droning of the electric fan as we tossed and sweated through the nights. There was a large and very noisy air-conditioning unit set into the dining room wall which was meant to serve most of the house but I rarely used it. I had left the hospital with a racking cough and I decided that either I had to acclimatise or else I was going to be really ill. Consequently the windows were left open and the fans turned on and the only sound of air-conditioning came from the simultaneous rattling of the units in all the other houses in the street.

We blessed Karen for being able to stay on during the six weeks of the radiation treatment. Joyce came when she could but her children were still young and needed her back in Buffalo. Karen's family had grown up and she decided to make the most of the opportunity to get to know her brother to whom, by force of circumstance, she had hardly spoken for years. Every day she came with the car and drove us either to the VA hospital in Hampton for routine blood testing and 'vital signs' or to the Riverside Cancer Treatment Center in Newport News for radiation.

We usually sat in the back of the car, most of the time Greg lay with his head on a pillow on my knees, with Karen talking and laughing as she negotiated the roads and the miles of commercial boulevards. Once we sat out a tornado together in a parking lot while the rain pounded down so hard on the roof of the car that we could hardly hear ourselves speak. As Greg often said afterwards,

'Karen was the best thing that came out of that summer.'

Fortune smiled on us once again at the VA when we met our new doctor, who most accurately resembled one of my more enlightened tutors at art school at the end of the sixties rather than an oncologist. Quietly spoken and very laid back, he gave me his home number to ring at any time if I was worried about anything. He stopped mentioning the word 'hospice' when Greg laughingly told him to check out my body language as I sat with my arms folded against my chest, legs crossed and feet only just not tapping impatiently on the floor. We were lucky in that we always felt supported by our doctors, whoever they were, as we met them.

Radiation began on August 4th after the initial appointment for making and fitting the plastic mesh mask that would permanently mark the area to be irradiated and would hold his head firmly in place during treatment. We met our radiologist, another doctor who didn't quite know how to meet our

140

eyes once he had seen the MRI scans. It was a good opportunity for me to look at the scans myself and ask as many questions as I could think of, while I sketched a quick diagram in the diary to show Greg later. I was shocked when I saw exactly how much of my husband's head was already allocated to Charles and under prompting the doctor was persuaded to translate the images for me. He pointed out the initial damage from the bullet wound and indicated how the tumour was putting the brain stem under increasing pressure and pushing it to one side.

'Doctor, how ever did he manage to go for so long with a thing like that in his head and not show more obvious symptoms?' I asked.

'I don't know. I can only say he must be a highly disciplined man,' he replied, unaware of my husband's history.

As I was helping Greg off the table and into the wheelchair, he called us into one of the side rooms.

'Before you leave I have to tell you both that radiation rarely cures this type of tumour. It may shrink it but they invariably grow back again.'

'I'm not going to have the treatment,' announced the patient once we were back at the house.

'But you must, Beloved, you must!' I said in panic. 'It's the only thing that will buy us time to find the miracle.'

'I won't have it. I'll have acupuncture instead. I won't be a guinea pig.'

'Gregory, until there is a definitive cure for cancer, everyone who has it is a guinea pig and it's their treatment that increases the wealth of knowledge available to help the next generation. With the best of intention I have never heard of an acupuncturist who has successfully dealt with a tumour like we've got.'

'I don't want it, I tell you. I don't want to lose my hair.'

'You won't lose all of it, only at the sides, and it will grow back again. Please have the radiation, please, if only for me. It's the only thing that will shut the tumour down for long enough while we find something else. I don't want to lose you. I love you. Please, please!'

Seeing my husband pinned to a bed by the mask clipped over his face and then watching the flickering on the computer screen caused by magnetic interference as the treatment took place was like watching something out of *Star Trek*.

'Gregory, I must say that of all the weird situations we have been in together, this has to be the weirdest. It's very strange to leave you behind that huge door.'

'It's very strange to be left there and nothing I particularly enjoy.'

'But you must stop talking about the Spanish Inquisition when you're in there. I don't think it helps the treatment if you go in with a negative attitude.'

'I guess you're right. Maybe I should give the machine a name and lay there practising metta towards it. How about that?'

'Then it has to be a female name, one that you can develop a deeply meaningful relationship with. You have my permission. Just this once.'

141

The radiation exhausted him and increased the early morning inter-cranial pressure during the first few days, putting the steroid up to forty-four milligrams daily. After the ninth treatment, Greg was showing so much improvement that I was given permission to try reducing it very slowly down to twenty-four milligrams. Radiation played havoc with his already erratic appetite and I could never anticipate from one day to the next what he might want to eat or what would satisfy him. During the third week he woke up with a dusting of hair on his pillow and three days later the back and sides of his head were completely bare.

Sometimes on the good days he looked at himself in the mirror and then at me and said,

'I don't know how you can love me but I am so glad that you do.'

'You're my husband, I can't help it. I suppose I should be used to you abusing me by now.'

'I'd rather you didn't have to be,' he said. 'I want to get off the steroid.'

'You will when you're better. It will be all right, you'll see.'

'Oh Mali, I hope so, I do hope so. I'm sorry it had to be this way. When I'm well you won't have to worry about anything again. I'll take care of it all as I used to.'

'I know you will,' I said.

He usually slept for most of the morning and went to bed for an hour in the afternoon after radiation. On one of our more difficult days after he had finally fallen asleep, I was standing in the living room looking out of the window at the houses opposite, the trees, the patch of blue sky. I was wishing for the thousandth time that the house would blow up and take us with it. I was feeling desolate. Sorry for myself and sorry for my husband. A man came walking down the street pushing a profoundly spastic child in a specially-adapted wheelchair. They went on past the house and disappeared behind the bushes of the garden next to ours, absorbed in their unique tragedy. Unaware of me at the window living mine.

'No matter how bad everything is, there is always someone worse,' I thought.

That child would never know the freedom we had known and might still know again. She would never know the love. We had so much to be grateful for. My poor beloved. He struggled so hard to recover for me.

'It's not time for me to die yet. There's still so much I want to do. And I want more time with you,' he said.

There were always the moments of tenderness. There was still the laughter. He could still appreciate my teasing and sometimes outrageous remarks. I started calling him my 'lamb' and 'lammie' which he hated.

'I prefer husband,' he said.

'I know but I can't help it, I'm so sorry that you're sick, beloved you,' I answered as contritely as I could.

'Lambert then,' he growled.

'Lambert? Lambert Klein? Really?' I said.

142

We both collapsed into helpless laughter.

Getting him into the bath tub was usually fun every morning and I was nearly always hung around his neck as I pushed him along in the wheelchair. If he saw a reflection of himself in a shop front and hated it, I would always point out the blonde hanging over the back.

'How many men in wheelchairs have beautiful blondes necking with them as they push, Gregory?'

'You're right but I want to get out of this chair!'

'I want you out of it, never fear.'

To that end we paced up and down Buckroe Beach for half an hour every day on the way to radiation, with Greg pushing one of the others sat in the chair as ballast. I steadied him with one hand firmly linked into the belt loops of his shorts. He wore sunglasses to keep the light from dazzling his eyes and a black, silk bandanna around his head to minimise the extra, natural radiation from the sun. In the beginning we got to the end of the beach and back mainly by good luck as I literally held him up while he concentrated on getting one foot straight in front of the other instead of going sideways with his legs crossed so that he almost fell over.

At weekends we went out alone, either pushing the chair around the maze of streets or taking our lives in our hands along the main road to the nearest shopping precinct. We were surprised to find houses empty and for rent in every street and wondered why we had never been told about them. I couldn't understand it and became increasingly wary and not willingly co-operative with the realtor, consumed as I was by the cryptic, nagging doubt about the house that continually destroyed any peace of mind I may have had the chance to enjoy.

As always money was a problem. Not content with clearing out our savings, the mortgage company needed more and I didn't have three months to repay the money I had borrowed. Without an established credit history we were financial lepers in America. We had no choice but to cash in an Investment Certificate that Jean had saved from the pension and made over to Greg before he went into hospital.

'At least I can buy you a ring now for our wedding anniversary,' he said and insisted on being taken to buy it almost immediately as though he was afraid that he might not be well enough to buy it in October. Karen and I left him for almost an hour sitting in his chair in the shop and keeping the assistants on their toes.

Gillian came for two weeks in August, bearing gifts and good wishes from the Sangha to add to the pile that were already decorating the shrine and the walls and all the shelf space.

'People love me!' he said with some surprise.

'So did it have to take a brain tumour to teach you that?'

'I guess so.'

I found myself desperately wishing we could go with her when she left.

A few days later, a chance remark at a dinner party showed us how, in her pain and fear for her much loved son, his mother was prepared to go to any lengths to keep him at her side. As she outlined the plans she had made for his living and his dying, with dawning horror we realised what we were getting into. We went back to the house feeling dejected and bruised. It was too late to say much about it then.

'Come to bed Mali. We'll talk about it in the morning,' he said.

He was soon asleep. Not I. It was still almost unbearably hot at night, even at the end of August, and the ceaseless droning from the fan was not conducive to peace. As the night wore on all my pent-up grief raged into focus. Where was life on our own terms? What had happened to the freedom to be ourselves? I was more than willing to live with the inexactitude of the brain tumour but in our own way and in our own time. I lay wide awake staring up at the shadows from the street lights on the ceiling, boiling in impotent fury. I had to talk to someone. I had to let this out or I would be insane by the morning. It was four o'clock, nine o'clock in England. My mother would never sleep again if she heard this but Gillian might still be at home.

Greg was deeply asleep beside me and made no movement as I slid out from the bed, pausing for a moment to listen to his breathing before I closed the door quietly behind me. Huddled in a chair in the kitchen with one ear aimed towards the bedroom, I talked for half an hour. To hell with the bill. All my brave plans and the brave face were history for that moment. I blamed myself bitterly for allowing us to get into this mess and there was nothing Gillian could do or say. I only needed her to have the kindness to listen.

'Well, at least maybe now I can sleep,' I thought as I crept back towards the bedroom. I almost fell over two thin, brown legs sticking out from behind the boiler cupboard. Somehow he had got himself out of bed, opened the door, crawled into the living room and propped himself up against the wall. In his disabled condition, how did he manage it without making a sound? I realised he must have heard everything I said. I was furious with him.

'What are you doing here? How did you open the door? How dare you listen to me!'

I almost spat at him.

'I had to hear what you really thought about us staying here. I knew you would never tell me directly. It was the only way,' he said.

'I was just letting off two months' worth of steam, that's all and for once that's my business. We're committed to this house now and I'm going to make the best of it. You won't have to hear anything like that again.'

'Mali, what makes you think I am prepared to stay here?'

'Well, aren't you? You've never said otherwise.'

'Mali, I'm not staying here. I wound up in Vietnam to get away from America. I'm not about to come back now.'

'You mean you've intended leaving all along?'

144

'Of course I have. We're getting out of here as soon as the treatment is finished. It's my life, our life, we're talking about and it doesn't end here.'

'But I thought you wanted your family to be with you if you died.'

'Mali, I told you before. I don't want to die but if that's the way it has to be, I only want you with me. No one else. I made my mind up to that while I was still a monk. Nothing's changed. My family know I love them but it's my natural inclination to worry about them when I'm with them and I don't need that if I'm dying.'

My mind conjured up an image of the Last Rites and a Catholic Wake.

'As an Ajahn you have lived, as an Ajahn you will die. Is that it?' I asked. 'How does an Ajahn die, Mali?'

'With dignity and grace. As he lived, Gregory. Do you mean I can start packing?'

'Yes, of course you can.'

'What about the house?'

'What about the house? I'm not going to close the deal. It's as simple as that. Buying this place was never our idea from the beginning.'

'Where shall we go?'

'Where do you want to go?'

'Not to England. Somewhere in Europe. Hey, how about the house in France? The one Sasha told us about? We could speak French and have sunshine and be near enough to civilisation in case you needed doctors.'

'Yes, we could do that. I'll write to Sophie after breakfast. Until then will you please come back to bed for what's left of the night?'

After eight miserable weeks I lay down with my husband again, the child on full retreat to the privacy of our intimate life where he belonged. The man re-empowered had clicked back into gear. Later he sat at the table and wrote the letter, his hand steady and needing no help from me while I washed the breakfast dishes.

'Read this for me please and tell me if I've made any spelling mistakes,' he said.

'Only two. There and there. They are easily changed,' I said.

He sealed the envelope and handed it to me.

'Get it in the mail box right away,' he said.

I sent for a large canvas holdall at the same time, as big as his pack and fitted with wheels.

'What do you want that for?' he asked.

'Because you can't carry a full pack any more and I certainly can't. But I will be able to drag this around airports. Things have changed Gregory. However well you get, you won't be able to risk putting a lot of pressure on that shunt. The last thing we want is to have it move again. And we're going to have to think seriously about transport in Europe.'

'We are not buying a car. They're too much of a liability.'

'So how do you suggest we travel to France? How are we going to do simple things like shopping with only me to carry the bags as well as helping you?'

'I don't want a car. It's as bad as having a house.'

'I don't agree. For us a car means freedom and without that we're sunk.'

We chased the argument around for some days. Finally he said,

'As you have obviously made up your mind, what sort of car are you thinking of?'

'Only a little one. But it's got to be tough and feel like it has four wheels cornering. I'd like a two door Volkswagen that's not more than two years old. We don't want it breaking down on us. It has to have a 1.1 litre engine for economy and preferably a dark colour, grey or black. And it can't cost more than five thousand pounds because that's all we can afford.'

'Okay, but there's one thing that's absolutely non-negotiable. It has to be a left hand drive if we are going to France. I refuse to buy an English car.'

He knew that left-hand drive cars were almost non-existent in England unless they had been specially imported and sold on. He remained adamant. I sent our last eleven thousand dollars to the bank in England to be turned into seven thousand pounds and filed my 'case' as half concluded. We had a far more pressing problem to deal with.

— ❋ —

Not closing the deal on the house was not as simple as Greg thought it would be. All hell let loose when the realtor knew what was going on. He started talking about suing and thousands of dollars. No one knew better than he that neither Greg nor I had read the papers when we signed them and Greg had still been so drugged that he could hardly hold the pen. We had already lost over three thousand dollars on the house and we had neither the time or the energy for a lawsuit. It didn't do a lot for my estimation of the American legal system. Here was a man in pain and desperately trying to survive the biggest tumour in a living brain and we were being threatened just to save a real estate agent's career. At last we heard the whole story behind the agreement to purchase and it was true that in some ways he was as much a victim of misunderstanding as we were but he had been very anxious to off-load a house that had been on his books for more than a year.

In this nightmare situation we couldn't afford to be gracious. After a week of arguing that put Greg on continual doses of pain-killer and sent the phone bill soaring, the only amicable solution was for us to close the deal as agreed and then to make the house over to the realtor on the same day for him to sell on, giving him power of attorney so that we would never have to hear of it again.

'You can have one month's mortgage payment and that's all you're going to get,' I said. 'If you haven't sold the house by then you can pay the next instalment yourself. You won't get another dollar out of us ever again and neither are we going to pay you to sell it.'

It was ironical that the monthly mortgage payment would be less than we had been paying for rent.

Greg took his Will to the bank to have it notarised. It was very simple and to the point, leaving what few possessions we shared exclusively to me, requesting that his ashes be interred at Chithurst and stating clearly that I was to notify no one of his dying until after his death had taken place. I knew the last clause would probably be the source of more difficulty than just a few headaches. He was my husband, he was categorised terminally ill and his wishes had to be more important than my feelings or anyone else's.

Sophie wrote back saying we could have the house in France all winter and another letter came in the same mail from one of the lay supporters in England, with a newspaper article about a new drug called Temozolomide which was reported to be having an astonishing success in reducing brain tumours. Best of all it was being currently tested in a hospital only forty-five minutes' drive from my mother's house and in the area of jurisdiction accessible to our doctor in England. During the final week of radiation, Greg had become increasingly unwell. He was having more headaches and had very little appetite.

We went back to Richmond as we had planned for a follow-up MRI scan, which showed some lessening in the overall mass compared to the original size of the tumour but not as much as we had hoped for, and it was still too large for the consultant to consider the stereotactic treatment. Greg had never wanted to see the scans until then. He was not encouraged when he saw the reality of what we were up against. We told the doctor about the news item from England and how we were sure we qualified for it.

'It sounds like your best chance,' he said. 'I was trained in London. They're sometimes five or ten years ahead of America on drug availability and there's nothing more we can do for you. Get back there as quickly as you can. There's nothing left for you here.'

In two days our travel insurance company had us booked to leave on October 7th.

Jean took it very well. Greg had been packing up and leaving for most of his life, but we needed a break before then, that elusive week away together that we had never had.

'Mali, I want to show you something that's beautiful in America before we go,' he said. 'Let's hire a car from the Base and go to the mountains.'

'I don't believe there are any. As far as I can see the whole country is flat and covered in trees.'

'That's not true. The Blue Ridge Mountains are not flat.'

They were covered in trees but they were not flat and they were blue, edged with the first tinges of the red and gold of the Fall. After the sweltering heat of the coastlands, it was wonderful to be shivering in the mornings and to have to wear sweaters. Our room looked west over the Shenandoah valley. I made a bed for us on the floor beside the window so that we could fall asleep watching the stars. Greg still needed pain-killer in the early mornings and the wheelchair came with us to the Skyline Caverns but that was the only time we took it out of the car. Otherwise he was fine, insisting on walking everywhere using me as a prop, and happily buying me a black bear to go with JBJ when I was disappointed at the picnic grounds because we didn't see any real ones.

We spent the weekend in Buffalo, driving all day on the Friday, staying long enough on the Saturday to ride in the 'Maid of the Mist' under Niagara Falls with Rick. We drove back to Shenandoah on Sunday for one last peaceful night before going on to Hampton to pack up the house. Greg had been wide awake and happy all day and late into the evening in Buffalo, with no need for pain-killer. It could only be an encouraging prospect for the future.

Chapter Thirteen

On a dull October day, England would have been depressing before Charles but I sat in the back of Gillian's car looking at the fields and the expanse of open sky with uncharacteristic fondness and relief.

'It's not so bad this time,' I said.

Greg and Gillian looked at each other.

'I don't believe it! Did you hear that?' he said.

'Considering all the things she used to say,' added Gillian.

'Obviously nothing's permanent, Gregory, including my dogmatic attitude when contemplating the dismal Isles of Avalon. It doesn't mean that I shall suddenly discover an abiding love for being damp, however, so don't get excited.'

We had left America with all of the medical records and a new, light-weight and highly manoeuvrable wheelchair that came apart for travelling. Greg had spent the whole of the six hours in the air deeply engrossed in continual in-flight movies and woke up the next morning relaxed and completely free of pain. At last free from the stress in America, our vast supply of narcotic pain-killer from the VA became permanently redundant. It was left to gather dust at the back of a cupboard until long after the tumour was gone.

My mother had gone to great trouble to make the little room at the back of her house perfect for us and in three days I had found the car we had talked about in America. A dark metallic grey, left-hand drive, two-door Volkswagen Polo Peppermint, one and a half years old with a 1.1 litre engine that had recently been imported from France and only costing four and a half thousand pounds, which left enough for the road tax and insurance. Ill as he was and still jet-lagged, I was so proud of my husband when he insisted on checking all over the car before we bought it and getting very carefully down on his knees to look underneath.

'It is our car Gregory. I know it,' I said.

'Yes I agree. It's just what we need,' he said.

We had an appointment at the hospital in Southampton for the following Thursday. Before we went, I read all of the medical records aloud to Greg including the scan reports and the summaries from each operation. It was not exactly light Sunday reading but we had to be sure that we knew as much as anyone did about Charles. We met our new doctor, whose eyes only widened slightly when he saw the scans. He told us that Temozolomide was taken orally, taken twice daily for five days once every month and was generally very well tolerated except that some patients felt nauseous for the first evening. Greg could begin the treatment whenever he wanted to but we would have to report to the hospital for each course of treatment. We couldn't just pick up a six-month supply and disappear into the blue.

'Okay, we'll commute then,' I said. 'We'll spend one week in England and three weeks in France alternately all winter.'

'Will I have to stay on the steroid?' asked Greg.

'If the treatment is successful and the tumour reduces in size then we can certainly consider reducing the steroid,' the doctor replied.

We went home to think about it and talk about it.

'Well, so far it's the only hope anyone is prepared to offer us,' I said.

'Yes, but however tolerable it is, it is still chemotherapy and I don't like western medicine,' said my husband.

'It may come down to a choice between two evils, the steroid or Temozolomide, whichever has the least obvious side effects. Unfortunately you can't manage otherwise. The positive case for the latter is that if the tumour could be reduced by twenty or thirty per cent, you would probably be able to walk again without assistance and without the steroid your face would go back to normal. And you could start exercising again.'

'That is a possibility, I agree. I wish there was some natural remedy that I could feel confident to try. There are so many special diets and cures and I don't feel like trying any of them. There's one thing we have to do. I want to go to Cyprus and try to see that healer we were told about while we were in Virginia. It means a lot to me, Mali.'

'Your wish is my command, my Lord. Shall we go for our wedding anniversary and your birthday?'

'Yes, that's a good idea. I'll tell the doctor that we will start the chemotherapy when we come back. And Mali, when I can run I can drive that car!'

'You're on!'

We went back to the Temple, where I had been trained, for healing once a week and booked ourselves a week in Cyprus with a hired car. A second appointment with the hospital was arranged for the day after we came back on November 4th. As Greg was still very tired in the mornings and usually slept until lunch time, I tried to do all the shopping and the chores while he was safely in bed but it was intensely lonely driving the car around by myself.

'I suppose this is what it will be like if he dies,' I thought. 'Only then he won't be lying in bed waiting for me when I get back.'

I couldn't bear it. I didn't want it. He couldn't leave me. After a morning driving around with tears dripping off the end of my nose, I left the shopping in the car, went into the house and marched straight upstairs into the bedroom. A twinkling eye and a big smile peeped over the quilt at me.

'Gregory, I've decided I hate having to do things without you so I'm going to write all morning as I used to and then take you with me when you get up.'

'You mean I have to come to the supermarket?' he groaned.

'Yes, there is no negotiation.'

'I hate shopping.'

150

'So do I. So we'll go and hate it together.'

He got into TV in a big way every evening which was a drag for me. Fortunately it didn't have the same deleterious effect on his sensibilities as it once had. Except that he put himself in charge of the remote control and was forever changing channels to find something more interesting. My mother and sister took it very well. It often had me screaming.

'Gregory, please! Give me that wretched box!'

'Just relax. We don't want to watch the ads.'

'But you don't always wait for the ads!'

I always sat with him whatever he was watching. Time was precious and who could know how much we had left? We saw Gillian usually once or twice a week and occasionally one or two others, but no more. In his weakened and disabled state Greg had no energy left for an image and he refused to see anyone he felt might still expect something of him.

'Mali, I'm ill and I don't want to have to be anything for anyone any more. If I don't want to see people I won't and that's all there is to it,' he said. 'If I thought about all the things I can't do now and may never be able to do again, I would go mad, so I'm not going to think about them.'

— ✵ —

We walked around the lanes near the house on dry days, enjoying the autumn smells and the colours of the trees. My mother kept him supplied with her best soups for lunch while I exercised my culinary skills to their uttermost to keep him in tasty and nutritious food at dinner time. Two days before we flew to Cyprus a huge bunch of roses appeared on the table in our room, twenty-four white roses and one red one.

'Happy Anniversary in advance, Mali baby,' he said. 'There's a rose for each of the years I promised you. Next year you'll have twenty-three white roses and two red ones, and so on until we get to twenty-five years and then you can have a whole bunch of red ones.'

They were beautiful but every petal tolled countless tears as the scream raged on in my psyche, almost within howling distance in every waking moment. Echoing through every night of fear. It ran before me as I took my solitary walks on the beach in Cyprus while he slept in the studio in the mornings. It filled all my imagining, curling it's darkness around my heart as I watched the sun go down while he slept again for another hour in the evening before dinner.

The island smelt like Rhodes and Limnos, that same eastern Mediterranean smell of hot rock and fragrant bushes, but it was not so beautiful. The British had been there for too long. Good beaches – with a view and no people – were few and far between. The only one that could have been perfect overlooked an oil refinery.

We booked a table and a special vegetarian meal at the five-star hotel next to our studio for our first wedding anniversary. Very proud of the emerald and diamond eternity ring that had been slipped onto my finger in bed that morning, I was wearing my green dress once again as my beloved escorted me into the restaurant. His silk shirt and dark trousers still fitted despite almost five months on a high dose of steroid. A little Buddha-rupa cast in eighteen carat gold hung from the bracelet on his wrist; I had commissioned it specially three months before. We followed the head waiter across the dance floor to our table.

'I wish I still had all of my hair,' he whispered.

'Who cares? You've still got the top and the sides,' I whispered back.

We never saw the healer. Several of the local people did their best to contact him for us until we gave up on the phone and went to his house in Nicosia only to find it closed.

But one night I had a very vivid and powerful dream. An elderly man with very dark eyes came to explain to me that there was nothing he could do personally for Greg but that karmically it was very important that he soon meet with Ajahn Sumedho to heal the breach between them. Then he brought a woman forward who he introduced as 'the Korean woman', except that she wore a black sarong and a short-sleeved white top, very similar to the Thai lay supporters at the monastery. She held a large, sharp knife in her hand and stepping over to where Greg lay sleeping, she made three cuts in his head, one at the back and two on the left side. Laying down the knife she massaged the cuts between her hands until a pale, blood-stained jelly oozed out of each one which she wiped away with a clean white cloth. Then she closed the wounds with her fingers, squeezing them together until no mark remained to be seen. The old man stepped forward again.

'She has relieved the pressure for him,' he said. 'We can do no more but that will help.'

Greg was not so disappointed when I told him about the dream.

'Don't worry, my love,' I said. 'There will be another way. Not every notable healer makes miracles with everyone he meets. We have three days left so why don't we go to Egypt on that cruise we have seen advertised?'

'Do we have the money?'

'Yes, just. Do you think you can make it?'

'Why not? As long as I don't have to go everywhere in the wheelchair,' he said.

We sailed to Port Said on November 1st, dining that evening with the ship's doctor who had us berthed in one of the best cabins on the upper deck at no extra charge. Early next morning we were sat in the best seats at the front of the bus for the two-hour drive into Cairo. Our guide was easily persuaded to take a photograph of us posed in front of the pyramids with JBJ sat in the wheelchair.

I led Greg through a bevy of little boys who were all trying to sell us souvenirs as we took our places in the queue to go into the pyramid. That was the bravest, craziest thing he ever did with the brain tumour. Crouching down behind me with both hands tucked into the waistband of my jeans for support, he scrambled down into the darkness of the narrow, unlit nightmare of disordered humanity stumbling and groping in a two-way traffic system that had originally been designed as single lane only. At the end of the sixty feet long passage there was only a musty chamber with an empty, stone sarcophagus at the far end and an old man yelling 'Come on English! Come on German!' to encourage us to keep moving. When he lifted his skirts and started fanning us because he thought Greg looked faint, my husband turned me firmly back into the passage.

'Let's get out of here. Right now!' he said.

JBJ nearly got taken into slavery beside the Sphinx when a man selling silver bracelets tried putting two into my hand.

'I want that for my baby,' he said, pointing to JBJ's head sticking out of my bag. I stuffed him quickly out of sight and closed the zip.

'No!' I said.

'Yes, yes! You have these. It's a good price,' he insisted, waving the bracelets under my nose.

'No! Go away! No, no, no!' I shouted, grabbing Greg and pulling him away before we got totally surrounded.

Armed policemen escorted us everywhere we went and stood guarding the tour buses while we visited the Cairo Museum. Greg sat alert and interested in the wheelchair, listening to our guide's detailed explanation of the artefacts on display, while our fellow tourists shuffled and yawned, already feeling the effects of a late night's entertainment followed by a five o'clock start to the day. In the Hall of the Shrines, he paused and pointed out the image of the winged goddess, carved in sunk relief, her wings outspread to protect the dead king.

'See the wings,' he said. 'They represent eternal life.'

And in that single still moment in the babble of Cairo Museum I was reminded. There is no death, rather a continuum in Metamorphosis. I leaned over the back of the chair, folding my arms around my beloved, allowing the sweet peacefulness of the shift in consciousness to breathe healing into my frantic heart. Something so simple but it had shattered the vacuum of fear that had been my prison for four long months. In that moment I was released into a cool spaciousness of awareness and acceptance. Charles could do his worst but he could never destroy us. We had come together to create something more than ourselves and it was that something that would continue beyond the death of the physical body.

— ❋ —

'I hardly know how to tell you this but Temozolomide was temporarily withdrawn from circulation three days ago.'

The doctor gave a helpless shrug, spreading his hands and looking quickly from one to the other, watching our reaction to this latest disappointment. I did a quick calculation. It must have been on the day we sailed to Egypt. We were staring into the void again.

'Why?' I said.

'Because one or two rats developed breast cancer and it has been withdrawn pending investigation. It doesn't affect anyone already on it but no new patients can start the treatment. I asked if an exception could be made in your case on compassionate grounds but it was refused. I'm really sorry,' he said.

'Is there anything else left to try?' I asked.

'Not really. You could try a course of two treatments of a similar drug from which Temozolomide was developed but I have no idea what success we might have, if any. And of course it has to be administered intravenously here in the hospital. It is generally well tolerated and you could have the first course next week.'

Greg said nothing, staring hopelessly out of the window.

'Can we talk about it and let you know?' I said.

'Yes. Of course you can.'

We agonised over it for the rest of the day without conclusion. The Temozolomide had been a possible alternative to the steroid, and oral chemotherapy with a partial success rate was a more attractive option than being hooked up to an intravenous drip without a lot of hope.

Early the next morning just two letters came through the door, both addressed to us and from entirely unrelated people. Both contained articles about the North American Indian Essiac formula. Reputedly, it had proven successful in either alleviating the symptoms of cancer or curing it completely in some cases. Greg had had so many healers and healing techniques recommended to him that he had shelved them all on the grounds that too much of a good thing did him no good at all.

'I have to follow my intuition in this,' he said.

'So what about this Essiac formula? Do you think it's some kind of a sign? Both articles appearing together like this and today of all days?'

'What do you think?'

'Well, it looks simple enough. There are only four ingredients and according to the article it has had results.'

'Let me read it again,' he said.

'Shall I telephone around and see about the herbs?'

'Yes, you could do that.'

Finding a supply of Sheep's Sorrel turned out to be the only problem. It was not available anywhere in the UK which was strange because I knew that it grew as a weed all over the country. But a phone call to Debbie in California located a pound of it that would be sent to us as soon as a willing courier could be found who would bring it back in their hand luggage. It couldn't be posted as we couldn't be sure that it wouldn't be subjected to routine radiation en route, rendering it completely useless before it ever reached us. In the meantime Greg decided to have one treatment of the chemotherapy, if only to find out what he didn't want, while we were waiting for the Essiac ingredients to appear. Truth to tell I was glad because I was becoming increasingly concerned about his condition. He had stabilised on twenty-four milligrams of steroid daily without pain but he was getting sleepier, becoming more lethargic and less steady on his feet.

'Is he shutting down on me already?' I thought. 'Please no. At this rate he'll be gone by Christmas.'

The Essiac offered all that there was left of hope.

He had his single dose of chemotherapy on November 11th, Veterans' Day. It took an hour to drip into his vein and he vomited almost all of that night.

'I'm not doing that again,' he said.

I was not going to argue. I had taken him through the entire six weeks of radiation on emotional blackmail and I felt I had no right to insist on any further treatment simply for my sake. But three days later we all noticed that he was very much better, he was brighter, laughing and going out for walks again without having to be almost pushed out of the door first. He refused to believe that it had anything to do with the chemotherapy but then it didn't matter, it was as though the Holy Ones were giving us time to find the Essiac. The wheelchair went back into the cupboard and I booked our tickets for Iceland and New Year.

— �֍ —

Ajahn Sumedho had invited us to visit Amaravati, offering us accommodation in the house that was usually reserved for parents and similar guests, so that we wouldn't have to be on public view and where the members of the Sangha could meet us in comfort and privacy. Greg held out against going for weeks.

'Why are you being so difficult, Gregory?' I asked, mildly exasperated.

'Because I'm ill and I don't want people to see me like this.'

'But this is the Sangha and they love you. Why should they be anything less than kindly towards you? What about practice, Gregory?'

'What about practice, Ajahn!'

'You can say what you like, we're going! You'll enjoy it once we're there. Besides I want to see the nuns. I'm going to telephone and find out when is the best day to go.'

I heard him muttering as I left him but he was so much better that I decided it had to be now or never. Five minutes later it was arranged for November 24th, from the Thursday through to the following Sunday.

'The diary says that it's Thanksgiving Day which has to be auspicious,' I said.

'I'll go on one condition,' he said.

'And what is that?'

'That you take a tape recorder with you when you visit the nuns. I don't trust you all together.'

'Not in a million years, Gregory!'

Our visit was a great success. I was exhausted at the end of it but Greg was very well, seeming to draw energy from the compassionate contact with his spiritual family again. There came one poignant moment as he sat cross-legged on the sofa, holding court to the circle of monks and nuns gathered around him.

'There's one thing I want to say to you,' he said. 'Remember always to be yourselves. Don't get caught up in being anything else other than who you really are.'

We took the traditional offering of flowers, incense and candles to Ajahn Sumedho to request his forgiveness formally for any pain we might have caused him personally. Not because we had to do it but because we wanted to. Our elegantly planned ceremony designed to last a gracious ten minutes became a unsynchronised muddle stretched over two days when we gave Ajahn Sumedho the offering on the first day and had to call him back for the forgiveness part on the second day. There were smiles all round but it was taken in the spirit in which it was meant. We visited Chithurst a week later and Greg's dearest wish came true when we had tea together with the nuns in their cottage without the need for a tape recorder.

Within a few days of beginning to take the Essiac on December 7th, my beloved was showing a profound improvement all round, far exceeding the earlier results of the chemotherapy. There was no more pain when he ate, the pupils of his eyes, continually uneven in size since July, were returned to normal. He rarely slept through the morning and he began to read again, covering not just one or two pages at a time but getting into whole books. His walking was much improved and he could manage for up to twenty minutes without my arm to steady him. Paradoxically it was this improvement that caused our one serious fight.

We drove north and east to Norfolk to visit friends for a weekend and to do our Christmas shopping at the US Air Base. I had been noticing the occasional steroid pill appearing on a chair or on the floor but I thought I must have dropped them out of the spare supply that I always carried in my pocket. We were driving back towards London and were just about to go onto the motorway when I remembered Greg was due for his lunch time medication. I pulled over into a lay-by and took the bottle out of my bag.

'I don't need them,' he said.

'What do you mean? You always have them now. Didn't we agree not to start reducing the steroid again until after Iceland? To give the Essiac a chance to work first?'

'Yes, but I have started reducing them myself.'

'What!'

'I knew you wouldn't agree so I did it myself.'

'But I'm responsible for you!' I shouted. 'Supposing you had a relapse? How would I have known how much steroid you were taking? It could have been critical! How much are you taking now?'

I was shaking with rage, gripping the steering wheel with both hands because I couldn't trust myself not to hit him.

'I'm down to twenty milligrams a day. I'm counting them very carefully,' he said.

'And in how many days?'

'I think it's three.'

'Don't you remember that steroid has to be reduced very gradually? Don't you remember what happened when we tried reducing it too fast back in Virginia? You were ill and the pain came back! How could you do this to me? How could you be so sly? How could you deceive me? This makes a complete mockery of everything about our relationship!'

By now I was screaming at him and thumping my fists down on the steering wheel.

'Mali, relax. Don't take it so personally,' he said.

'Don't take it personally? You bastard! You absolute bastard! How can I ever trust you again? As if there isn't enough to fear in this bloody business! What have you been doing with the pills I've been giving you?'

'I palmed them and threw them away.'

'Yes, on chairs and on the floor! I hate you, I absolutely hate you for this!'

I hit him. Without another thought I smacked him hard across the side of his face. He grabbed my hands and I scratched him with the long fingernails he was so particular I should cultivate, leaving long, bloody gashes all over his fingers and wrists. He held on tightly while I struggled and screamed. At the first pause for breath he countered with sweet reason but I could tell by the tone of his voice that he had been badly frightened by my reaction.

'Mali, I am very sorry for the lie. You must believe me, please Mali,' he said.

I was incensed. On the edge of exhaustion I was beyond rationality. I screamed at him for the next three hours until we pulled into the drive at my mother's house.

Always the master of facade, he greeted her as though we had just come back from a picnic but I was in no mood to act. I left him sat on the sofa talking calmly to my sister while my mother followed me out into the kitchen.

'What are all those scratches on Greg's hands?' she asked.

'I did them,' I said. I told her why.

'But he could have made himself ill again,' she said, horrified. 'And he has been so well recently.'

'Exactly! Fortunately there don't seem to be any ill effects so far, save on me. I can't tolerate the deception, it reminds me too much of the bad old days,' I said.

We were friends again, as always, when we got into bed.

'Mali, I will never deceive you again. I promise you,' he said. 'For a moment back there I was really frightened. I had no idea you were so strong. But you have to admit that I've been fine these last few days and you did say we could try reducing it soon.'

'Yes, in January, Gregory! Okay, compromise. Let's go down to eighteen milligrams and stay on that for three weeks, note the emphasis on three weeks, and if you're still well after that we'll try taking it down again when we're in France.'

'It's a deal. Do you still love me?'

'Of course I love you, damn you! Why do you think I got so upset? I'm terrified of losing you. Absolutely terrified,' I said.

'I know, I'm sorry. You won't lose me, I promise you.'

I had an early appointment the next morning. I left him in bed to sleep off the combined effect of the long journey and the storms of yesterday.

'Promise me you won't get up?' I asked him. 'Stay where you are and sleep so that I can be easy in my mind for the next two hours. I don't want to come back and find you in a heap at the bottom of the stairs. And don't go sending my mother out to buy me flowers as a peace offering. It will take a tiara at least to let you get away with this one!'

I came back to see my mother grinning. Greg was fully dressed and beaming his way down the stairs. Before I had time to open my mouth he sang,

'Da, de dah!' the next best thing to a fanfare of trumpets and leaning over the banister, he dropped a crown cut out of Christmas paper and glued together on my head. He was impossible.

'You came back too soon,' he said. 'I was just coming down to ask Mom for some coloured pens to make jewels.'

What could be done with such a man?

'I suppose you're showered and shaved?' I said.

'Yes, all that and I haven't fallen down.'

'Obviously not,' I said from under my crown and reaching up for a kiss. 'So are you well enough to come to Petersfield with me to book us onto the ferry for France?'

'Absolutely! When are we going?'

'January 11th?'

'Let's go!'

We always did everything together and however happy and well we were, our ever-practical minds did not completely exclude the possibility of death sooner than we had originally hoped for. Greg had asked Ajahn Sumedho when we were at Amaravati for permission to have his ashes interred at Chithurst. The subject of a gravestone came up soon after. Accordingly, one week before Christmas, he amended his Will and we visited a local funeral director to chose a stone. Greg's unsteadiness when walking offered some proof of our predicament but the sombrely polite gentleman in a dark suit was clearly unused to dealing directly with corpses who were still breathing and articulate. Especially when one of the couple didn't look like she was about to die in the immediate future.

My husband chose a simple, polished black stone to mark the place where his ashes were to be interred under the grass beside the oak tree at the entrance to the monastery. Mine were to follow suit when the time came. He directed that the inscription should read 'Greg and Mali Klein, Mettacittena', using only our names and the Pali word meaning 'a heart full of loving kindness'. He considered dates unnecessary and refused to have any mention of Ãnando to ensure that there would never be an excuse for anyone to turn the site into any form of a shrine, which he felt would be extremely inappropriate to practice. It was to be left plain, unadorned and unplanted just as it was.

We had a wonderful family Christmas with my mother and sister and Felix, Gabriel and Gudrun. We didn't talk about it but as we were both aware that it might be our last Christmas all together, Greg was determined to do it in style with plenty of presents for everyone, a tree, photographs, puddings and pies. With all the trappings of a traditional English Christmas. We had sent out over eighty Christmas cards using the picture of us standing in front of the Pyramids with the wheelchair and printed inside with the legend 'Have brain tumour, will travel!' in cartoon lettering. It was intended as a small gift to thank the many friends who had wished us well and also as a fingers-up gesture in pure defiance to Charles. If some people had found our slightly macabre humour concerning cancer and all related beings too much to take, they had to laugh at the Christmas card. Like I said,

'Some people have a baby, we've got a brain tumour.'

— �֎ —

We said goodbye to 1993 watching a spectacular hour of fireworks igniting the Icelandic sky, and New Year began with an unprecedented glass of champagne. Greg's condition was improving every day. We celebrated my birthday swimming with Lóa and Gunnar in the geo-thermal Blue Lagoon thirty kilometres south of Reykjavík. I reminded Greg he was not supposed to dive with a shunt in his head but he promptly forgot and did it any way. He was so happy to be independent and mobile, showing some of his old panache as he swam about in the warm sea water, pausing only to sing 'Happy Birthday' to me with Lóa before he vanished into the steam again, cheerfully ignoring me trying to keep up with him in my role as guardian/protector.

In the brief four hours of sun allocated to that midwinter day, occasional glimpses of a clear blue sky through the hot vapour swirling all around us brought up memories of dancing days of unequivocal delight. Our yesterdays of summer, of sand and sea and nectarines and love. It was hard to believe that the lava all around us was covered in snow.

Back in England I had four days to pack the car ready for the journey across France. Our doctor telephoned to tell us that Temozolomide was back in circulation but Greg refused to consider it again. Even with the Essiac to alleviate any unpleasant side effects, he was no longer interested in orthodox cancer treatment. He had the right to decide for himself. At the same time I couldn't help wondering what the effect of the Temozolomide and the Essiac combined would have.

'I don't mind commuting you know,' I said, the only comment I allowed myself to make.

'No, it won't be necessary. I don't want it,' he said. 'I want to stay in France.'

'Do you realise that you are putting the entire responsibility for the tumour on me?' I said.

'It's all right. You are my wife. I have every confidence in you,' he replied in the tone that invited no further discussion.

Did I have confidence in myself, I wondered?

I carried on with the packing, trying to envisage exactly what we might need in every event we might have to deal with. At the same time I was determined to take our few household possessions. The house waiting for us in Lacoste might be our last home together and I wanted it to be as perfect as possible with our own china and utensils in the kitchen, all of our music, our favourite books and a beautiful and powerful shrine. Greg wisely resisted interfering until he saw me put a urinal in the car. He was not pleased.

'Why did you buy that? I don't need it,' he said.

'Gregory, you might be glad of it on the road. We have a long drive after Calais. Or have you forgotten that Provence is in the South of France?'

Part Three

A Future
Beyond the Sun

Chapter Fourteen

He got into a quiet, tuneless whistling as he went about the house, perfectly content, finding books to read before getting settled on the sofa for the day. I spent the mornings at the computer in our little room across the hall, sitting always where we could see each other.

'Mali, what have you got for me?'

'Wait just a little while, Beloved, and then I will come and read it to you.'

When the pages were printed, I cuddled up to read to him on the sofa under our multicoloured Icelandic blanket. I made a practice of always reading the manuscript aloud so that he could hear how it read and suggest alterations and additions. His memory of his time as a monk was still excellent, his mind still lively and alert. He could still reason and discuss dhamma with me. The only time we came near to blows was when his whistling threatened to take him down the twisting stairs to the basement to inspect the central heating system without me behind him. I could never be persuaded that he might not fall, even at his least ataxic.

After seven months of being public property we were back in the routine we enjoyed the most, being together with no distractions and with all the time in the world only for each other. No appointments, no telephone calls, no doctors. Just us and music, laughter, talking, silence, making love. The only differences were that we needed a car for shopping, we had a basket full of pills in the larder and several bottles of Essiac in the fridge.

The house was on the outskirts of Lacoste, one of the hill villages in the Luberon, a ridge of low mountains dominating the heart of Provence. With a view across the orchards and vineyards in the valley to the roofs and spires of Bonnieux five kilometres away to the east, it was home the minute we stepped through the door, greeting us with a warmth and spaciousness reminiscent of Sasha's beautiful spirit in every room. What was to become our exclusive corner was immediately obvious when we saw the little room just inside the front door. It had a big window facing west, a huge farmhouse-style oak table against one wall for my desk and a bookcase with a conveniently empty top shelf for the shrine.

I went around the house opening all the shutters and came back to our room to find Greg sat on the floor, busily unpacking the bags exactly as he used to do. He should have been exhausted after two days and a thousand kilometres in the car but he had been so glad to be back on the road, scrutinising the map, choosing the music and once very grateful for the urinal on the Autoroute. I left him to arrange the clothes in the wardrobe while I set up an elaborate shrine of coloured candles, crystals and pictures. We offered some incense in gratitude for a safe journey and a secure refuge at the end of it. Our beautiful Marrakech bowls and plates took their places on the dresser in the kitchen, the computer and printer were set up on the table. We were home for the winter and the spring.

Provence, even in January, is a gourmet's paradise for vegetarians who are prepared to feed themselves. We filled our trolley in the local hypermarket with fresh fruit and vegetables. We bought nutty, walnut bread for breakfast, moist, black olive bread for lunch, huge mushrooms, delicious rounds of Brie cheese and slabs of Emmental and several packets of our favourite green pasta with a couple of bottles of cheap, white wine to cook it in. We never drank the wine but Greg would sit at the kitchen table grating the cheese and grinning as he watched me tipping the bottle liberally into the saucepan.

'Who said anything about water?' I laughed.

We agreed that the plates had a greater chance of extended life if I always did the washing up but he didn't want to sit about and be waited on. He needed his own list of regular chores to do. So he emptied the rubbish every day and vacuumed and tidied the living room once a week. He helped chop and mix the vegetables for salads and stir-fries, he made sure the cassette player was continually supplied with sound and whenever he could get downstairs into the garden, he picked up the pegs that were always popping off the washing lines over the balcony.

The nights were cold. I opened the shutters in the morning to see the sun rising over a fume of mist and frost in the valley. The afternoons were often warm enough for us to sit out on the balcony wearing only shorts and tee-shirts to eat our lunch. Greg was tanned in a week.

'Gregory, you don't look in the least like a cancer victim with that tan,' I said.

'I don't feel like one except if I try to run and of course there are all those pills.'

'But you only have them twice a day now. It's not so bad.'

'I agree.'

I began to dare to hope that the Essiac might be the key to the miracle. What miracle? Could a tumour so large and aggressive really be expected to disappear? Shouldn't I be content with the miracle of our continuing days of joy? He was so well that the likelihood of our seeing a second wedding anniversary did not seem as remote a possibility as it had done two months before. He had passed the six month prognosis. Easter was the next target and then the family party planned for July at Joyce's cottage on Lake Eyrie.

'I'm going to do my best to make it,' he said. 'But who knows what may happen? I feel that I have done all that I can for my family. I have said goodbye to them if that's how it must be. Either I will get well or I will die, there's no other way. But, Mali, I want to start reducing the steroid again from this evening.'

'Okay, I'll take it down by two milligrams and see how you are,' I said.

We walked for an hour or so every day, often climbing down into the valley and walking towards Bonnieux. Mostly we kept to the roads and the main tracks. One afternoon we went exploring and got hopelessly lost. After some abortive wandering around and arguing about the route, we found a path leading in more or less the right direction back towards Lacoste. It was perfect until it came to a temporary halt at a stream.

'Stand back. I'm going to jump it,' said Gregory, pushing me to one side and bracing himself.

'Wait a minute! How can someone as unco-ordinated as you jump a stream?'

'Just relax,' he said, and took off.

The landing was a shambling mess of arms and legs with me a second behind him and yelling as I grabbed at his coat in a hopeless attempt to stop him falling down. We were covered in mud and leaves. I had one wet foot, he was laughing. I was furious and laughing all at once.

'Gregory, you terrify me!'

'But we made it across didn't we?' he said, trying to atone for his sins by brushing me down.

'Yes, but look at us! I refuse to come this way again, ever!'

'Maybe it would be better to find another way next time,' he said.

'Absolutely!'

Some days we walked around the village and up to the Marquis De Sade's ruined chateau that stood out like an old, broken tooth against the surrounding hills. It was not a romantic ruin, no elegantly tumbling turrets or intricately traced stonework. Just four, square, stone walls with gaping window holes. The village, with its old houses and narrow cobbled streets, was delightful. As the afternoon sun slanting low over the rooftops lit a last golden glow on distant snowy Mont Ventoux in the north we would turn for home and hot spicy tea, drinking it curled up together on the sofa before adjourning to the kitchen to prepare dinner. We studied our French course for half an hour every evening after the meal was cleared away and we were usually tucked up in the sleeping bag by eight o'clock for me to read aloud from our travelling collection of Sir Laurens Van Der Post books. When one of the female characters in *A Story like the Wind* turned out to be called Lammie, my husband roared,

'That settles it! Lambert Klein!'

I was giggling helplessly.

'Gregory, I'm truly sorry but I really can't manage that as an alternative. It's too much.'

It was so nice to be as noisy as we liked in bed. With his renewed vitality, elements of our actively crazy passion for each other crept in again. We made love every night and spent the days basking in the afterglow of our intimacy. Travelling always stimulated him and we made one long trip at least once every fortnight. We visited his old haunts in Nice, another time driving towards Digne and the Alps, always looking out for the place where we might start the retreat centre he had been talking about for the past two months. The amendment to his Will had included instructions for setting up a beautiful place in the mountains for others who found themselves in the same position as we were, faced with terminal diagnosis and needing somewhere to go to think, to not-think, to be and to scream if they needed to. Not to die but to choose how to live when they came back down the mountain, back into the world.

He was down to a daily sixteen milligrams of steroid, still feeling well and showing no change in his condition after three days on a further reduction to fourteen milligrams. At twelve his walking was not quite so steady. It was hardly noticeable but I found myself putting a hand out to steady him more often.

— ✳ —

How swiftly things change. We wrote to Rick on January 29th daring to hope that the miracle might be in the making. The next morning I rolled out of bed careless and happy after a wonderful night and a morning just like old times. I walked across the hall to the kitchen to turn on the oven to warm the bread. If it took thirty seconds it took no more, but in that time he had stood himself up on the bed and, for no real reason, crashed back down on to it directly on to the old wounds on his back. Hearing him shout out, I ran back to find him holding his back and writhing in pain. He had fallen back against the pillow and hadn't hurt his head but there were angry, red marks across the scars just below his waist.

The next three days were hell. Terrified that he would lose clarity, he refused anything amounting to strong pain-killer. And something seemed to have happened to the tumour. If it had been asleep before, it was awake again now.

The first indications were a slight muddling of speech and an inability to follow conversation. Although he had no pain, his unsteadiness increased and his concentration wandered a little. We had told everyone that we were 'on retreat' for a month or so and we were glad that he would not be making phone calls until we had this sorted out. After several days of private nail-biting, watching every move he made, I dared to suggest increasing the steroid back to sixteen milligrams for a few days to see if he was better. Surprisingly he agreed and in twenty-four hours he was much improved if not quite so well as he had been before.

Imperceptibly he had lost ground that, try as he might, he couldn't regain. He became increasingly restless at night, possessed of a different, more aggressive energy. We had kept the 'gnomes' as we called them under control with a mild sleeping pill since November but as the energy became more dominant, the pill became less effective and the incontinence which had troubled him in Virginia came back to torment him. After mopping up the floor for the second night I suggested he use the urinal instead of trying to get to the toilet.

'No. I don't need it,' he said.

166

'Look Gregory, I'm willing to empty it if you're willing to fill it. Is that a deal?' I said, employing my most provocative smile that he could rarely resist even in a situation like this.

'It's a deal,' he said.

We were booked to go to Switzerland on February 19th for three days to visit the monastery and Kandersteg. I was looking forward to seeing the mountains and the snow. Greg was more reluctant to go. He was concerned that his occasional forgetfulness would make him appear more ill to the monks than he felt he was.

'I know my conduct is deviant but I only know it from you and your reaction to me,' he said. 'You must help me when we're there. You must make sure I don't do or say anything out of context.'

'I will. Don't worry, little one,' I said. 'Shall you be disappointed if Charles wins, Lammie?'

'Yes.'

'Why?'

'Because I see the Essiac as a worthy vocation to help people who are sick.'

'But don't you think you are already doing that by taking it and talking about it? By still being alive now?'

'Maybe.'

'Will you mind dying?'

'Yes, because I'm not finished yet. I still have a lot to do.'

'What have you got to do?'

He paused.

'Get enlightened for one thing.'

'What else?'

'That'll do for now.'

He smiled, such a smile that was always for me.

'At the point of every death there is the possibility of enlightenment, Beloved,' I said gently.

'Thank you.'

'For what?'

'For reminding me.'

'So what have you got to do, beloved husband?'

'Die peacefully holding your hand.'

'And with my arms around you as well?'

'That too.'

We were reading Van der Post's *About Blady* at that time which, as it happened, turned out to be very relevant to our present situation. It reminded me of all my reading and research into Chiron and the myth. 'Only the wounded healer heals.' How often had I quoted that in years past?

'Is that what Charles is then, Gregory? Our greatest wound so that we can heal?'

'Maybe.'

'And the part in the book about the dream, when the son knew that the cancer entered his body. Could it be that the tumour started into active growth during the autumn of 1989, after you were ill on the tenth anniversary day at Chithurst? When the voice in my head told me to come to the monastery?'

'That could very well be so.'

The next morning we were sat together in the bath tub, enjoying our Saturday morning soak. He had soaped and shaved and we were at the steamy, bubbly stage of complete relaxation.

'Mali, I want to cut down on the Dilantin.'

I had been dreading this.

'Please not yet. Let's get the steroid sorted out first.'

'We're getting that sorted out. I don't want to take all this medication.'

'I know but the Dilantin cuts down the possibility of epilepsy.'

'But I haven't had a seizure since last summer. I want to cut it out altogether. I don't want my teeth to fall out.'

'Gregory, I can handle you lurching all over the place and jumping streams but my nervous system can't manage epilepsy right now.'

'It's me we're talking about, not you,' he said.

'It is me we're talking about, as well as you!' I countered desperately, fear echoing blood banging in my ears. 'You're nicely unconscious when you're smashing about on the floor and foaming at the mouth with your face a seductive shade of grey-green but I'm not! I need nursing myself for shock when you come out of it.'

He put out a hand to stroke my cheek, looking at me, saying nothing. Eventually he said,

'I'm sorry, my Mali-Mali. Okay, we'll sort out the steroid first.'

I allowed myself to relax again and ran some more hot water to top us up. The bathroom was warm, the sun came shining through the windows, the nightingale sang in its cage in the garden next door. It was all a great improvement on England in February. Greg lay back with his chin level with the surface of the water and looked from corner to corner around the room.

'Where is the heater in here?' he said.

There was a huge, hot green radiator on the wall opposite.

'It's the radiator over there,' I said.

What was going on now? I listened as he talked about different sorts of heaters, in England, in America but he was very vague. He couldn't really describe them in any detail. He rambled on until he lost contact with what he was trying to say. Suddenly he looked at me and started laughing.

'You're looking very sceptical,' he said.

'Why is that do you think?'

'Because my ability to articulate has gone down,' he answered.

I was so relieved.

'I'm glad I wasn't like this in America after the operation. It would have been discouraging,' he said.

We called it 'talking Russian' and laughed when it got too absurd. Better to laugh than to cry. One of the best was when he stood up and announced very solemnly,

'I'm going to fold my robe,' and proceeded to close the shutters.

It was always easier if I packed when we were travelling. I sped around the house tidying and cleaning, filling bags and preparing food while he watched from the sofa. His little bag of toiletries was carefully zipped up and lying under the radiator where he had left them for me to pick up by the front door. It was the little things like that, the little gestures of care and concern for me, his wanting to be useful and to help me so that I wasn't too tired, the little things that brought the tears swimming to my eyes then and afterwards.

He was very sorry and very concerned when he terrified me by taking off his seatbelt and opening the car door to look for something he had dropped on the floor while we were at maximum speed in the fast lane on the autoroute north of Valence. I grabbed at him as I ground my foot down hard on the brakes and pulled over on to the hard shoulder. My heart was crashing against my ribs. Fortunately the road was empty.

'Gregory, Lammie, Beloved,' I began as soon as it felt safe to breathe. 'You have to promise me that you will never do that again. You could have fallen out onto the road, little one, don't you see?'

'Yes, I see. I didn't think. I'm sorry, Mali,' he said.

After Grenoble the weather conditions deteriorated, rain turned to sleet and then to snow. We crawled up the mountain roads towards Chamonix.

'Gregory, what day is it?'

'Let me see. It must be the eighteenth.'

'You're only one day out, that's perfectly allowable. So what month is it?'

'It has to be September.'

'Here? In this weather? Try again. Is it the first, second, third, fourth, fifth month of the year? Which is it?'

'It's the second month,' he said, without hesitation.

'And the second month is –?'

'September.'

'It's February. Remember the first month is –?'

'January.'

'So the second month is –?'

'September.'

'No, it's February, you funny man. What year is it?'

'Let me think. It's 1993.'

'You're just six weeks out. It's 1994. Don't you remember Iceland and the fireworks?'

'Indeed I do,' he said.

We made a game of it as we went along but he couldn't remember February for more than ten minutes at a time. I had only ever heard of one other case of a *glioblastoma multiforme* on the cerebellum and the lady had died within five weeks of becoming forgetful.

The void was opening at my feet again, the scream howling in my ears. Please no. It couldn't be five weeks. He couldn't leave me!

After a weary nine hours on the road we drove into a Christmas card village covered in thick snow and booked ourselves into a little hotel near to the monastery. In the morning the weather cleared, the sun shone and we walked the two kilometres to visit the monks. We stopped with great glee at the entrance to Dhammapala to take photographs when we found another, freshly steaming manure heap exactly where I had waited for my beloved nearly two years before.

The next day we took the chair lift to the upper slopes with two other guests from the monastery in support. The ski slopes and toboggan runs were crowded and Greg was immediately in his element, striding along while we did our best to keep up with him. Until I realised that it was he who was helping us along rather than the reverse.

'Can you believe it?' I said. 'And he's only wearing trainers.'

'Mali, I was born on snow,' he said.

When he started talking Russian, no one was shocked any more when I said,

'Gregory Klein, get your brain cell in gear!'

It was tragic but we had to make it funny, we had to find a way to laugh at it. I took endless photographs to make photo-collages to send out to our families. Greg grew increasingly exasperated whenever he saw the camera.

'Mali, you don't need so many pictures of me,' he said.

'I do. Now if you would just stand here –'

He looked at himself in the bathroom mirror, at the roundness of his face, at his arms, at the slackness of the muscles. He hardly believed me when I told him how much worse it could have been.

'Yuk!' he said.

'Hey, you may think you look like a fat old man with a brain tumour, you may feel like a fat old man with a brain tumour but you don't have to act like a fat old man with a brain tumour,' I said.

'You're right. Oh Mali-Mali, will it ever end?'

'I don't know, Lammie, I really don't know.'

— ✸ —

Anxious that his wishes be strictly adhered to in the event of his dying, he had sent a letter and a copy of his Will, both the original and the amended version, to his family before we left for Switzerland and he had been waiting for a reply. There was nothing in the post until a card came from Joyce at the end of the first week in March. He sat reading it several times over, immediately suspicious because it made no mention of his last letter.

'Will you try to telephone them?' I asked.

'No,' he said. 'I don't want them to know about my lack of articulation.'

'Will you write to them? I can type a letter for you if you want me to.'

170

'No,' he said.

It was all so difficult.

'I don't want to be carted off,' he said suddenly.

'You won't be, believe me. You do understand, don't you? The only person who will do any carting is me and then only if you want it.'

He looked past me out of the window for a moment, across the valley to Bonnieux.

'It's all right, it's all working out as I planned,' he said quietly.

I felt so sorry for him, for them, for us all. Eventually under the pretence of working on the manuscript that was already completed I went against the vinaya and wrote a letter to Joyce, only confessing about it two days later when it was safely in the post.

'Are you angry with me?' I asked, after I had read a copy to him.

'No. Your intention was good enough. It's all right, it doesn't matter,' he said.

Three days later he got up at eight o'clock as usual for breakfast and sat down for his hot chocolate and walnut bread. After a few mouthfuls hunched over the plate, he pushed it aside and held his head in his hands, eyes half closed.

'I feel wretched,' he said.

'Do you have any pain?' I asked.

'No, but I feel terrible.'

I led him to the toilet and straight back to bed. He lay for nearly three hours in a deep sleep, very still, almost comatose. Suddenly he got up and staggered out to the bathroom, shutting the door hard behind him.

'Lammie, are you okay?'

'Go away,' he said.

Instinct took me back to the bed. I put my hand into the sleeping bags and found them soaked. Fortunately I had come to France prepared for this. I already had a large supply of padding hidden in a cupboard. In a few minutes I had the sleeping bags washed and dripping over the balcony and an improvised bed made up on the sofa. I walked into the toilet and knelt down on the floor in front of him.

'Don't worry, little one, beloved you. Everything's done. Would you like some lunch?'

'No, I don't feel like it.'

'Hey, Gregory Klein, you've terrified me this morning and you'll terrify me still more if you stop eating. People do that when they go into comas. Can I make you some soup?'

'If you want to.'

'Can I increase the steroid for three days? Just to see if you're okay?'

'Only for three days.'

'And I'm going to put the Essiac up to three doses a day.'

'All right then. Mali?'

'Yes Lammie?'

'You have my heart.'

That almost broke mine. I held him and cried all over him, forgetting he was still sitting on the toilet and that I had gone in there to help him to stand up.

A strangely sinister, almost demonic energy gave us no peace and very little sleep that night. Our gnomes were becoming gremlins.

'What is going on in me is neither right nor appropriate,' he whispered.

'What can we do about it?'

'Nothing much in the end,' he said.

'Will you try one of the new sleeping pills the doctor sent?'

'Yes.'

He sat up and put the pill on his tongue and then to my amazement immediately pushed it out of the opposite corner of his mouth and into his hand before he drank the water.

'What are you doing?'

'I'm taking the pill for you.'

'But you're not! You're spitting it out!'

'I don't want it.'

'Why did you say you would have it then?'

'Because you wanted me to have it.'

'Only because I wanted us to sleep. How can you expect me to look after you if I'm not allowed to sleep? I can't manage without any sleep! Do you hear? I can't, I can't!'

I was weeping in fury.

'I'm sorry Mali, I'm really sorry,' he said.

After months of nights of interrupted sleep, now that he was beginning to worry himself by his behaviour, I knew it could only be a matter of time until my sense of humour ran out and I would be no use to him then. And I was afraid. Who in the end would dominate, the monk or the Marine? Both were equally imprinted into his psyche and I knew the tumour would take him down to his most fundamental instincts before we were through with it.

'Lammie, I'm getting a bit tired you know. It's hard for me to have to do all the washing, the cooking and the cleaning as well as be wonderful for you. If Gillian could come and cook for us, would you mind very much?'

'Let me think about it.'

We walked up to the village later that morning but after ten minutes he was leaning heavily to the left and showing a considerable lack of co-ordination and balance. I had barely the strength to support him and gratefully accepted a lift back to the house.

'You can telephone Gillian if you want to. I don't want to wear you out,' he said.

'Are you sure about this?'

'I haven't got much choice after this morning, have I?'

'Do you want to go back to England?'

'No, I want to stay here.'

'Then I'll telephone her now.'

— ❋ —

When I went back to the living room to tell him she was flying to Marseilles the next day, I found him already asleep on the sofa. I left him as he was and walked quietly back to the kitchen and shut the door. I picked up the phone and called Jan and Judy, our English speaking neighbours across the village. Judy answered.

'Hello, this is Mali Klein. Judy, can you do something for me please?'

'Yes, if I can. What do you want?'

'I need to know the procedure if a foreign visitor dies in Provence. I need to know all the necessary formalities. I need to know about cremation, the price, how I take the ashes out of the country. Where I get the death certificate officially translated.'

Understandably she was very surprised.

'Do you mean for your husband?' she asked. 'Is he so bad then?'

'Yes. We are living with a very large *glioblastoma multiforme* that should have killed him two months ago. We have already arranged somewhere for us to go in England if he has to die but we are happy here away from everyone and at the moment he doesn't want to go back. So I thought that if it was not impossible, maybe we could do it here. I think I should know in case something happens unexpectedly.'

'I'll look into it and ring you back,' she said.

In another half hour I was secure in the knowledge that it was not difficult to die in Provence and in many ways the process of cremation was much easier and more to our personal preference than the procedure commonly employed in England.

I didn't tell him then, he didn't ask. Maybe he heard me talking, maybe he didn't. He just looked up at me with a long, loving look, putting up his hand to stroke my hair as I climbed in under the blanket beside him. I held him tightly. How would I ever let him go? Saying nothing, he continued lightly stroking my hair and under the spell of that gentle touch I became almost mesmerised. He was smiling when I came fully back into consciousness and looked at the clock to find that two hours had vanished out of my life. It was the only opportunity I had to be truly relaxed in all of our time in Lacoste.

Chapter Fifteen

How long does it take to die? When does the dying process begin? In Buddhism they tell us that it begins as soon as we are born but it is always something out in the future. Indiscernible, ungraspable, vague, something to think about at some other time. But when it comes, how long does it take to die?

We put Gillian in the back of the car and drove to the Pyrenees for a few days. On the last morning Greg fell onto his back again in the bathroom in the hotel, not so painfully as before but I noticed that he spent most of the five hours driving home with his face screwed up to the left and only using one eye.

'Gregory, tell me something wonderful,' I said.

'I love you,' he said.

'That is definitely wonderful. Tell me something more.'

'I love you.'

'I love you too, beloved you. Two eyes, Lammie!'

He opened the other one, slightly surprised, but it closed again in a few minutes until I gave him his sunglasses. Obviously his eyes were becoming overly sensitive to the light again.

We made love properly for the last time on the evening of March 20th, the Spring Equinox, and by the next day there could be no denying that he was sliding, slowly, inexorably downhill.

'I've been having vindictive dreams. But not about you, not about you,' he said as I sat him up to take his Essiac.

I didn't dare ask who they were about. He seemed to be working all his remaining anger out in his dreams and occasionally by refusing to co-operate with me.

We were sitting on the sofa together, Gillian was in the kitchen cooking. Rock music always made us cry. Bryan Adams, *Dancing in the Dark* – we couldn't dance together any more.

'Don't worry, little one. If you die and have to give up this body that won't let you dance with me now, we'll boogie in spirit. I'll never dance with anyone but you, you'll see.'

We turned the music up loud to cover our tears and conversation.

'How are we going to do this dying thing, Gregory?'

'As best as we can.'

'Can I ask Jan to call the local doctor and ask him to come and see us just in case we need him sometime?'

'Yes, that's okay.'

'But I'm not giving up hope. I can't give up hope. Not yet, not ever. I can't!'

'Don't,' he whispered. 'I love you.'

'Charles isn't going to separate us. What stops us? Nothing!'

Gudrun came on March 23rd, amazed at the sunshine and the heat after a damp and shivering England. She was not happy about Greg.

'What's happening here?' she asked.

'What you think?' I said. 'He's doing his best but he's dying. He's just dying.'

'Do you remember what you said to me when you first told me about him?'

'No. What did I say?'

'I've never forgotten it. You said you were leaving with Ajahn Ānando and that one day he was going to get sick because of the gunshot wound in his head. Whether it is sooner or later, you said, I'll be the one to take care of him.'

'Oh Goo, why do all the ghastly things come true?'

We continued our heliotheric activities for an hour or so every afternoon. Greg, Gillian and I as usual on the balcony, Gudrun down below in the garden. In five days she had reddened to brown, spread out beside the swimming pool, not quite at ease about the scorpions living under the cover.

The wisteria trailed along the front verandah and hung in soft, lilac froth around the basement pillars. Then came the clouds and with them the Mistral. Days of rain and nights of frost. What had been a wonder of the palest of pink and white blossom as an incandescent haze across the valley turned overnight into a withering brown mush. The farmers were out at four in the morning in the orchards and vineyards, anxiously shaking their heads over the apricot harvest and fearful for the grapes.

Some necessary changes had to be integrated into our lives. By choice we had each always been floor sleepers but now accommodation had to be made for a more traditional sleeping arrangement in our lives. Even with my assistance, Greg could no longer pull himself upright from a kneeling position on the floor. I had found the widest single bed in the house, firm enough for his back but with a thin foam mattress to protect his skin. My nights were spent perched on the edge of the bed, snuggled into his right side as I had always been.

Since it had become difficult for him to shave himself properly, I had taken to doing it for him directly after lunch while he was sitting up at the table in the kitchen. Unless I had him laid out on the old metal travelling chest in the bathroom, while I shaved him and washed his hair over the side of the bath. He turned his head to watch me squeezing the shaving foam into my hand.

'I'm thinking about what I'm doing to you.'

His voice was a whisper for most of the time now.

'You're not doing anything to me. It's only Charles and he's doing whatever he's doing to both of us. Don't worry about me, little one.'

'I want to get well,' he said.

175

'I want you to get well too. I love you so much. Sometimes I say to myself it will all be okay tomorrow. He will get up, well and strong. We'll open the door and go out for a long walk, laughing and holding hands as we used to do.'

'It would be nice,' he whispered.

'Do you know what depresses me most about this tumour?' I said. 'It's that it always has to be me who has to do the nasty things to you. Like giving you your pills when you don't want them, taking you to the toilet when you're too tired to want to be bothered to go. In some ways it's like it was when the children were little. It was always me who had to deal out the discipline and say 'no'. It's hard on me sometimes, Babe.'

He watched me carefully, just looking at me for several minutes afterwards. For the rest of the afternoon he took great care to smile at me and kiss me, squeezing my hand and insisting on necking with me when we were shut in the toilet together.

We had always been lucky with doctors and when Doctor Parraud came the next afternoon, we all liked him immediately. He was friendly and kind and in no hurry to leave. Greg was encouraged when his heart-rate and blood pressure reported normal. But the steroid was slowly increasing. I was able to tell the doctor that we were on twenty-six milligrams daily but a week later with increasing flash head pains in the morning we were up to forty a day and only just holding. Whenever I asked Greg how he was feeling I always got the same reply after a few seconds of consideration.

'I'm feeling very well.'

'Do you have any pain?'

'No, not at all.'

There was nothing wrong with his mind. He could still hear, think and see although it had been more than a month since he had last picked up a book. He was very amused one evening when Gillian and I got into a heated discussion on the meaning of Dukkha, a word I realised had never appeared in the manuscript for 'A Dangerous Sweetness'. It is one of those words some might associate with the Christian concept of evil; in Buddhism it means dis-ease, discontent, suffering, defilement.

Some people might see what was happening to us as Dukkha or less wisely as some kind of a karmic come-back for the previous year but I could never see it that way. As Greg said, he needed the tumour, therefore I needed it too. It was all practice and everything was okay just as it was. It only hurt more when we chose to see it as pain. And if I cursed and swore occasionally it was only as an active relief from the tension that continually built up from having to deal with something that was almost more than I could handle. Even then that didn't mean to say that either the tumour or the cursing were bad or unwholesome, but I could not deny that I was concerned at what I might be suppressing within myself in the daily, tortuous heartbreak of watching my husband slowly die.

176

I was torn between acknowledging it as an honour and a privilege to be with him and at the same time not wanting to have to live without his physical presence, his voice, his warmth, holding his hand, wetting that wonderful chest with my tears, his heartbeat. A dreaded scenario rose to taunt my imagining, hour by hour drawing nearer. I hear that final breath, I see myself dressing him, sealing the coffin and driving to Orange and the crematorium. How will I feel? What will it be like? Will I be able to drive or will someone have to take me there?

There can be no real life without him. All my life was an illusory dream state until I drove him away from Kandersteg. Then everything came into focus, into sharp, vivid reality. Without him, no matter what course I take, essentially I will be in that same dream state again. Waiting at the Gates of Time until I can go too. I know I will never get over his dying but it's all right. It's not a crime or a weakness to miss someone forever. It's nothing to feel guilty about.

For ten years I had lived and worked on a farm, ostensibly looking after horses but so much more was involved. Physically I was never very strong but, like my husband, my rock-hard will saw me through ten years of work enduring demands often far beyond my physical capabilities. I stayed there so that the children would have somewhere nice to live as they finished their growing up. While emotionally I became increasingly introspective and as the boredom and depression grew greater so I made my work more dangerous.

If anyone had really known me they would have been able to gauge my level of despair by my horses. I was not a natural horsewoman, I didn't start riding until I was twenty-seven years old but I soon found I really enjoyed the risk. In 1986 I bought my first colt foal and kept him entire. A dark brown, almost black Anglo-Arab, he was both angel and devil and, through the five years of our association, my injury quota increased until he almost ripped my right arm from its socket the day before I sold him. With care the damage was ninety per cent rectified but weeks of supporting my beloved and now lifting him in bed were beginning to tell and renewed back spasms, old ghosts from last summer, came back to bedevil my nights.

On the last day of March I had woken up feeling very tired and dizzy with temporary blood loss from my monthly period. I sat Greg up and hung on to him while he tried to use the urinal. My arm and shoulder were raw with stabbing nerve pain and after forty minutes I gave up and dragged him to the toilet. Poor lamb, he wasn't being deliberately difficult but I was short on energy and patience that morning. I called to Gillian.

'We have to sit otherwise my day might as well end here and now.'

I lit the candles and incense and went back to sit on the bed, kissing him and stroking his hair as I found my cushion. He stroked my knee as I was getting settled and then made anjali and joined in the chanting as firmly as he knew how, not missing a word from beginning to end. We were always immediately all right. No matter how awful it all was, he could always console me. Right from the beginning, even if it had been something that he had said or done that had made me cry, there was always the look, the little gesture, the smile, the kiss. Even now, so ill that he could only speak in a whisper, he could still reach me with that same look or a hardly perceptible nod. Sometimes just the pressure of his finger on my foot as he lay on the sofa in the afternoons while I sat on a chair reading the manuscript to him, with my feet cosily kept warm under his legs.

— ✳ —

Gudrun left on Thursday, April 6th. I drove her to Marignane airport having seen Greg safely to the toilet first. I was praying there would be no delays so that I could be back in time for when he wanted to go again. As I roared the car along the road, the rain came crashing down making it almost impossible to see anything beyond the wall of spray.

'This reminds me of the tornado in Virginia,' I said.

'Was it as bad as this?'

'Oh yes.'

'How are you going to manage without me?'

'The same as we did before. You have to get on with your life. You have to get a job.'

'But what happens if he gets worse?'

'We'll manage, I'll manage. Somehow.'

She walked into the airport in tears and I drove back on to the autoroute very conscious that I had already been an hour and a half away from home and resolved to be back in little more than an hour.

'She'll be back in a fortnight. I know she will,' I thought. 'She'll hate being back in Guildford after Provence. She's completely penniless but somehow she'll manage it.'

Sophie came for the weekend. That evening Greg celebrated by absolutely refusing to take his sleeping pill. Ironically I had decided to halve the dose because he had been much quieter in the last few days but he would have none of it, spitting it out and clenching his teeth tight shut. He sat on the bed between Gillian and me, resolutely immovable. I was angry and beginning to panic because I couldn't see how I would manage the days with absolutely no sleep. We tried persuasion, even tears. He remained unmoved.

He knew I was upset. When I came to bed a few minutes later I carried a cocktail of half of one of the mildest sleeping pills and some pain-killer on his night tray.

'If you're not going to take a pill, I'll have to. One of us has to get a few hours of sleep,' I said.

I squeezed myself on to my six inches of bed.

'Are you going to kiss me goodnight?' I asked before I switched off the torch.

'If you want me to,' he whispered.

Silly man, how did he think I would manage to sleep without my good-night kiss?

He made a determined effort to sleep. Every time he fidgeted and I cried, he held my hand firmly to his chest until we dozed again. We woke up at one thirty so that he could use the urinal and then fell back into a blissful four hours of uninterrupted sleep. Two days later I had increased the steroid by another four milligrams and we spent a cold and uncomfortable night between the nylon mattress cover and the blanket with two completed changes of bedding left soaking in the bathtub. Both times I had missed giving him the urinal in time. I came staggering back from the bathroom for the second time and went to the cupboard for the padded liners. After he was washed and sprayed with cologne I held out a pad.

'I'm so sorry my lamb but I have no more bedding. Can you bear to wear this at night for now?'

'Okay,' he said.

He held out his hand for it, trying to help me to put it on him, telling me with every look and every gesture that he was sorry. I climbed back into bed, cuddling him and kissing him. The padding was still dry in the morning when I sat him up but he couldn't use the urinal. He shook his head.

'Oh dear, oh dear,' he said.

'Do you have pain?'

'No.'

'It's just everything, isn't it?'

'Yes.'

'Poor little you. It's only bodies, the body not able to cope with the brain tumour.'

I called Gillian and together we got him to the toilet intact.

'Well at least you have some bladder control left,' I said as he sat down in obvious relief.

'Yes,' he said.

'Gregory?'

He looked up.

'Kiss me or I'll scream!'

He smiled, happy to oblige me, knowing I was quite capable of carrying out the threat to the full no matter where we were or what we were doing.

He chanted with me though the morning meditation. My mind went spiralling into unlimited fantasies about miracles. He could look almost comatose for several hours while he slept in the morning and then be bright and smiling in time for lunch, able to use the toilet all day and take part in the conversation over dinner. Nights like the last one seemed to be out of context, part of something and somewhere else and only the sheets decorating the balcony reminded us otherwise. I made an amendment to the Sermon on the Mount that morning.

'Blessed are those who sit, for they shall remain sane, ' I said as we put away our cushions ready for breakfast. 'If Jesus had said that I would still be a Christian.'

I made a serious inventory of all our bedding, laying everything out ready but after another night we had to admit that he was completely incontinent at night and that it was useless for me to try to help him to use the urinal. I had tried once more for his sake to make do without the liners and rely only on the padding over the sheets. When I woke up for the third time at three o'clock to find him already soaking the sheets I went back to the cupboard for the liners again.

God was not a woman, women's bodies are too poorly designed. Why was I having another full period after only eight days? I did not have the energy to bleed.

'I'm so glad we are vegetarian and don't drink,' I said.

He looked slightly amazed at such a statement, coming as it did then in the middle of the night.

'And why, you may ask? Because it gives us practically odour-free urine. Believe me I know. My nursing days may be long gone but they are not forgotten.'

He smiled at that.

'Beloved, I'll have to start putting the liners on you at night and just wake up once to change you halfway through. I'm sorry but I can't manage it any other way.'

'It's all right,' he whispered.

In another hour he woke us both up. He was shivering so violently that the bed was shaking. He soon settled down again with one of the sleeping bags piled over the blankets and me with my arms tightly around him.

He was tired all morning but so sweet, doing his best to co-operate as we got him out of bed and trying his hardest to take as much of his weight as he could, with only the two of us to support him, while he walked across the hallway to the toilet. My super-lift never failed to swing him straight on to the seat, Gillian shutting the door on us while I sat down on the floor in front of him.

'I–I–I,' he said, trying to formulate the words and leaning towards me with that little, twisted smile.

'I love you,' I said.

He nodded and leaned towards my mouth.

'I love you,' he said.

Tears filled my eyes.

'Why do you have to die? That's what you're doing isn't it? Very slowly you're dying on me.'

He just looked at me. That little smile. The tenderness in his eyes. He didn't say no.

'What sort of a life will I have without you? I'm only forty-three. Years and years of just missing you. How is that life? How can it be life?'

180

He stroked my hair. What could he say?

'Promise me you'll haunt me. Don't leave me. Please don't ever leave me.'

'I won't,' he said.

We had had a few days of sun and wind. All the washing dried in a few hours and came in ready aired for the night. The pain in my back was becoming a more immediate problem. Gillian spent half an hour a day massaging and rubbing cortisone cream into rigid muscles. Greg was very worried when he saw me laid out on the floor.

'What's up?' he whispered.

I explained about my back, blaming my apparent hormonal imbalance, while Gillian carried on rubbing. Both of us were acutely aware of him watching and thinking 'That's my job, I always do that for her.' Tears trickled off the end of my nose just thinking about it. There was such an opportunity for endless heartbreak in all this.

Gillian left me asleep on the floor for an hour or more while she made lunch. Greg dozed on the sofa. When I got up at one o'clock I noticed the sky was covered in a lowering, heavy cloud. The hills beyond Bonnieux had disappeared. It looked cold, dreary and depressing, too much like England before a storm.

I had a constant rule in getting Greg up which was to get him moving and then to the toilet as quickly as possible. This time we took so long taking care of my back as we were moving him that he was starting to be wet before we got there. I rarely ever raised my voice except in laughter. Now I was swearing and shouting and furious with myself.

'We are here to look after him, not me! We will not waste time fussing like this again!'

'Don't shout,' said Gillian.

'I will bloody well shout as much as I like and especially when I think it is necessary!'

The door closed and I sat him down. I collapsed into tears with my head on his knees. Ānando would have given me a desana on conduct and my use of colourful language. Greg/Ānando leaned forward and kissed the top of my head while I talked and cried.

'I wish we'd bought that bike we talked about last year and driven it off a cliff. Then none of this would have happened. Look at us! You're sick to death and all I face is the prospect of missing you for the rest of my miserable days. We could take a load of pills. There are plenty of them in the kitchen. Or I could put you into the car and drive us into a wall. Or off a cliff. There are plenty of them around here.'

He said nothing, made no response. He just looked at me steadily and I knew the answer. I hated Gillian at that moment for being there and feeding me, forcing me to survive. What for? To write another bloody book for everyone else to read? I was just a hand and a pen. My heart was surplus, it didn't matter any more. I wasn't grateful to her at all.

Maybe she should be grateful for the experience of us and our damnable situation. Wild and desperate with grief, I looked up at him.

'I want you back, I want you back! I want you back! This disease had has its way with us for too long. I want to go to bed right now and make passionate love with you, screaming, crazy love and go to sleep and when we wake up you're well. It's not true, this tumour. It's not real! It's not real!'

He sat stroking my hair. When I stood him up, he put his arm around me and held me tightly as I sobbed into his shoulder. I had iron pills and pain-killer with my lunch. When he was comfortable on the sofa for the afternoon, Gillian went out for her walk. I played our tapes, Mozart and Pachelbel, the smooth saxophone tones of Kenny G, and lit the candle under the little steam pot on the shrine. The room was filled with the woody fragrance of sandalwood.

The sky lightened and lifted for an hour, maybe less, and then the cloud came down again. Beating rain and hail smashed against the windows and the wisteria. A rainbow appeared over the farm in the valley. As I closed the shutters in our room that night, I saw a single star gleaming over the trees on the hill.

The weather was strange, brooding, setting already strained nerves on edge. Without the sun it was almost impossible to relax and be mind-empty. Gillian felt it too. She battled with her own fraught energy as the cloud only lightened with the coming day and we wondered how the washing would dry. My fears and fantasies about him getting better crowded my mind by day; at night, sleep, when it did come, was dominated by urine, by dreams of scenes in toilets, getting him onto the toilet, getting him off. I would tell him about it in the morning and we would be laughing as I changed the bed. At least we could still laugh. He could barely string six words together in conversation but he could still manage morning chanting and the blessing at the end.

He had been very restless at night, with occasional flashes of pain. How much more steroid could he take I wondered? We were up to fifty-two milligrams daily and despite it all his face and body were remarkably unbloated, neither were they overly fat. He was hardly changed since the drug had taken its initial toll the previous autumn. His hair was beginning to grow back, his eyes were very clear and his skin was in extraordinarily good condition. The discomfort he had experienced when eating had never recurred since he began taking the Essiac but now he was having increasing difficulty in swallowing any quantity of liquid. It would make him cough and retch so we were careful to include as much 'mush' in his food as possible. We made Miso soup thick with vegetables at lunch time, he had yoghurt with his pills, and little drinks as often as he would take them.

182

Chapter Sixteen

We used to say, 'It's always toughest in the first year with everything still settling down. It will be better in the second year when there's more time and no divorce and everyone's forgotten us.'

That was something we were never to have, the sweet, soft familiarity of years, but somehow we had had it from the beginning as though we had just picked up again from where we had left off.

Gudrun came back on evening of Saturday, April 16th, staggering off the bus in Bonnieux with her rucksack and the remains of her tan after twenty-four hours by coach from London. Greg was not sure whether he was pleased to see her or not, being more concerned about her future than the need for being nursed. He was waiting on the sofa when she arrived, ready with a smile and a kiss hello. We took him to bed soon after but as I climbed in beside him, he gave a strange little start and a shudder. During the past few weeks I noticed his body would suddenly be shaken by tremors that would last for two or three minutes. Sometimes he was cold, sometimes not. He was not cold now.

'What's the matter?'

He didn't answer.

'Do you want me in bed with you?'

'Yes. Oh yes,' he said, turning his face towards me.

Greg wanted me in bed with him but Charles did not. For two hours we lay together in our narrow little bed getting hotter and more uncomfortable. Greg started pulling at the padding around him.

'Do you want to use the urinal?'

'No!'

This went on for another half an hour. He continually pulled at the padding while I begged him to leave it alone because I didn't have enough dry bedding to change him. Finally he pulled the padding away from himself and immediately wet all over the bed and the blanket. There was nothing I could do and he wouldn't let me change him.

'For once, just for this moment, I hate you,' I said. 'I will have to leave you as you are until the morning and sleep on the floor.'

I inflated one of the sleeping mats and curled up in a single sleeping bag, sobbing bitterly. I couldn't help it. I knew there was no going back. After a little while I heard him turning on to his side towards me and I put up my hand to him. He held it tightly in both of his.

'I love you,' I whispered.

'I love you too. I do, I love you too,' he said quite clearly and fell asleep.

Three days late we woke up to yet another grey morning in this dark and bitter Spring. I was so relieved to see him open his eyes when I kissed him.

'How are you today? Do you love me?'

He nodded faintly with a ghost of a smile, the best he could manage. It was as though some dark force had been watching us, waiting to pounce. In a few short minutes the evening before it had caught us.

For the first time Gudrun had been out visiting on the other side of the village. I had spread a plastic foam mattress out on the floor to sit on beside the sofa, where Greg was enthroned as usual to listen to me reading our evening story. Gillian sat behind me massaging my neck and shoulder while I read *Out of Africa* aloud for over an hour.

I hadn't felt well all day. My back was in spasm, my shoulders a mass of tension and knots and I had a splitting pain in my head. I couldn't bear sleeping on the floor. The physical separation was becoming all too real. No more loving arms around me, no soft, even breathing against my hair, no strong chest to soak up my tears. How would I ever enjoy life again bereft of his sweetness?

Then the telephone rang. Gillian got up to talk and I put the book down until she came back. I felt better and Greg looked comfortable. It was only an hour or so since he had been to the toilet and didn't look as though he needed to go again yet. I got up and walked out of the room across the hall to our bedroom to start remaking his bed. Barely inside the door, I felt rather than heard a quiet movement behind me and turning I saw Greg face down in a heap of pillows and covers. He had fallen off the sofa on to the mattress on the floor with his head on his slippers. One good look told me he was all right but I realised he must have been wanting to go to the toilet.

Why hadn't I known? Exhaustion made me irrational. I had to save the bedcovers. The morning's washing was still hanging around the house doing its best to dry without the assistance of the weather gods. One more wet bed before the morning and we were finished. I tried rolling him over but he was stuck. A golden trickle of urine appeared, soaking into the colours of the blanket and the sleeping bag below. I didn't know what to do. An all-unreasoning anger took hold of me, not aimed at him but at myself, the damned weather, the wet covers, another damned miserable night.

I shouted for Gillian to come and I freaked. Why was I so stupid? How could I have let this happen? Why wasn't I more careful? Somehow we got him rolled over. I sent her out while I changed him and then she came back to help me get him by main force back on to the sofa. He was as quiet as I was vociferous, both of us equally shocked by his falling. I hated myself for giving way to my misery. He sat very still and unresponsive as I tried to talk to him and apologise. Something about the look in his eyes was disturbingly familiar. I switched on the light to look at him more closely. He was staring past me, focused on some unseen spirit as I had seen him once before on a morning in the previous July in Richmond, Virginia. I called to Gillian who had resumed her conversation on the phone.

'Gillian! Come in here! He's having a seizure.'

184

Mercifully it lasted less than two minutes and not half as dramatically as before. The convulsions were relatively minor and he did not foam at the mouth. I hugged him until his breathing came back to normal and we laid him on the floor on the mattress wrapped in my sleeping bag. Gillian telephoned to Judy and the doctor.

He came out of it remarkably well, my beloved survivor, sleeping all night on a shot of Valium. I wept into my pillow until three Tylenol and half a Temazepam released me for a few hours from remorseful self-hatred and the raging, unrelenting despair that had nipped at my heels for almost ten months. Sometimes I could almost hear its howling agony echoing through my consciousness, a dark power that would not close in for the kill until death claimed my beloved. Then it would rip out what was left of my heart.

No, I wasn't grateful for Gillian or Gudrun. Without them I would have finished 'Dangerous Sweetness' and then probably loaded us both into the car and put an end to this misery over a cliff-edge into the sea. They were forcing me to survive, to do the 'decent' thing. To become a heart-broken widow. His slippers were laid, as always together, side by side on the floor in the hall. How would it feel when his feet were dissolved into ash and would never go walking across the hall again? I could wear his clothes and his jewellery but what about the nights? Who would I laugh with? Who would I cry with? I wouldn't have to be anything to anyone again but what would I be? Only the gods knew and I couldn't trust their kindliness towards me.

He stayed in bed for most of a long grey day, only getting up for meals. I lay beside him all afternoon on my six inches of bed space. He was warm and smiling as I cuddled up to him. The dark angel had not taken him yet.

'I love you,' he said.

He was dry in the morning when I woke him up. I washed him nevertheless. We walked him to the toilet, half expecting a flood on the way. But it didn't happen. He was in control of himself all day and talking more. It was as though the electrical short circuit of the seizure had redirected something in his brain and it stayed that way. Urine took a back seat in my dreams for the rest of our time with Charles, leaving only the odd flash of pain and the slowly increasing steroid to prompt me out of any possible complacency.

'This reminds me of transition stage in labour,' I said to Gillian. 'Did you have that? The bit where everything seems to stop before the dam bursts?'

And we got into another conversation on obstetrics as women do.

If the weather had relented it would have been a truly perfect day. As it was, the claustrophobic grey had us all watching our minds and our tongues by lunch time and made our usual banter as we walked him to the kitchen harder to keep up. The birds seemed strangely silent, even the nightingale in the cage next door barely twittered a note. Nerves as taut as a bow string,

I found myself entertaining fantasies of driving into the mountains, walking by the sea, loading the car and getting away from here. But then where was he? Was he with me physically or only in spirit?

The next evening he bumped his head very slightly on the wall as I sat him down on the toilet, hardly a knock but the shock was enough to make him start and I realised that it would take very little to send him back into a seizure again. In accordance with the doctor's advice he had finished his course of Valium but he was very fragile now. I cradled his head, stroking his back and his shoulders and singing to him as he sat until his breathing slowed and he relaxed against me. His temperature was normal when I checked it later but a flash or two of pain during meditation the following morning put the steroid up to sixty milligrams at breakfast.

It was the evening of April 23rd. I looked out of the window at the moon approaching full, riding high among the clouds and stars and the blue-black sky over the bright pinpoint lights of Bonnieux. I never thought that I would see another Full Moon with him still breathing beside me. We had had a happy evening, he on a steroid 'high' of sixty-two milligrams daily and the four of us enjoying the beginning of *Brideshead Revisited*. Gudrun was bored until Sebastian Flyte walked out of the pages, with his teddy bear under his arm, and then she was fascinated and instantly in love.

'Did you like the story this evening?' I asked as I put him to bed.

'Yes,' he said, his face clear and alive with interest, his eyes bright. Minutes later, as he lay on the pillow, his eyes closed and his mouth set, I knew what he would look like when he lay dead. I had seen that look coming during the last ten days. I would enjoy the high, we would laugh and tease, sunbathe between the clouds, lay together in the afternoons, read together in the evenings.

There was no need for Ajahn Sumedho or anyone to harbour guilt and remorse about the events of the autumn of 1991 at Chithurst. Greg was meant to leave. Ãnando, always almost arrogant about his health as a defence I supposed, would have found this illness too much to bear while so much was unfulfilled in him and he would have dropped dead on the spot if he had known exactly what was in store for him. A wheelchair, helplessness, at the mercy of much-despised western medication.

But Greg/Ãnando always conducted himself with grace and humility. He hated being ill but he accepted it and his regular several times weekly rebellion over his pills was the only way he could effectively express his point of view, now that his ability to articulate his theories had been lost. And he had an adoring wife who could do the little things, the intimate things, for him in a way that no monk or nurse could ever do, with no loss of human identity or manhood. He was still my husband and flirting together even over a wet bed was a necessary part of our relationship. Only a wife could neck with him in the toilet with Gillian laughing and holding him up from behind while I pulled up his trousers. Gudrun would be waiting to help as soon as we had cleared the door and Greg was satisfied that we had turned out the light. Stress had always made me either ironical or comical and there were still times when all four of us would be laughing so hard, usually at some outrageous observation that had escaped my lips, that it was little short of a miracle that we made it safely to the sofa or the bed.

My husband still took mischievous delight in imitating my English accent. When we were moving him I usually guided each step he made while Gillian and Gudrun supported him on either side. Sometimes he forgot he had feet. His legs went sliding sideways and everything came to a halt.

'Darling, you are like a little frog,' I observed one morning as I pulled him upright.

'Daahling, you're like a little froog,' he repeated, looking around in delight as his guides convulsed themselves.

'Gregory, please! It's bad enough when I say it but it's ten times worse when you repeat it.'

I took photographs of the Full Moon that I had never expected to see with my beloved still breathing beside me. He smiled and kissed me after I had repeated our wedding vows and bowed to him. I stood in the kitchen later waiting for the moon to rise, watching for the white glow over the trees, missing him not standing beside me. I wanted to call him.

'Greg! Come and look at this! It's wonderful!' And he would come and stand behind me, his arms around me, leaning me back against him. Kissing my neck and blowing into my hair.

'Yes, indeed it is.'

I remembered watching the same moon rising over the hill on Limnos and chanting as the silvery light flooded the sea. Why all this damned nostalgia? Why even now was the reality of Charles so hard to accept?

Nick will be coming in two days and he is needed, we are all reaching the end of our physical strength. Already the house is becoming a community except that there is no room here for personal feelings and preferences. Everything evolves around Greg, nothing else is either welcome or tolerable. We have the practice and it is at times like this that you realise how necessary it is to be surrounded by people of the same religion, whatever it is. There is a common bond, everyone speaks the same language and, more importantly in this situation, we had all been brought up in one way or another by Ānando. Nick had lived at Chithurst for four years as a layman, an anagarika and briefly as a monk. He had continued the meditation practice ever since he had disrobed. He would be a welcome addition to the morning sitting.

— ❋ —

The sun came back at the waning of the moon with not a cloud in the sky and hot enough to tan me very brown in two separate hourly sessions on the balcony the next afternoon. I found Greg laying wide awake when I went in to him but oddly unresponsive to my teasing. We hadn't discussed the actual amount of steroid he was taking for almost a month. It had become one of those tacit agreements, understood but too painful to talk about while I agonised over and over in my mind, muttered occasionally to Gillian and he counted the pills on his tongue before he swallowed them. Earlier I had made a telephone call to the doctor in Southampton with the kitchen door closed and that was a mistake.

'Tell me something wonderful?'

No answer.

'Do you love me?'

'No, I do not!'

He had never said that to me in all our time together. I knew why he had said it but that didn't stop the immediate rush of hurt and pain.

'How can you say that to me? How can you? How can you?' I said and burst into tears.

'Oh Mali!'

'So you can say my name! You haven't called me by name for more than a month!'

'You don't tell me – you ...,' he began.

He held out his hand. I pushed my head under it so that he could stroke my hair while I blew my nose.

'I know. I know why you're angry with me. Okay, I'm putting on a brave face. I would have told you later but I didn't know where to begin. I talked to the doctor in Southampton for the first and only time without asking you this afternoon. I had to know how much steroid he usually prescribed in a case like ours. He said twenty-four milligrams a day. You're on sixty-four and counting. Doctor Parraud says that we can go up to one hundred milligrams with a terminal case. It might make you feel temporarily better but wouldn't necessarily improve your quality of life and you might begin to experience more of the unpleasant side effects of the drug even with the Essiac to help you. You might live a few more days or a couple of weeks but you won't get better. We've run out of ideas. Charles is winning.'

He stopped stroking my hair, leaving his hand resting lightly on my head, looking straight up at the ceiling.

'Do you have any more ideas?'

'No.'

'Do you want me to raise the steroid dose?'

'No.'

'Do you want to go back to England?'

'No.'

'We can stay here. I asked Jan and Judy to find out what the formalities were, just in case. It's not difficult to die in Provence.'

Feeling his hand tighten over my head, I moved to slip under his arm. I held him while he shook convulsively for several minutes.

'Beloved, don't see this illness as personal failure,' I said softly. 'You haven't failed me by getting sick. I mind, oh yes I mind because ultimately I haven't been able to really help you, only help you to bear it and make you comfortable. But don't see it as personal failure, please.'

188

His face had been very straight as I was talking. As I finished he turned to me and smiled and made to kiss me.

'Are you afraid to die?'

'No.'

'Are you afraid of losing me?'

Silence.

'I will always be your wife. Do you know why?'

He looked at me intently.

'For three reasons. The first because I love you. Secondly because a relationship with anyone else would be inappropriate and could never possibly satisfy me. I've had the best of the best. Who and what can follow that? And thirdly because no one is ever going to know me or have power over me again. You are worth it. No one else can ever be. But for heaven's sake, please don't die on me at Wesak. It will be in such poor taste.'

He started laughing.

'I couldn't live with the legend and some people will be convinced you are a saint. And no holy springs under the oak tree where the ashes are supposed to go!'

'I won't,' he said, raising both his hands and running his fingers over my hair while I laughed and cried and snivelled into a tissue. 'I love you,' he said.

So we turned to face the guns, at bay and snapping our fingers at the dark angels. Come on Death! Where are you now? We had been married exactly eighteen months to the day.

Leaving no stone unturned I had Jan check with Doctor Parraud to be sure that he was prepared to administer a morphine pump here in the house if it should be necessary. I told Greg the result of the telephone call.

'It's all fine Beloved. The doctor will help us here. You won't have to go anywhere. We can stay right here and then I can make you into a beautiful urn and take you back to Chithurst. Is that okay?'

I was crying. He was smiling.

'It's fine,' he said.

His whole attitude had changed completely. There was no trace left of that fierce, angry will to survive. We were in this together. It would be all right. For the rest of the day he was as attentive to me as he could be, stroking my hair, my legs as I stood up beside the bed to arrange the bedcovers before he settled down to sleep.

'Sleep well, beloved husband,' I said.

'Oh I will,' he whispered, again with a smile.

We went to sleep that night holding hands, his hand hanging over the edge of the bed and it was still there for me when we woke at five the next morning.

Greg and Mali were somewhere else having fun. They were fine. It was just Charles who was dying now, taking with him the outer shell, like a snake shedding an out-grown skin. Greg and Mali were emerging damp and shining, iridescent and glowing, essentially the same but renewed, refined. That's how it was for us, in metamorphosis.

Chapter Seventeen

It was strange, this process of dying. Sometimes he was peaceful, sometimes so angry that I could feel it pouring out of him and into the room. There were times when I found it hard to feel appreciated. No matter what I did, I felt he was critical. He would look at me but refuse to answer my questions and barely co-operate as I nursed him. I knew he was angry with me too, angry with me for not dying with him, angry with himself for dying so soon, so young, so quickly when we had just found each other. When challenged he admitted it, that old anger and jealousy searing his heart even now.

'Don't hate me because you're dying and I'm not, not yet. Don't hate me.'

He didn't want to share me with anyone else ever, he wanted me for eternity if it was possible but he hardly knew how to trust in the possibility of that eternity. Every night I cried silently, the tears bubbling into my ears and running down into my hair, missing his tenderness and sweet attention, until the blessed pills gave me an hour or two of sleep.

I knew that he was afraid. It was all so unknown and now that the reality was coming closer every day I wondered how much of that old Catholic conditioning still lingered. In despair, desperation, bravado, we were facing the guns. The steroid would go no higher, Charles could go his own way now. We were no longer running but walking hand in hand towards the Time Gate, the vision of colour and light that had come to haunt my days and my dreams. We had found a way around the early morning inter-cranial pressure by sitting Greg upright for fifteen minutes, with Nick supporting him, to allow the shunt to work at maximum and so far the spasms immediately disappeared. There was no need for pain-killer. We would keep him going as long as we could for who could say that the new Messiah wouldn't come walking past the door? I could invite him in so that a touch of his robe could bring about the miracle.

Nick had arrived in time for Gillian to show him the routine before she went home early on Sunday morning, May 1st. She had done all she could do and I took advantage of the change of energy to consciously alter the vibration in the house. Greg's varying mind states had been communicating very strongly to me during the past several weeks. Probably not helped by the large increase in steroid, there were times when they could be very negative, almost malevolent. Deciding to keep it simple, we cleaned through the house, clearing all the kitchen surfaces and putting everything we weren't actually using in cupboards. Greg lay in bed listening to what was going on and watching in some surprise when he saw me pushing the wheelchair out into the hall.

'We're changing everything,' I said. 'And after lunch we are putting you in the wheelchair and walking you to Bonnieux. There is no negotiation.'

He rolled his eyes in exasperation.

'I know you don't want to,' I said. 'I can hear you saying that you are too tired, too lazy, you don't want to be seen in the wheelchair, the sun is too bright, you don't want the bother.'

He nodded, his face still set in the 'Oh Mali!' expression.

'But you're going nevertheless, even if we have to drag you up the steps. I promise you will enjoy it once we get going.'

And to his surprise he did enjoy it. Between the three of us we got him safely up the steps and into the chair. We were out for nearly two hours walking almost to Bonnieux and back. Nick did the hard work managing the wheelchair, Gudrun and I walked either side each holding a hand. The weather was warm but with enough of a breeze to keep him comfortable. He came home tanned and relaxed and happy to do the same again tomorrow.

'Nick, if you are willing, we will take him out every day for as long as he enjoys it,' I said later. 'It will have to be the same route every day because all the other roads are too steep for the chair but he is much better for being able to get out. None of us thrives sitting around waiting for death.'

We walked a little further along the road every day, taking advantage of his absence of pain to make the most of the days. He was much more sleepy at night and during the mornings but fine when we were out. He always tried to help with whatever we were doing, putting most of his weight onto Nick to spare Gudrun, giving me a foot for a shoe. It was so nice to be able to discard the padding and dress him in shorts and trainers for a few hours. Nick talked to him about cars and plumbing and on the third day we got deeply into a discussion about enlightenment as we went along. Greg listened with avid interest, joining in with a nod and a squeeze of our hands. Gudrun had finally discovered that enlightenment was all that some people lived for.

'What is it then?' she asked.

We each had our own ideas. For me it could only be akin to the joy I had experienced when I saw my grandparents meet after death. For Nick it had to be like imagining the best time he had ever had and then multiplying it a thousand, thousand fold. We were all agreed that at every death there was a possibility of a point of enlightenment. The discussion developed until we decided that we weren't nursing Greg who was dying, rather we were making a conscious attempt to assist him in his effort to win to enlightenment. Just a simple variation in the use of language and we noticed our whole perspective become newly sensitised in a very positive and dynamic way.

'Greg, what do you think of that?' Nick asked.

'Okay,' he said, quite clearly and nodding to emphasise the point.

It eased the underlying tension of the situation, that unnameable fear. If I felt sorry for myself there was always a little voice in the middle of my mind reminding me that I was privileged and honoured by being with him, bearing his name, helping him to die. He was barely articulate but I was so grateful that there was nothing at all wrong with his mind. He could still evaluate, rationalise and, most importantly, communicate his thinking to me.

— ✤ —

The last of the petals have dropped from the wisteria and the pink of Judas trees has faded to a dull brown. The brilliant red of the poppies along the road remind me of Limnos and this morning, May 4th, I heard a cuckoo calling as I opened the shutters. My beloved had a very restless night with a few slight pain spasms early but the swallowing reflex is becoming the major problem. He managed his early morning Essiac and his pills and yoghurt but only half his bread and half his mug of tea and he is much sleepier; I saw him nodding quietly behind his sunglasses as we walked this afternoon. His grip on our hands was as strong as ever.

I had all the problems the next day. Only women bleed but it's rarely convenient. I dragged myself out of my sleeping bag, exhausted and irritable, and decided that today I was absolutely fucked off with the brain tumour, fucked off with what it was doing to him, fucked off with what it was doing to me and I said so despite the vinaya. For all of my life of clean living, if someone had offered me a joint or a line of cocaine right then I would have taken it. Anything to escape for a while.

Another lift would finish me. It felt like I was at the end of my strength as I rolled him over in the bed to change the padding and the sheets. While he choked and stumbled his way through breakfast I found myself entertaining fantasies about feeding him pills, forcing the final horror on to us, feeding myself pills, needing to scream, needing to cry, wanting to go out and buy myself some new clothes to convince myself that I have to live. Maybe I could take him completely off the steroid and let him become totally himself once more before he died. But what do I mean about 'being himself'? He is himself just as he is now and no lessening of the drug will magically turn him back into the image of the man as he was a year ago. Before they gave me back the pieces and said, 'Here you are Mali, here's your husband. At least he's alive, make the best you can of him.' All my worries came uppermost, money, bank statements, how long we could have the house, where we would go when it was needed for people and holidays. I was talking about it as we walked.

'I have to talk,' I said. 'You will just have to put up with me. It's the wrong time of the month and I feel disgusting so just let me curse and moan and howl until I feel better. No one is to worry about me or about anything I say and no one is to take anything personally.'

He squeezed my hand in understanding and love and slowly lifted it to his lips for the softest, sweetest of kisses. How would I ever manage without that? I know I will never be spiritually lonely again but how can I go on

192

living without hearing his voice, without the comfort of his touch? Every night I go to sleep fantasising that in the morning we will wake up and he will be smiling at me.

'Come Mali, back into bed with me,' he will say. His face will be clear, he will be well and all this will be a bad dream.

Saturday, May 7th, was the last day we took him out in the chair. The pain spasms were stronger this morning before we sat him up but he still refused all pain-killer. He was very tired and sleepy over breakfast, better at lunch time but too tired to hold his head up properly while we were walking. We didn't go so far today and it took all our strength to help him safely down the steps and into the house. He is much heavier to lift now and when I gave him his afternoon Essiac, the effort to swallow brought on a few spasms of pain. I called in the doctor that evening who prescribed some Valium drops which Greg promptly refused to take until the morning, when he had seven and a half milligrams and slept soundly until lunch time.

He was bright enough to sit in his usual place at the table and chant the grace twice through without missing a word. He had never lost hand/eye co-ordination and helped himself to Nick's orange juice without hesitation but he slept all afternoon with me lying beside him and he was so sleepy at dinner that we put him straight back to bed as soon as he had eaten. He was fine until nine thirty and then the spasms began again as he tried to drink. At twelve thirty I fought him to try to get ten milligrams of Valium into his mouth. The spoon clicked hopelessly against clamped-shut teeth. Why did the drops have to have such a distinct and disgusting taste? Tasteless and they would have gone down with the Essiac without a murmur. It would not have been an honest solution. After a restless night I lifted him upright at five o'clock and sat with him, propping him up until Nick got up at six.

Sometimes I'm frightened and angry but I can't help but admire him. Almost completely helpless now and disabled by the tumour, his mind is still clear, he is still my man, my stubborn, wonderfully impossible husband. Even now he sticks by his principles. He has no control over anything else, why shouldn't he have some control over the drugs?

I left Gudrun and Nick to look after him while I drove into Apt as soon as I knew the Pharmacy was open. He had not had a bowel movement in two days and I couldn't bear to think of him sitting on the toilet trying to function and all the while risking pain in his head from the effort if he did. I came home with some particularly dynamic suppositories as I imagined only the French would sell. I padded him up, slid one into him before he had time to object and, happily disregarding all looks of alarm, harvested the result half an hour later. He was pleased too. He had no pain spasms and one less potential problem to worry about. He smiled and almost laughed when I told him how wonderful he was, he could still enjoy my capacity for the ridiculous.

We got him up for all three meals but he was very sleepy all day and it was hard work getting food and drink into him although he took his usual medication and his vitamins washed down with yoghurt without protest. During the afternoon as we lay together I talked to him again about his drugs, just to be sure that we were both still in agreement.

'I know this may seem like a crazy question, ' I said. 'But I feel I must ask you in accordance with your early Catholic conditioning. As we are living in a Catholic community, would you like a priest to come here to see you before you die?'

He shook his head.

'Would you like me to tell your family how sick you are?'

Again he shook his head.

'There's just one thing I wish you could promise me. When I die, please, please be there for me. Be waiting for me as my grandfather was for my grandmother. Let that joy be for me as well. Let me feel the joy as my spirit releases.'

His eyes filled momentarily with tears. He nodded and turned towards me for a kiss, holding my hand very tightly. I know I am loved. I will always be loved.

I feel the energy in the house changing. It is becoming very peaceful, softer. The acceptance of the inevitable. I check his bedding and the padding regularly. Gudrun helps me treat his pressure points. Nick is the strong arm, making it possible for us still to get him up and out of bed but every time it is more difficult. We each make sure that we have at least half an hour of exercise outside, walking or running every day. Healthy bodies don't take kindly to prolonged inactivity.

Tuesday, May 10th. He slept until four in the morning with the help of ten milligrams of Valium. The spasms began again soon after he woke up and barely lessened even with fifteen milligrams more. He managed to get up to eat a small breakfast but lunch was a disaster. He would neither eat nor drink, sitting slumped in his chair until we took him back to bed again. I was worried because it was almost twenty-four hours since he had passed water and I decided to call the doctor in again, this time without first consulting Greg. Kind Doctor Parraud came and examined him carefully. The blood pressure was still normal, the heart still strong. The bladder was not yet under stress but we would have to consider fitting a catheter if he didn't pass water soon. He verified that the swallowing mechanism was deteriorating and confirmed what we had all been thinking about the breathing. Termed 'Cheyne-Stokes breathing', when one strong breath follows a series of smaller ones continually on and on. The tumour was no longer allowing the brain to remind the lungs to breathe properly.

'The prognosis is not good – but it is a good way,' he said.

I asked him to prescribe some morphine in case we should need it and while Nick and Gudrun went to Bonnieux to collect it, I sat on the bed with my beloved. He listened carefully while I told him everything that was going on, everything that had been said and how he would die.

'Are you cross with me for calling the doctor?' I asked.

He shook his head.

'I love you and I'm so proud of you. You are doing so well, so very well. I'm helping you now and I know that when it's my turn, when my time comes, you will be there to help me too. Don't forget, be there for me,'

He nodded and squeezed my hand. I know he will. His eyes are as clear and bright as ever. Why does he have to die? Why? He will take my flame with him, leaving his own burning bright in my heart. I know he will.

The sun came streaming in through the window, I played him some of his favourite music as I sat and held his hand all afternoon, only getting up to change the padding when I joyfully discovered it well and truly wet an hour or so later. We made no attempt to get him up for dinner. Gudrun made some of her best Miso soup, thick with carrots and leeks, and he ate it all with a bowl full of yoghurt to help swallow the pills. Later, as he dozed we all sat with him, talking until the light was completely gone. Holding his hands, talking about Ānando and Chithurst and then about Greg. How we lived in the little house on Rhodes. The happy times, the funny times, the good times.

Wednesday, May 11th. He is changing, his skin is very clear, his face very soft and peaceful even though the mucus that he cannot swallow is building in his throat. He was restless around two a.m. although not so much in pain. He let me give him ten drops of Valium, I think more for my sake than his, and when I got out of my sleeping bag that morning he was still asleep. As I kissed him my mind was overwhelmed with the vision of us standing together in front of a vast, swirling, multi-coloured image of light and energy. We had arrived at the Gates of Time but he was well, standing upright and strong and holding me in his arms. Both of us waiting, just waiting for when it was time for him to pass through.

The bed was dry. It was over twelve hours since he last passed urine. When I called him to wake up there was only minimum response. We propped him up on cushions and pillows and he slept quietly, without any of the restless movement, for the first time for weeks during the morning sitting. When it was finished and the chanting done, I decided to crush his pills into the yoghurt and see if he would take them that way; it was the first time that it seemed necessary. With coaxing he woke up enough to swallow one mouthful of the yoghurt with just over half the medication but that was all he would take. The rest just trickled out of his mouth and down his chin. Talking to him all the time, I washed and shaved him and straightened the bed. I was so happy when I found the padding wet at nine thirty; desperately I didn't want him catheterised.

He was so sleepy and unusually unresponsive, his breathing short and shallow but pulse still strong and even. After telephoning Amaravati and the healers asking them to chant for us, to pray for us, I switched on the cassette player and started playing our favourite songs. His eyelids began to flicker and to try to open as he heard the *Unchained Melody* filling the room. I sat beside him, holding his hands and singing it as we used to sing it together.

Baby I need your Loving, Dancing in the Dark, Unchained Melody again and I knew he would have sung them too and smiled if he could.

Gudrun made our lunch and then she and Nick went down to the basement to play ping-pong; I could hear the flick and snap of the ball and the murmuring of their voices. The warm, bright early afternoon sun crept round to our window as I resumed my seat beside him, holding his right hand, playing a tape of our favourite Pali chanting. He knew I was there, making little almost imperceptible gestures in response to my voice and to the chanting and when I tied one piece of the string that Sister Thānasanti had sent us from the Easter retreat at Amaravati around his left wrist. I knotted the other around my own.

And so we went on until three fifteen when suddenly his breathing went into a spasm and I knew the inevitable battle had begun, the heart and lungs making a last desperate effort to function normally. Taking both his hands in mine I began the chanting, all our usual chanting and more. His momentary agitation calmed as he felt my hands and heard my voice that somehow remained strong. Even with my throat full of tears the strength came from somewhere.

'Come on Beloved, you can do it, you can do it,' I repeated, encouraging him, loving him.

Gudrun and Nick came to join me, Gudrun at the foot of the bed, Nick down on the floor beside us, and we all three chanted, keeping up a continuous round until after five thirty when the battle seemed to be over and his breathing quieter. His pulse had been racing and now it began to slow, so very slowly to slip away. In the vision that had been filling my mind throughout the day, he was increasingly merging into the light, no longer standing beside me but before me and beginning to merge into the vortex of energy. We sat on, talking to him, holding his hands, feeling for the pulse that became more and more difficult to locate. Gudrun sat cradling his feet, keeping them warm, her eyes fixed on his face.

'There's nothing wrong with death,' I said. 'It's just a natural and normal process. Don't you remember all the times we sat in the stables at the farm, waiting for the foals to be born?'

'Yes,' she said.

'And don't you feel the similarity in this?'

'Yes.' Her eyes widened as she considered this new idea.

'It is more like waiting for a birth than a death, isn't it?' she said.

'Yes. That is what it is, as well as a release from the confines of a worn-out body. The final freedom.'

At nine o'clock we bedded ourselves down. From lying on top of the bed with his arm around me, I slipped under the covers pulling up my tee-shirt to feel his warmth against me.

'I'm coming in with you Beloved,' I said. 'Back in this bed where I belong except that for the first time in our life together, and now of all times if you please, we're sharing a room with two others!'

196

Gudrun and Nick were making their beds on the floor where they had been sitting. Nick laughed.

'Have you never done that before?' he asked.

'Absolutely not! The Kleins are very private people!' I said.

The light faded from the room. I lay curled around his right side, my head against his shoulder, my hair spread out over his chest. Him breathing ever more shallowly, us talking.

'Do you know why we are so relaxed?' I said. 'It is because we are still so secure because he is still breathing. It's not normal breathing and from where I am I can hear so much going on in him but I know that I want even this to go on all night. I don't want to hear it stop and neither do you.'

'He almost seems better now, as though he is going to get well,' said Nick. And it was true, he was so much more relaxed. His skin was still damp and tinged slightly bluish from the battle but clean and clear as though there were no longer any drugs polluting his system. They were all burned away in the ferocity of the spasms that were so like the pangs of birth. As we begin, so we end.

At ten his breathing paused. We looked at him, at each other, relaxing as he drew breath again, and then once again with a longer pause. I looked at the clock, two minutes after ten. We waited, hoping against hope to hear him breathe again. I found myself saying,

'One more breath for me Beloved, oh please, just one more breath for me!'

After an eternity it came, his final gift to me. One last sighing breath as the clock ticked over to three minutes after ten, already early in the morning of May 12th in Vietnam, exactly twenty-seven years to the day since he lay near death on the field of Operation Union on another May 12th.

And the vision was complete. He was standing within the vortex at one with the colour and the light and the energy, smiling his everlasting smile and holding cupped within his hands a little flame, my flame, leaving his with me as a light and a heat in my heart that was almost too strong for my exhausted body and mind to bear.

Our tears, so long held back, poured down our faces as we bowed and chanted the final blessing. He was dead but he looked so beautiful and so young. There no lines on his face, his hair tousled on the pillow as though he had just fallen asleep. The camera was on the table and I picked it up, the moment was too precious to be lost. My hands were shaking but the picture when it came was clear and a slight fault in the processing of the negative had given it an unearthly quality that was extraordinarily appropriate to the time and place.

Chapter Eighteen

The Death certificate read:

'Cause of death – [immediate] progressive loss of vital functions due to alteration and disappearance of cerebral functions, coma, then respiratory arrest followed immediately by cardiac arrest; subsequent to [initial cause] after-effects of a bullet wound [occipital region of the skull affecting the cerebrum and the cerebellum] received in Vietnam 1967, gradual development of cancer of the cerebellum spreading to the cerebrum.'

— ✳ —

After the doctor had gone and I had spoken to his brother Bob in Duluth, we began the time-honoured ritual of laying him out. Nick and Gudrun were sent out while I made sure there would be no leakage from his bladder. Then, having packed him and padded him and dressed him in his best emerald green briefs, I summoned them to help with the washing. Nick shaved him while Gudrun and I laid out his wedding clothes and his favourite Icelandic red socks. They helped support his body while I went back to work with my cotton wool and cuticle stick. Still my capacity for outrageous remarks did not fail me as I gave an impromptu desana on the difference between the back passage of a man in comparison with a woman. Despite ourselves we were all laughing and when we turned him over, by some trick of the settling of the body, he was smiling too.

His wedding shirt and trousers still fitted him well. It seemed that no amount of steroid could make him dramatically overweight. I combed his hair and we rubbed sandalwood oil into his face and hands. Sadly I took off his wedding rings and slipped them on to the ring finger of my right hand. Nick fastened his bracelet with the little golden Buddha around my wrist and the emerald, now faded and dull, lay on the shrine. I left his earring in place. The gold was so thin and fine that I doubted that there would be much to retrieve from the ashes. Finally I laid his hands over his breast, looped together with the purple and white silk scarves, with my little mala bracelet on his wrist and holding the single red rose that had stood all day on the shrine. Another photograph and we made him secure with cushions and pillows, tying the black silk scarf around his chin and knotting on top of his head. I apologised profoundly and told him it was only for the required number of hours but the look on his face said quite plainly 'Oh Mali! Do I have to look like this?'

I kissed him gently before I settled down to sleep beside him as usual for the last time, kissing his forehead, his nose, his lips, his chin, as always and as dear to me cooling and still as he had been warm and breathing.

'Goodnight beloved husband. Sleep well, rest well. I love you.'

He was dead, physically he was certainly dead but all the time I was so aware of his vitality, his smile. He seemed to be more vibrantly alive than ever before. Except for the silence. The overwhelming silence. I never realised how vitally his breathing, his heartbeat had filled my sound of silence until they were no more.

In the morning the formalities began. Jan, our good neighbour, came into his own so that I had to do very little. It was Ascension Day and a national holiday in France but death stops for nothing and by midday the death certificate had been made and copied and was already in the hands of the official translator. The cremation had been arranged for eleven fifteen the following morning in Orange by the two local men who served all the villages in this way. We were allowed to keep him with us but on a cold bed neatly covered to the waist with a sheet and surrounded by roses from the garden. A screaming babble of tears rose into my throat, swallowed back and rose again until I could find space to be alone and let them wrench themselves free.

'Why did you have to leave me? Why, why, why?'

The answer came whispering.

'Oh my Mali, I am with you always. Remember, there is no separation. Only in your own mind.'

'But I can't help this. I can't bear this silence! I want you back, not sick but well! I want you well and with me! I want you back!'

'Be kind to yourself Beloved, it's not wrong to cry. Be with it Baby, just be with it and it will pass away. Remember, don't fight it, just watch it and let yourself cry. You will be well.'

'But I don't want to be well. I want to die too! How could you go where I'm not allowed to follow you yet? How could you?'

In answer I felt a heat growing at the base of my skull and circle of heat forming around me as though two arms were encircling me, holding me close. So it remained all that day and into the next.

I went to the bathroom and ran a tub full of hot water and lay soaking my weariness. Thinking, trying not to think. As I pulled the plug I realised the towel was still on the radiator on the opposite side of the room. I always hated dripping across the floor to reach it. For no reason at all it suddenly fell on the floor as though it had been pushed or picked up. My momentary irritation evaporated into laughter.

'Thank you, Gregory,' I said.

That night we moved him on the cold bed into the main living room in front of the household shrine. The refrigerator unit gave off a distinct and continual hum and an energy that caught at my throat. It was impossible for me to sleep in the same room so we combined both shrines, two Buddha-rupas, all the candles, flowers and incense and left him lying in state in front of it with JBJ perched on his knees to keep the vigil.

It was so terrible, this between-worlds atmosphere, time in slow motion. I would look at the clock thinking that at least half an hour had passed but it would only be five minutes since my eyes last wandered that way. Food felt dry and uneasy in my mouth. It was so hard to swallow. We ate a lot of mashed potato, purely comfort food and I was glad of my cocktail of pills and a mug of hot milk when night finally came.

The weather which had been so fine and warm turned to cloud and howling wind within an hour of his death. I was glad that it was cooler so that there was no excuse to send him to the mortuary. Somehow it was so appropriate to hear the wind crashing and howling around the house, to hear the rain come flooding down and then to look out at the magnificently dramatic skies that followed.

'As we will be clouds together ...' the quote went over and over in my mind as I watched the majestic clouds forming and reforming, white, silvery grey, black, shot through with shafts of white sunlight and flashes of silver and blue. 'As we will be clouds together when the wind comes to remove the last prints of Greg and Mali Klein from the sand.'

Our two sturdy men reappeared at nine fifteen the following morning, May 13th, exactly three years to the day since the death of my father. We had turned the refrigerator off during the morning sitting and our meditation had been punctuated by the drip-drip of ice melting onto the floor. We hoped that they wouldn't be offended; he was so soon to go to the fire. An hour would make little difference.

Our friends, Betty and Pichou, had bought a great sheaf of broom flowers, all green and gold and smelling so beautiful that the room was filled with their perfume as they were laid over him. The broom and the roses went with him into the coffin, together with a lock of my hair, my nail clippings, the Valentine card I had last given him, with the poem that I had written for him on Rhodes added to it. Gudrun drew a dolphin and a rainbow on a card written all over with love for the father she had known so briefly but loved so well. The village policeman, who was usually to be seen on the back of a tractor, appeared in his official jacket to supervise the sealing of the coffin after the last kiss, the last minutes stroking his hair, the last 'I love you, mortal remains of my beloved husband. Goodbye to your precious body that I have loved and enjoyed so well.'

I watched his face as the lid went on. It seemed odd to see him set against white satin and lace and then he was gone. Just a knowledge that what was left of his body now lay in this stiff, wooden structure with its heavy recyclable handles and four brass coloured knobs that screwed into place and shut him out for this incarnation from our mortal sun. A large and serviceable screwdriver appeared out of a pocket to screw down the last two screws, one at each end and then to be melted over with dull, red sealing wax and stamped with the official seal. The wax caught momentarily as they sealed the head end. A little yellow flame danced lazily over the liquid wax, in flickering anticipation of what was to come.

They were so kind to us at Orange, to our little funeral party of five, the three of us with Betty and Pichou. There were no morbid theatricals involving revolving stages and curtains in time to canned organ music. His coffin was placed on a simple low, wooden trolley in a circular room devoid of any religious bias, with a high, vaulted wooden ceiling and simple stone flags on the floor. We knelt and I began our chanting that we had made together so many mornings within our Sangha of Two, calling the Devas and the kindly spirits to be with us as we said farewell to our friend, our teacher, my husband. The Holy Ones were kind, my voice didn't falter. Barber's *Adagio for Strings* went echoing up into the roof, nine and a half minutes of farewell to the Marine, the karma with Vietnam finally laid to rest. We chanted the final blessing, made our final bows. I opened the door to tell the solitary employee hovering in the reception office that we were ready.

I had to see the smoke. We went into the garden and stood among the flowers and the polished slabs of stone, named and dated, some with portraits sealed into the stone, others with effigies of the Virgin and Jesus. The sky was covered all over in high, unbroken cloud. I stood watching almost frantically for the shimmer of the heat over the building. I was terrified of missing it. There was no chimney to be seen. Within a few minutes I saw the wavering, melting air begin to form and I knew it had begun.

Tears streaming down my face, I trickled the beads of his mala bracelet through my fingers as the shimmering grew stronger and fiercer until the little wafts of black smoke went curling up into the cloud. And I was glad that the tumour was melting, burning away, defeated. A death unto itself and peacefully, without the tubes and morphine, the usual paraphernalia these beings enjoy. We had had our final miracle. Painless metamorphosis.

Everyone has their share of miracles. He had been shot twice twenty-seven years ago, lying four hours on the field with an open head wound and survived. He did his best to give himself as a monk for almost twenty years and then without a single moment of regret he laid the monastic life aside and gave himself to our relationship, maintaining all the clarity of the holy life as a lay man, as a beloved husband in our Sangha of Two. A brave Man, a brave Monk, a brave Marine, never less than worthy of respect and now a brave Spirit. We are even stronger, our love unsullied, unspoilt, untouched and until it is my time to pass through the Time Gate, we will go on, working from both worlds. Our deep love and commitment to each other gave us the freedom to be ourselves, no facade, open to each other in every way, in complete honesty and with nowhere to hide. The total surrender of body, mind and spirit. I know the love goes on.

In less than an hour I was carrying a hot urn out of the crematorium to the car, feeling the heat from his ashes burning through the double layer of card of the carrying box and into my legs as I held it on my lap while we drove back. We went past the turning for Lacoste and on into Apt. It was difficult to know what to do with ourselves. We were hungry but with no great enthusiasm for food. I had the two last films in my bag so we decided to take them in for processing, forcing down salad and bread in the Café Grégoire while we waited for the shop to open. I put the still hot box down on the counter while I searched through my bag for the films. As usual the girl asked after my husband.

'Il est mort,' I said. 'Il est ici.'

I put her hand against the side of the box.

'Oh!' She looked at me in amazement as she realised what she was touching. Instinctively she drew her hand away and then touched the box again, curious more than shocked.

I sat with my box beside me, watching the people in the café with their cigarettes, their children. The pretty waitress, so slim with her long black skirt split up to her thigh, the men in their jeans and leather jackets, all the body language, the intense concentration on living, being alive. What was it all to become but a box of hot ash or something going green and liquefying six feet down in the local cemetery? All those hopes and dreams, all those seemingly important values. New clothes, a smart car, a new baby. Look at me, I'm beautiful, I'm expensive, I'm fertile – and all of it to become ashes and dust in the wink of an eye of Time.

Some gypsies were beginning to set up a stall ready for the market next morning. They were advertising pancakes and toffee apples, talking hard at each other, busy, organising, intent on their profit. What would it be like, I wondered, to incarnate into a life where everything evolved around financial security, where values were nothing more than how much you had or didn't have in your pocket or in the bank? Here was I, sitting with my box of ashes but my husband had taught me very well. He had given me a spiritual inheritance that was priceless if only I could find the strength and the wisdom to be fully aware of it.

— �֎ —

The morphine went back to the Pharmacy unopened with the rest of the Valium. Nick left early on Sunday morning and Gudrun stayed on to help me with the house, to feed me and make sure I stayed alive. We stood on the balcony and waved as he drove away

'And then there were three,' she said, giving me a significant smile.

'Yes,' I said. 'Now there are three.'

I spent the rest of the morning writing a letter to send out to as many of the people as I could remember who had been chanting for us, praying for us, doing my best to express our gratitude for their caring and their love. The interment of the ashes was already arranged for July 17th at Chithurst and I wanted all the ladies to bring a single stem of white lilies to spread out a magnificent feast for the rabbits at the end of the day.

That afternoon we went out for a long walk through the valley where Greg and I had last walked in January. I showed Gudrun where he had jumped the stream. It was another day of magnificent cloud and dramatic sunshine. The streams and little rivers were bubbling full with the recent rain, the fields and hedges lushly green and crowded with flowers. In the orchards some of the fruit on the cherry trees was beginning to ripen and we gathered as we walked, spitting out the stones. Talking and laughing, both of us very much aware of him striding along with us, at last enjoying the freedom of completely unhindered movement and living on prana as he had always wanted to do. It was impossible to feel sad that afternoon. I made a conscious effort to cry and could only smile. I stood still and closed my eyes.

'Gregory! Kiss me or I'll scream!' I shouted.

I could almost feel his lips and his laughter as he responded.

On the seventh day we got the key to the church from the girl in the Post Office and lit seven candles for the Seventh Day Rite. That evening I sat meditating for an hour at ten o'clock, talking to him and crying. By the next afternoon I was only aware of a sudden and unreasonable rage. I didn't want to remember the tumour any longer. I didn't want this death. I wanted the man who had been gone for so long, the man who took such care of me. His devastating sweetness. I walked my tears of anger to the village to post the letters, wanting the good times again, Limnos, Rhodes, the sea, wanting him, wanting him back. Anger gave way to depression, lethargy, grief. This terrible grief.

'Be with it, Baby, just be with it. You were my blessing, I am yours. Be kind to yourself.'

'I don't want to be. I can't bear this. I'm not brave. I don't have a good attitude to death. It's all a lie. I want you back. I want you back!'

The evening meal restored me. Gudrun served up pasta cooked in white wine with mushrooms and garlic. I was surprised at how hungry I was. We sat on at the table after the plates were cleared, watching the clouds out of the kitchen window, watching the evening light over Bonnieux.

'If the power of thought is supposed to be stronger than the spoken word, then does Greg know everything we are thinking?' she asked.

'In theory I suppose he could.'

'But I have such crazy thoughts. I don't like to think that he can see them,' she said.

'We all have crazy thoughts. It's not unique, neither is it a crime.'

'But you know, I've been worried that I haven't been crying as much for him as I thought I would. I usually cry all the time when someone dies, for days, but this time it was only at the beginning. I'm worried that I didn't love him as much as I thought I did.'

'Consider this. When your friend Adam died and your grandfather died, where were you? How involved with their actual dying processes were you? How much experience of death had you then?'

She looked at me, head tilted slightly to one side, waiting for the answer.

'Ask yourself why did you cry? What were you crying for? When you look at it carefully you can see that the tears come as result of shock, a feeling of personal loss. I'm never going to see that person again and also the tears are linked to a deeply unconscious fear of an unknown that one day, sooner or later, you know you will have to face yourself.'

'Go on,' she said.

'You have done something for Greg that most daughters never have the chance of doing in this modern culture, where everything is usually handed over to a hospital and a mortuary. You have nursed him, laughed with him, loved him, helped him to die, prepared him for cremation. If that is not an act of selfless love for another human being, a father, I don't know what else it is. You have been as intimately involved with death as anyone ever could be and you have seen that it is nothing to fear. You have seen it for what it is, a release. Don't doubt yourself.'

She was content with that.

The days drag on. He didn't want to die. Desperately, passionately he wanted to get well and be there for me. The loneliness comes and goes. The afternoons for some reason are the worst. I lie on the balcony in the sun desperately hoping for some terminal illness, wanting to die and never come back. Seeing him so strongly beside me as he was when he was well, wearing his dark blue sweatshirt and jeans, his beautiful eyes without the slight puffiness around them from the steroid. Smiling, lying down and laughing beside me. I can almost feel him again, stroking his face, running my fingers through his hair. Beloved you, why is this so painful?

He didn't want to be a Buddhist monk any more, he lived with me and through our relationship we did find out what love was all about. This fragile human love that grows and strengthens and becomes invincible through lifetimes, through eons. The one thing that never dies.

But how many years will I have to wait? I remember the shape of his back curving tanned and smooth to his waist, watching the way he walked in front of me on the beach at Limnos, picking his way through the rocks and stones and the thorny balls of vegetation. He has taken to appearing in his blue sweatshirt since the sadness got worse. Yesterday almost in anger I dismantled the large shrine that we had made in the living room the night before the cremation and put the room back as it was when we first came in January. He was immediately beside me, suddenly very practical, walking about and asking me where I wanted things put, just like he used to do. I was comforted by his presence, his love and concern. Finally I picked up the urn and shook it gently, surprised a little by the sharp grittiness of the sound of the ashes against the metal.

All my thoughts of suicide, wanting terminal illness, wanting out. While I'm driving I find myself entertaining really strong fantasies about crashing the car, putting down my foot and speeding into oblivion. Dying would be so easy that way as long as I took no one else with me. But I hear him saying,

'What about your enlightenment Mali? That's why you are incarnate. Shouldn't you be thinking about that now? Why put it off any longer?'

204

I don't want it to, but it does make sense. Thoughts of my personal enlightenment have never had priority. A life of service and contemplation, worthy of his name and worthy of respect, would help to pass the time. But I just want him back!

The nights are not so bad. I turn on to my left side and I can almost feel him beside me, slipping his arm under my shoulder, holding me. I take my cocktail of pills and fall asleep thinking of him, dreaming of him; he seems even closer to me then. Two nights ago I know he was lying beside me, I could feel his energy in the bed with me, so much that I put my hand out and felt the heat where his chest should be, his arm. Sometime during last night I came out of sleep just enough to be aware of a huge glowing crystal on the table beside the bed. It made me smile. He never could resist them.

The Full Moon flooded the eastern sky on May 24th, the festival of Wesak in Buddhist terminology, the dreaded first Full Moon of saying the wedding vows without being able to enjoy his physical response. I could hear his voice echoing after mine repeating the words and I found myself smiling between the tears. In meditation my concentration is terrible, two or three breaths and then a host of random unrelated thoughts.

'Watch the breath Mali, the breath.'

'I'm a mess, Beloved. Now you can see what a mess I am. I can't concentrate for more than two minutes.'

'Be kind to yourself. Just watch the breath.'

I tried but my mind went sideways into visions of us together in so many ways at so many different times. He was still there with me. I could feel the heat in my palms and my fingers. As the meditation was ending I heard him say quite distinctly,

'Oh my Mali, I love you. We are one flame, one heart. I will never leave you.'

'I love you,' I whispered into the room.

'Practise, Mali, the practice.'

I hear the word all around me and as I write the tears are running down my cheeks and my nose. I know that he would materialise right now beside me if he could and just hold me.

I always cry alone. I try to be positive especially in the afternoons but by five o'clock I am tired and in tears. Our wedding photograph on the shrine helps to remind me of all the bright energy of Greg and Mali Klein but yesterday Gudrun put *Baby I need your Loving* in the cassette player as she was working in the kitchen and the tears became a flood, soaking silently into the pillow.

The strange thing is that the silence is no longer an unbearable torment. It seems to be filled with him and I want the silence. I'm reaching out into it, waiting for him, listening for him. I need the silence now. When the pain and the tears threaten to overwhelm me I school myself to sit cross-legged just as we used to sit, knees touching, holding hands to meditate and then he is so real again. My hands tingle and grow hot, my concentration wavers but it is growing stronger and I feel better, lighter. No longer alone.

All the next day Gudrun and I were cleaning and packing up the house, ready to leave some time the following morning. Not an unfamiliar lifestyle for Greg and Mali Klein. In one place for a few months and then moving on but after all that had happened here, this was a major leave-taking and for the first time without him sitting beside me, sorting out the music, reminding me to put on some lipstick. We arrived in Lacoste in love, happy to be alone together again, almost hoping that the Essiac might make the miracle. We leave with a pocketful of memories and an urn full of ashes but all around us the sense of his vitality, his joy.

It was after midday before we were ready to leave. The bags were in the car and I went through the house saying farewell and thank you, room by room, lingering finally in the little room where we had laughed and cried, slept and made love, where we finished 'Dangerous Sweetness'. Where he had finally entered metamorphosis. The bed had been moved since then and the shrine was in pieces in the car. I noticed some ash from the incense on the shelf that I couldn't bring myself to dust away. I straightened the picture of Saint Francis on the wall. It was impossible not to cry.

'Come, brave spirit, beloved husband,' I said aloud as I turned to close the door. 'Travel with us, be with us, be with me always.'

The key turned twice, the lock clicked shut. A handful of poppies growing out of the wall shone scarlet in the sunshine. Gudrun was waiting to close the gates after the car.

Chapter Nineteen

It was a hot, lazy afternoon. Gudrun lay in a rubber dingy in the middle of the swimming pool. I was circling round and round the edge of the pool, doing walking meditation and promoting my tan all at once. The old injury to my neck had finally succumbed to weeks of lifting and stress. It was far too painful to attempt to swim.

'You look like a nineteen-sixties starlet in that bikini,' observed my daughter.

I didn't know whether to be flattered or insulted. We had the pool to ourselves. Betty and her husband Paul were asleep in the house. Occasionally Feeling the dog came past on patrol to make sure we were well. Our welcome at Eguilles was all we could hope for, food, love and rooms in the Retreat Centre.

The second day was hard, lazy, sad, no energy, missing my 'home' in Lacoste. I spent most of the day lying on the bed in semi-darkness. It was not worth unpacking anything familiar for the few days we were there. I was glad that Greg and I had made the little room in my mother's house our own. At least that would have some kind of comfortable familiarity about it. In complete desolation of loneliness I cried out into the shadowed room, into the echoing expanse of the Universe.

'Gregory! Greg! Where are you?'

'Right here, right now!'

'I want you back, I want you back! You promised to protect me, to look after me. You made a vow when we were married. You wanted to be the strong one for me. Why did you go and die on me? Why?'

'Mali, I can protect you in many more ways now than I could before. I will always look after you, you know that. I love you.'

All the tears came again. The sniffing became unmanageable and I had to grope around beside the bed to find a paper tissue.

True peace is such a personal thing. There can be no real peace in a world full of conflicting views and opinions. Many people had been kind to me but I needed to hide myself away for just a little longer from the more fanatical element in my husband's followers. I was talking about it to a Tibetan monk who came to stay with Betty, the evening before Gudrun and I were due to leave.

'Did you see Greg as a Master or a husband?' he said.

'He never considered himself to be enlightened and never understood how anyone could see him as a spiritual Master. I always respected him, for his practice, for his intention, for what he was trying to do. But he was always a husband to me, never a Master and he didn't want it any other way. He still is a husband to me, a husband and spiritual companion, completely that. I feel no sense of separation from him at all. I keep asking myself why I am now Greg and Mali Klein, both of us in one body? What is it all for?'

'You have to go on. You have no choice. In Buddhism there is no death as such, no separation, just a change of state. He will go on teaching through you.'

'But do I want that? Why was it all dumped on me?'

'You have no choice.'

— ✳ —

We arrived in Kandersteg on June 1st, driving over the mountains in a blistering thirty-five degrees of heat with all the windows wound down and the cold air on full. Quickly absorbed into the compassionate silence, we had the monastery almost exclusively to ourselves with only a single monk in residence and two laymen. A two day retreat for twenty people was scheduled for the following weekend.

That evening during meditation, my husband appeared in front of me holding a bowl like a monk's bowl, filled with light. Again I remembered the image of the Grail as before when I saw my father pass. Greg/Ānando handed me the bowl, closing his hands over mine as I held it. We merged so completely that we were one, there was no dividing us from each other or from the bowl or from the light that was of it and from it. The light that was our inheritance, the foundation of this uniting.

What is the symbolism of the Grail, or the Bowl? Why in the vision after my father's death did I offer it to him and then why did Greg bring it to me for acceptance into our Being?

I got ready for bed and was about to prepare my usual knockout cocktail when he said quite distinctly,

'Mali, you don't need that any longer. It's quite unnecessary. We don't need that.'

'But what if I wake up in the night? I need sleep.'

I hesitated, more than half willing to obey him. At the same time my nagging mind dreaded neck pain and exhaustion.

'You will be fine. Trust me.'

I woke at six and turned off the alarm clock. It was Saturday, June 4th. The retreat was due to begin after the morning meal, the weather was turning colder and raining before the end of the day. Difficult for Gudrun and me after a winter in Provence.

The monastery seems full now, a concentrated and unfamiliar energy, and it is not easy for me to have so little privacy, no place to indulge in tears. I am so conscious of my beloved within me that it creates a sense of space and peace naturally. Perhaps this is my first lesson in making my own space no matter where, no matter how.

When we were sent out to do walking meditation, my first idea was to go to the waterfall. Idyllic, romantic, perfectly in keeping with my widow's state. Instead the Being within sent me out to the back of the house, walking up and down twenty-five paces between a peg and a pine cone under the washing lines beside the woodpile. I couldn't help remembering another Saturday exactly two years ago when the monastery was full and busy with a similar retreat, and I was waiting in Gruyères with a hired car and a bag of new clothes. Even so I feel no sense of loss.

'Once I knew Ãnando, I know him still and better now, my husband and lover, my wonderful lover.'

Maybe death only separates as much as we want to be separated. By thinking that the connection is gone, that everything is finished, maybe so it is and then a wonderful opportunity for loving and learning is lost. The Wise, the source of all wisdom, are generally thought to be discarnate or to have some connection with higher, finer dimensions. Why should we fear connection with discarnate beings? Why should we fear such insight into the potential of human love?

I have no sense of clinging. He has shown me that we are as powerfully connected now as we were before the death of his physical body. I could never reject him in life, how can I reject him in death?

And so it rains, and the mist fills the valley, the mountains almost completely lost in the cloud and the wet that turned to snow on the higher ground. I have a curious sense of being in two worlds at once. I keep seeing my body walking about, doing things but always at a distance. While I am standing entwined with my husband in a great form of light. Watching, communicating beyond the limitation of words and yet I hear his voice.

'Listen to the voices of the incarnate, my Mali. To us they are indistinct, like the sounds of mice scratching in the wall. Occasionally one voice rises above the murmuring when words manifest wisdom and clarity. But remember, for every hostile word there are countless, kindly hearts who wish you well. Allow yourself to grieve but also allow the healing of the woman, which has already been accomplished by the man, fully into consciousness. The woman isn't destroyed at the metamorphosis of her mate. She is complete and ready to go on. You are not alone. You are all one.'

'But I want a relationship with you, beloved husband in spirit. Is that so wrong?'

'You only have to reach out.'

— ❋ —

Back in England, arranging the formal interment of the ashes. Finding the gravestone from under the pile of clothes in the cupboard where my mother had hidden it. We had never intended it to bear any resemblance to the Vietnam Veterans' Wall in Washington DC but that came immediately to mind as I traced my fingers over the black, polished stone.

'Greg and Mali Klein, Mettacittena.'

I would be one of the few living to dig her own grave.

'Only people in concentration camps do that,' I thought.

No one knows quite what to do with me or what to say. The living are only concerned with the living. No one wants to know about anyone being dead. Widows are by tradition slightly apart from society, the hangers-on at the edge of the community. Perhaps I should go out into the snow to starve? It's too late to throw myself onto the funeral pyre.

It's strange how all the post doesn't come, people can't ring me and machines go wrong when I am around. It's the little things that mean so much in love and the little things that hurt so much in sorrow.

I have URW after my name now on my military ID card.

'What does that mean?' I asked the Sergeant.

'Unremarried widow, Ma'am,' he replied.

I drove away from the Base in tight knot of pain. SP for spouse was so much nicer.

I need time to recover from the cancer, from the wayward, compelling energy that insinuated its predatory tentacles into my psyche for so many months. I tell myself 'Don't cry, don't cry. Tears are for your pillow and your intimate grieving. Your conduct, Mali.'

How many times did I hear that?

Desperately he sought peace of mind and heart. From woman to woman he sought it in the perfect relationship. When that failed him, he renounced a world he was disappointed in and bored with. For the Holy Life. He saw no better alternative to despair and maybe one day to a bullet that wouldn't miss.

'I doubt I would have been alive by the time I reached thirty if I hadn't been a monk,' he used to say.

To renounce in despair is one thing. To renounce life and love at its sweetest and best is quite another. Lacking fulfilment, he sought fulfilment in the Holy Life but that proved no sure road to enlightenment. His true renunciation came when he chose to die.

We spend the whole of our life incarnate preparing for death. How we conduct ourselves, how we live from moment to moment preconditions those final moments of metamorphosis. I know that three factors contributed to the quality and ease of his passing. Equally his twenty years of spiritual practice and the nature of our relationship combined with the palliative element of the Essiac herbal formula. Finally he had what he always wanted. His heart and mind at peace with his beloved wife at his side while he was still young enough, yet physically, emotionally and spiritually mature enough to savour the sweetness and the joy.

Some wounds never truly heal. Our frail flesh bleeds and knits and mends but the damage goes deep. While scarcely more than a child he had faced death on the battlefield. When death came for him again, he made the true renunciation, trusting in the conviction of his spiritual training and in the love of his beloved companion to help him win through to the final freedom.

By choosing to stay in Provence we were fortunate in that the French custom of cremating within twenty-four to thirty-six hours allowed us to keep his body with us so that we could pay our respects and honour the dead in our own way while the remaining life force detached from the host. It was important for us to be able to handle his body after death and to prepare him for cremation.

Our cultural conditioning looks on a corpse with fear, aversion, a shrinking revulsion until it has been made 'safe' by a competent mortician, embalmed and dressed, painted and coiffured into something resembling the person we once knew. Most people think nothing of standing in a butcher's shop and waiting to be served surrounded by hunks of meat dripping in trays around them and hanging over their heads. Many think nothing of falling on their knees before an image of the Christ, tortured in crucifixion and painted to emphasise the wounding by thorn, nail and spear. Yet when a member of their own family lies dead before them, as worthy of respect as any Buddha or Christ, they turn away and thankfully pay strangers to do what has to be done. In a society that encourages the keeping of a body for a week before burial or cremation, obviously it has to be kept in some state of preservation but why are we afraid to see our loved ones pale and cold? What conditions that fear?

There is no mystery, no great art or hidden skill demanded in washing and packing a corpse before *rigor mortis* sets in. Gudrun at eighteen saw it as an honour and her natural right as his step-daughter to be able to support his head and prevent his mouth from falling open while I worked with my cuticle stick and cotton wool. When the undertaker came in the morning and asked to be left alone with the deceased for two minutes, he opened the door in less than one.

'Bon,' he said, satisfied that everything was correct. As they lifted my husband's body on to the cold table only twelve hours after his last breath, I caught the first faint whiff of decay, the natural processes already at work once the spirit had departed. There was nothing revolting, upsetting or morbid about that either. We breathe, we eat, we excrete, we die and as we honour the breath that gives us life so we must honour the process of decay that sends our out-grown remains to the earth or to the fire.

'Let my freedom be for ever your love'. For both of us so it is. I gave him the freedom to enter into death empowered and on his own terms. He has given me myself.

'Oh my Mali-Mali, I love you still but I'm offering you an alternative viewpoint on our relationship. It all begins with the breath. Tune into the rhythm of your breathing, your heartbeat and you will enter the parallel world of unlimited vision.'

Together we lived and investigated a noble teaching so what does it mean to me now? What can the Four Noble Truths teach me right here, right now?

Q. What in my present state gives me the most dissatisfaction and dis-ease?

A. Fear of the loneliness of widowhood and all that it entails.

Q. What makes that dissatisfaction arise?

A. Social conditioning, others' reaction to me.

Q. What makes it cease?

A. Contemplation of what we were put together for. The awareness of the unique value of our experience.

Q. What is the path leading to the cessation of that dissatisfaction?

A. As always, the practice.

'Practise Mali. Watch the suffering rise and pass away. Be with it Baby.'

Q. What have I lost from our relationship?

A. Physical companionship.

Q. What have I gained?

A. Spiritual companionship and an excellent fundamental training. He taught me by example. By example he teaches me still. The spirit of our relationship has not died. If anything it continues to grow and to expand. By choice what remains of my time will be my own to investigate and develop all that I have been taught and know to be true for me.

Q. What is conducive to peace?

A. Consciously and completely to let go. Letting go is the key to enlightenment. The conscious effort to let go of old grief, remorse, anger, ill-will and to realise that we don't have to come back at some later time to sort things out at a later date. Loving Kindness to all the world. Calling up the old pain and letting it go. Wishing all the people well whom we have hurt or who have hurt us. No matter when, no matter who.

By saying 'I'll sort it out in another life' we chain ourselves to the perpetual wheel of rebirth. We have to realise that ultimately we sort it out by simply letting it go. I helped Greg harvest the fruit of his incarnation. At the same time he was helping me prepare the ground to nurture the young sapling that is my incarnation. He was ready to go on. He had done a lot during his twenty years as a monk. I still have a lot to do with my mind.

'Mali, do everything in your power to further your own enlightenment,' he says. 'Free yourself and you free the pair of us.' What is he telling me?

I gave 'Dangerous Sweetness' to a retired psychiatrist and listened as he described the stark reality of the personality disorder my husband had done so well to live with for so many years. It gave me some comfort, however cold. For if we had managed to put the tumour into remission for longer, what then would have been the cost?

'Better dead than insane, my Mali,' that heart-achingly familiar voice.

Beloved, is that why you chose not to live?

Some days it's almost unbearably lonely without you. I write about you and the tears fall faster than the pen can form the words. I am young, I should be dancing, I want you back but at the same time I have this overwhelming feeling that you have never left me. As you say, one flame, one heart and that's how it seems to be. I am so aware of you, all of the time.

The other day I read a passage in the chanting book:

'Give gifts then for departed ones, recalling what they used to do.

No weeping nor yet sorrowing nor any kind of mourning aids departed ones, whose kin remain unhelpful to them acting thus.'

I'm not crying for you, Gregory Klein, I'm crying for me. And when I'm not crying for me, the tears fall just remembering the little things you used to do. Even when you were so sick. That devastating sweetness, your dangerous sweetness. Worthy of love when it was before me, worthy of love in recollection. And more than recollection, a fundamental transubstantiation of spirit, mind and heart. The heart that still hears your voice.

You have bequeathed me an unrepeatable spiritual inheritance, teaching everything you could teach me condensed into two immeasurable years. You shared with me a unique experience of love and life, of sickness and death. Passing on everything necessary to give me the opportunity to put what I have learned and what we have learned together into practice. You taught me well, you teach me still but only by my own efforts will I unbar the door.

— ✳ —

Laid out on my beach mat on deserted Agios Giannis again, the tavernas closed, the short holiday season over on lazy Limnos. I can still see the faint outline where we built our foundation for the tent just two years ago. And are the white, sea lilies more abundant now? Or is it only my imagining?

I saw my grandparents meet and spiral into light five days after my grandmother's death. I saw the same spiral of light take the spirit of one of my horses thirty-six hours after he had been shot. I saw it again six days after my father died. The same colour and energy I saw magnified a thousand fold at the moment of my husband's passing. Each time a flash of the same indescribable joy. My grandmother would have described herself as a Christian but neither my father nor my grandfather subscribed to any religion, and certainly not the horse. Yet I saw them all pass into light accompanied by the same spiralling sensation.

So what does it all mean?

Sitting in the sun, laying pebbles into patterns in the sand, tracing intricate spirals of smooth, multicoloured stones to the edge of the sea. Floating the question in the ocean of my mind. What did they all have in common other than the gift of life?

Maybe it was that they had all done their best in the time they were given and whether I agreed with my father's conception of life or not, I know that his intention towards me was always for the best.

We are not limited to the invocation of a deity. There is no hot line to an omnipotent God. Our liberation into the continuum depends entirely on how we conduct ourselves in living out our time. Our conduct towards ourselves and our fellow beings and finally our courage and peaceful acceptance as we approach our own passing. Because it matters how we die. No one should be denied their death experience.

The hot Meltemi wind comes spinning off the sea, whipping my hair into my eyes, drenching my lungs with life. The little church is swept and clean again. How can I live the Septembers of all my years and not be on Limnos?

But all conditions are subject to change. Don't depend, don't cling. Take refuge in the truth and in love. Everywhere I go he is with me. I have his shining spirit before me, beside me, within me. Dancing on the waves, splashing me with light, my husband, an extraordinary Being. Some people 'supernova'. He did. Equally living incandescence and a man of shadows, many loved him. But he gave himself to me to be my beloved.

All my life I had a dream. I knew that one day I would meet the one man who would be my completion. My fulfilment. I met him and there can only be one. For who can follow Greg? Who can follow Ãnando?

Glossary of Terms

Ajahn Thai word, literally 'teacher'. Applied to Buddhists monastics in the Western Sangha who have achieved more than ten years ordained.

Anagarika novice/postulant technically still a lay person living in the monastery under the discipline of the Eight Precepts.

Ānando Greg's ordained Pali name, meaning 'spiritual bliss'.

Anjali with head bowed, hands held, palms together, fingers pointing upwards, in front of the chest as a gesture of respect.

Ataxia loss or lack of muscular co-ordination.

Bajan Hindu call and response chant.

Bhavana Pali – 'development'.

Buddha-rupa statue representing the Buddha.

CAT scan Computerised Axial Tomography (CT scanning).

Dana meaning 'generosity', most generally applied to the daily offering of food to monastics.

Decadron (dexamethazone) synthetic corticosteroid drug used for its anti-inflammatory action and its value in reducing oedema of the brain.

Desana formal Dhamma talk given by a monastic.

Dhamma Pali term for 'truth' as discovered and taught by the Buddha. [Sanskrit-Darma]

Dilantin trade name for Phenytoin, prescribed to counteract symptoms of epilepsy.

Dukkha meaning 'hard to bear', dis-ease, suffering, the sorrow of humankind.

Enlightenment achievement of perfect purity of mind and the development of penetrative insight into all phenomena in their true state.

Four Noble Truths As taught by the Buddha to describe four recognised states of being:

i There is suffering.

ii Suffering arises because of attachment.

iii Suffering ceases when the nature of attachment is understood.

iv The cultivation of Wisdom, Morality and Concentration is the path leading to the cessation of suffering.

Glioblastoma multiforme Astrocytoma Grade IV. Diffusely invasive of normal brain cells so tumour cells are usually left behind during surgery.

IV Intravenous drip.

Karma action or cause, created or recreated by habitual impulse, volition, natural energies. [Pali – Kamma]

Lay supporter follower of the Buddha who is not ordained but supports the monastic community.

Mala beads Tibetan Buddhist prayer beads.

Metta Loving kindness.

Mindfulness Attention.

MRI scan Magnetic Resonance Imaging.

Pali ancient Indian language surviving in the Theravadan Buddhist Scriptures.

Patimokka Buddhist Monastic rule, the 227 rules for the ordained Buddhist monastic.

Practice developing awareness of the present moment, developing the willingness to listen, to observe and to make the conscious effort to change.

Prana the Force of all light, Jesus called it the Light, the core ingredient of the power of all creation.

Precepts Five, Eight and Ten, the basic ethical codes of conduct recommended by the Buddha for his followers.

Puja formal, daily practice.

Sadhu 'It is well'.

Samadhi concentration or one-pointedness of mind, meditative absorption.

Sangha Buddhist monastic community.

Semper Fidelis US Marine Corps motto, abbreviated to '*Semper Fi*'.

Sit to sit meditation.

Stupa Buddhist shrine, usually a large, domed structure.

Tai Chi Chinese-based series of movements to train the body and the mind.

Theravadan Buddhism the southern school of Buddhism, traditionally the interpretation considered more close to the original interpretation of the teachings, emphasising monastic life. Predominant in Thailand, Sri Lanka, Cambodia, Laos, Burma.

VA Veterans' Administration, USA.

VOA Europe Voice of America, European Broadcast.

Vinaya Discipline.

Wesak Buddhist feast day of the Full Moon in May, observing the Birth, the Enlightenment and the Passing Away of the Buddha.

Fisher Miller Publishing provides a service for authors. We arrange editing, typesetting, printing or a complete self-publishing package, at cost but to professional standards, tailored to your requirements and your pocket. We specialise in short print runs and books which mainstream publishers find uneconomic to publish. You, the author, keep control, and you receive the profits. If you are interested in our services, please contact us at Wits End, 11 Ramsholt Close, North Waltham, Hants RG25 2DG (tel/fax 01256 397482).

The Clouds Trust (Registered Charity Number 1064289)

Clouds has been set up to carry out Greg's final wishes, namely:

- to research and supply the herbal tea known as the Rene Caisse formula, or Essiac, as a worthy vocation

- to establish a place of retreat in the mountains above Nice in the south of France for others who are faced with a terminal diagnosis as Greg and Mali were. A place where they can find peace and space to make their own choices, without pressure or prejudice, as to how they wish to conduct their own way of living, and their dying if it has to be. No one will come to Refuge Des Nuages to die but to choose to live. To choose how they are going to live, what are they going to do with their lives when they go back down the mountain, back into the world. Terminal illness does not mean confinement. There is still freedom, there is infinite potential. No one knows what they can do until they try. Only fear bars the door.

Clouds needs:

- people who can say 'yes'
- enthusiastic, optimistic and active supporters
- input and feedback, ideas for fund raising
- anyone willing to distribute information leaflets or sell the books
- volunteers to help with the annual Sheep Sorrel harvest.

For further information about The Clouds Trust
please write c/o 38, Dennis Way, Liss, Hampshire, UK
Tel/Fax +44 (0)1730 301162